Editing for Print And Electronic Media

Editing for Print And Electronic Media

Vivek Sehgal

CYBER TECH PUBLICATIONS
4264/3, Ansari Road, Daryaganj New Delhi - 110002
Phone : 011-43559448, Fax : 011-23280028
Email : cybertechpublications@gmail.com

Editing for Print and Electronic Media
CYBER TECH PUBLICATIONS
4264/3, Ansari Road, Daryaganj
New Delhi - 110002 (India)
Phone : 011-23244078, 011-43559448,
Fax : 011-23280028
E-mail : cybertechpublications@gmail.com
Website : www.cybertechpublications.com

First Published : 2008

ISBN 978-81-7884-351-3

Price,` 1200.00

Printed at :

New Green Print Solutions, New Delhi 110078

Contents

Preface

Editing is tough and News Editing is tougher, as it demands extra skills for presenting a common item in a special form. In fact 'News' is a strange term, which carries with it diverse feelings, for example, happiness, sadness, wonder, etc. The intensity of happiness or sadness depends upon the way, any news is reported. There may be a thundering news with no or little effect, if it is not narrated properly. Similarly, a plain and simple thing can be transformed into an interesting one, if a proper method of narration is adopted. This proper method of narration is actually the art of news editing. In news editing, words are to be manipulated wisely. A little deletion of the unnecessary ones and addition of the necessary ones, double the effect. Besides, there are certain other things, which have to be taken into account, while editing news. For instance, if we talk of a daily newspaper, it is very necessary for a news editor to know, where to put, which item of news? Banner news is of prime importance both nationally and internationally. Generally speaking, the front and back pages are very important. These two pages are supposed to carry all important news items. All these aspects constitute the subject matter of this small but compact book. This modest work is an exhaustive book on the subject.

We expect a warm welcome to this work from all concerned circles, including press and universities.

—*Editor*

Preface

1

News for Editing

The news is the timely report of events, facts, and opinions and interests a significant number of people. It is a new piece of information about a significant and recent event that affects the audience and is of interest to them. The definition of a news item is dependent on:

(a) the size of the community,

(b) the periodicity of the publication,

(c) the social character and economic base of the community,

(d) the focus of attention of community.

Jhon Bogart pointed out that unusual events fall under the purview of the news. Later, Joseph Pulitzer, publisher of New York World defined news as "original, distinctive, dramatic, romantic, thrilling, unique, curious, quaint, humorous, odd and apt-to-be-talked about". Walter William, the founder of the first school of Journalism, defined news as, "News in its broadest sense, is that which is of interest to the readers-the public....."

The former-managing editor of the New York Times said that the news was "..... anything you can find out today that you didn't know before."

Thus, the news is Perishable; of interest to a large number of people; of unusual events and happenings; what is new to the public; an event put forward by a reporter.

Hard News and Soft News: These are the two main categories in which the news is mainly divided.

Hard News is mostly event-centered. It is a narration of an event. The Hard news items are centered on, "what, when, where and why".

No doubt, the major thrust of a daily newspaper is the hard news. The main task of the dailies is to provide information to the readers. Mere accounts of events however do not satisfy the readers. They would like to enter beneath the upper crust of hard news. This type of news is called soft news. Thus, soft news goes beyond what has happened. It analyses, interprets and draws logical conclusions. It is becoming a very important segment of the daily newspaper.

Reporting of News

Here is a description about news reporting and the main components of a news report-the body and the lead.

The Lead: The lead should contain the essence of the story. It should give the reader an idea of what the story is about and help the copy desk to pick a suitable headline for the story. A good lead should arouse the reader's curiosity and force him on to read the rest of the story. It should be precise and made up of short, simple sentences. The lead should answer the five W's-Who, What, Where, When and why and How.

The Body: While the lead should arouse the reader's interest, the body should sustain it. The body should flow smoothly and logically from the lead. The body should be as complete and as tight as possible and should provide all the relevant information within the shortest space possible.

The essence of good journalistic writing is brevity and simplicity. Do not use a complex or long word where a short word would do.

The Components

Timeliness: News must be timely and new. It loses interest if it is already known.

Nearness: People are more interested in what happens under their nose. They are more concerned in the occurrence of an immediate impact on them.

Conflict: People gather in a street if and when there is a fight. Conflicts of all kinds are part of life and make good copy.

Prominence: What happens to important persons makes news. The value of the news increases with the prominence of the person involved. What the prominent people say, is also grist for a reporter's mill, particularly if they make some announcements which have an impact on the common people.

Government Action: The passing of a law or other orders concerning general people, Cabinet meetings, Parliament and assembly sessions, notifications about new rules and regulations are news worthy.

Development Projects and Issues: This is not news about government action, activities, though sometimes it will also qualify to be covered. The intention of a high yield variety rice and its success in changing the lifestyle of a community will be of interest to people who will financially benefit from it.

Weather and Sports: Both the weather and sports have great news value. Also entire page is devoted to sports in many newspapers.

Follow-up: The news item become very interesting for the general public when the issues are followed and updated. It is important to remember that follow-up of news events will keep the interest of the readers alive.

News Values: News values differ from community to community, country to country. News values are also different for developing and developed countries. For the industrialised and individualised societies of developed countries, communally provocative speeches and incidents may be reported word for word, blow by blow. But the same treatment would be suicidal in a developing country. One should take all possible care in reporting such developments keeping in mind the volatile nature of the audience and the reach of one's publication. One must follow some journalistic ethics and at times some self-censorship. Freedom of the press is not a licence to damage or destroy any one's reputation.

Fundamental Qualities

Accuracy: Accuracy is basic to any news item. When you fail in accuracy, you lose credibility. Cross check your facts and information. Check figures, names and facts. Make sure that the meaning is not changed and the statements are not quoted out of context. Exclude rumours or gossip from your report.

Balance: To be balanced in reporting, is as important as being accurate. While writing about a controversy, both sides of the story should be given. A story may appear to be 'imbalanced' and thus biased, if it has too much of government views, or tends to give too much of foreign news which has little relevance to readers.

Objectivity: Your opinion should not be mixed in the story. Report only facts and other peoples opinions. You should be a disinterested observer, reporting events without taking sides.

Clarity: Your introductory sentence should be short and in active voice to the maximum extent possible. The ideal length of each para may be 3-4 lines containing one-to-three small sentences to facilitate easy comprehension.

Impact: Whenever you do a news report, consider the impact your story should have. Will it induce some changes somewhere for the better? Develop a "nose for news", particularly news that will make an impact.

News Sources: A reporter, to be successful, should have a variety of reliable and highly placed contacts. There are some of the useful 'sources' for his information. Among the news sources, some are available to all reporters, such as public meetings, monitoring of radio and television programmes, press conferences, news briefing, seminars and other functions. But the contacts are sources of exclusive information for the reporter. They may be in the government, public or private sector business or just anywhere. Some of the contacts may like to be quoted for the story as it gives them publicity. In case of a critical story, they may not risk their neck. In that case, the story may have to be distributed to 'sources' only. It is the responsibility of a reporter to ensure the truthfulness of a report. In such cases, it will be advisable to keep some documents or audio tape to prove your story.

In the business of collecting the news, particularly of critical and investigative nature confrontation with the government is inevitable. A journalist chronicles daily events, places facts before the public, and tries to communicate that he considers truth. This may not suit the politician all the time, hence confrontation may occur. In case, a confrontation becomes inevitable, a reporter should face it. He should also treat his sources as 'sacred'. There may be pressure on the journalist from the government and the judiciary at times to disclose the sources. Protecting one's source is a cardinal principle of journalism.

Varieties of Reporting

Objective Reporting: A reporter is essentially a short story teller and he should tell the story in an objective and truthful manner, without lacing it with personal opinions or subjective comments. He should be fair and impartial and present both sides of the story. Complete objectivity is a mere concept. The reporter is a human being and he has certain ideas, feelings, attitudes, opinions and prejudices. However, a good reporter should try to rise above them and tell the facts as he has collected them in his search for truth. Objective reporting is, of course, not synonymous with dullness. It means fair and impartial reporting that is free from personal bias or prejudice.

Interpretative Reporting: It combines facts with interpretation. It delves into reasons and meanings of a development. His the interpretative reporter's task to give the information along with an interpretation of its significance. In doing so he uses his knowledge and experience to give the reader an idea of the background of an event and explain the consequences it could led to. Besides his own knowledge and research in the subject, he often has to rely on the opinions of specialists to do a good job. Interpretative reporting goes behind the news, brings out the hidden significance of an event and separates truth from falsehood.

Investigative Reporting: It is difficult to define the term 'investigative' journalism. In one way, of course, investigative journalism is a redundant concept, since all stories require some kind of investigation on the part of the reporter. However, the investigative reporter is expected to dig deeply beyond the facts stated in the hard news. Though, we may face difficulty in defining the term, we can not ignore the concept of investigative journalism. Investigative reporting has made great leaps in western countries. In India, it is still in its infancy. Attempts at investigative reporting, to quote one eminent Indian editor, arc like drilling for oil. A fair amount of wastage of effort has to be taken for granted. But when the oil is discovered and becomes marketable, the sense of achievement is usually more than in any other sector of journalistic enterprise. In India, investigative reporting started making a mark after the end of internal emergency in 1977. With governments becoming increasingly secretive and corruption spreading its tentacles far and wide, the need for investigative reporting can not be over emphasised.

Investigative reporting requires hard and sustained work. The investigative reporter should be combination of a crusader, super detective and blood bound and should have the necessary time and finance to carry out his work. The best thing of Investigative Reporting is that which keeps the public interest in mind. It may highlight an injustice, expose corrupt practices or unmask dishonest politicians and bureaucrats.

But experience shows that unless an investigative reporter or a crusading reporter gets the support of the judiciary, the executive or the legislative, can not bring his reports to logical ends.

Crime Reporting: There is tremendous public interest in crime stories and no newspaper can afford to ignore them without damage to its circulation and credibility. Crime is a part of life and it is newspaper's duty to inform the readers of what crimes are going on in their city, state or country.

Crime reporting is a highly responsible and specialised job. The reporter should not only have the ability to shift the grain from the chaff, and the truth from lies, he should also have good contacts in the police and other departments of the administration as well as working knowledge of the penal codes and law on libel and other relevant matters. Besides, he must observe a code of honour. He should not suppress news of public interest. Nor should he seek to settle personal scores with police officers or lawyers or judges. And he must be careful that in the course of this work, he doesn't necessarily invade a citizen's privacy. The crime reporter must never violate standards of decency and good taste.

Crime as News: There are several types of crime news-murders, fires, accidents, burglaries, fraud, blackmail, kidnapping, etc.

Fires: The reporter must get his facts correct about the essential elements of a fire story-the number of persons killed or injured, the extent of damage, to property, the loss of valuables. He should question eye-witnesses about any act of bravery or cowardice. All these are essential ingredients of a fire story.

Homicides: In cases of a major murder, the reporter should rush to the scene as soon as possible and gather all the relevant facts. Their dependence on police information often hampers their search for truth.

In reporting dowry deaths or alleged dowry deaths, the reporter should refrain from levelling uncorroborated statements by one party or the other.

Accidents: Most accidents are reported on the basis of police bulletins or information supplied by police spokesmen. However, wherever possible the crime reporter must rush to the scene of a major accident to give authenticity to his story.

Positive Sides

A journalist must possess and uphold certain noble qualities in order to be professional. Integrity of character, commitment to the truth and a reasoning power of mind are essential to any reporter. These qualities also contribute to the credibility of the reporting organisation. Besides, a journalist has to be truly responsible. A journalist is responsible to the audience as much as to the news organisation. Again a journalist is always responsible to the sources who reveal information. A reporter must also have a healthy respect for news values.

The Accountabilities

It is said that a reporter is both eyes and ears of a news organisation. It is not possible to strictly prescribe qualifications which a good reporter must possess. However, novice reporters must train themselves informally for the job so that they would be able to discharge their responsibilities with confidence, courage and competence. To be a successful reporter and to accomplish your job competently, you must be able to perceive, predict, calculate and plan your action appropriately in anticipation of a news event.

Sterling Features

A Nose for News: The reporter is the most important functionary of a newspaper. So one must know what constitutes news in order to be able to gather news. A reporter's job of discovering the news has been simplified in one, way and rendered difficult in another sense, in this age of information. While there are the usual press notes on which news reports can be based, there are other sources of information on a variety-of news event. But quite often, most of the material before a news reporter may just be a publicity matter.

Therefore, as a reporter, one must check the material and squeeze the news that would interest one's reader. A sharp sense of observation may also help one to gather amusing sidelights of interest to one's readers. This alertness will help one to discover contradictions and problems.

Outgoing Nature: Professional journalists are never arm chair writers. Introverts normally make poor reporters. Reporters have to move about meeting people, making their acquaintance and winning their confidence. This would help them to establish contacts, which in turn helps in writing well-investigated reports. This is the era of investigative reporting and readers are keenly interested to know what is going on behind the scenes. To get that kind of stories, one has no alternative but to be outgoing. One has to develop an affable temperament and an easygoing nature.

Ability to Establish Contacts and Develop Sources: An outgoing nature is the basic quality to establish contact and develop sources. You must have the ability to win the confidence and respect of those who may be potential sources of news. During the course of your regular duties, people may voluntarily offer you information.

Alternatively, this might not be the case when you are working on an investigative story. People may hesitate to talk on sensitive matters. They may like to reveal, yet are afraid to in case it were to affect them adversely. It may be quite difficult to win their trust. While you are establishing contact, there may be some among them who may want to plant information on you to serve their vested interests. Such information may consist of half-truths and even lies. So, you must have other independent contacts through whom you can verify the information. What matters is the alertness and ability to pursue your sources to get the right lead.

Ability to be an Unprejudiced Observer: The reporter must be an unprejudiced observer of events, one who presents the facts to the reader in a balanced, objective manner. It has been said that reporters mix comment with fact and so their reports are quite subjective. The reporters should not allow personal opinions at any place in the copy. One must be able to throw light on unclear aspects if any, of the news event. At the same time, the news reporter must endeavour to write a report which is only a statement of facts.

Thus, the first thing is to source your copy properly, to assure the reader that what you are passing on as news, is not your opinion. Even when you are not able to quote the sources, you must ensure that the story is balanced, by giving adequate coverage to all the sides of the subject. You should also ensure that the information you are presenting is true, which can be done by counter checking.

But remaining an unprejudiced observer does not mean adopting what is known in American journalistic parlance as 'man from the Mars' stance, i.e., seeing each event afresh, unconnected to any previous expectations or future possibilities and passing them on untouched by interpretation. In many cases, this would mean an irresponsible attitude, a refusal to make the reader understand the event in its proper context and realise its significance.

Clarity of Expression: Your command, as a reporter, over the language must be such that you can explain even the most complicated issues in simple terms to any general reader. In addition to specialised subjects such as science and technology, even government press notes are written in complicated language, burying the news point. You must be able to simplify it and bring out the news point.

Team Spirit: Except for routine coverages which can be handled by one person, many investigative stories have to be handled by a team. You must be able to work as a member of such a team. And you must pool your talents, sources and contacts into the team and work under a leader. In the course of time, you may rise to head such a team. Working under a team discipline will certainly be of help to you later.

Ability to Cope with Pressure: With investigative journalism seeking to bring out scandals and exposures, there is bound to be pressure on journalists to keep someone's wrong doings hidden from public view. The 'pressure' on journalists is exerted in the hope of preventing exposure. The concerned journalist may also be bribed with attractive favours in return for silence on the matter.

The pressure could be used to make you change the news or 'kill' a story. This constitutes censorship. Pressure could also be applied with the hope of inducing journalist to volunteer the change or omission which is then equal to self-censorship.

There are three ways of coping with pressure: fighting it, giving in or anticipating the pressure and taking preventive measures. Preventive measures to fight pressure could be legal steps, like seeking a court stay on any law or ordinance that could affect the freedom of the press.

Skills for Interviews

A very authentic way of gathering facts, figures and opinions on various issues is to interview the persons concerned. The interview is a very useful input for all the media-print and electronic. It depends on how one would like to use an interview.

It may be used as a programme to make the audience/reader get information/facts from the source directly. The interview can form the basis of an article, a feature or a commentary.

How to Prepare for an Interview: The most important part of the interview is to know youı subject as completely as possible. It is imperative for you to not only fully research the information you want from your subject, but also the person behind it. You should also have all the essential background information on the interviewee which will help you to build an instant rapport with the interviewee.

Research: It is most important to research your subject matter. It could be a subject in which you neither have any interest nor adequate knowledge. But once you are fully armed with the basic and important information acquired through books, newspapers, journals or magazines articles, you will be much more comfortable and should be successful in your venture.

You must know your subject matter as well as the person whom you intend to talk to about the subject matter.

Editing Interviews For Use: Two fundamental factors are to be remembered by all journalists-First, all interviews are subject to editing. So there is no harm in culling more information than you can use. The information that you need to buttress an argument or to refuse another or to make a point, can be used at the appropriate place. The rest can be stored for use in future.

Second, no statement made in the interview is allowed to be used out of context. If the authority interviewed does not generalise it, the reporter or, sub-editor is debarred from generalising it.

Strategy: It is important to establish contact with the interviewee much in advance of the interview. More often than not, where important interviewees are concerned, there is a channel you will have to go through. It could be the private secretary or the members of the family referred to as the "protector of the interviewee".

So, the first thing to do is to establish a rapport with the protector. To get to your subject-matter or the person, you must be able to play to the gallery to defeat all the obstacles imposed by the "protectors".

What You Want from the Interview: If the first thing is to establish contact and to build up a rapport, the most important part of the preparation is to decide what you want to get out of the interview. May be you want substantiation of a fact you have discussed; or the refutation of something; or may be you want the interviewer's views on some, proposition you or someone else is making.

It is vital for an interviewer to decide what he wants out of the interview. It is not a fishing expedition in which you net whatever you get. It is a hunt where you go after a target and get it.

Also one has to keep his senses on full alert and the antenna unfurled to each nuggets of news which have a knack of falling from the lips of the interviewee at the most unexpected moments.

Preparing Yourself: It is important and essential to make a deep study of the individual you plan to interview. Paying attention to his minute, apparently insignificant, matters really helps in conducing the interview smoothly. You must build a personal rapport to begin with, so you may start the interview comfortably.

Physical Preparation: If it is a television interview, then you need the cameraman, sound recordist, lighting technician and sound technician.

The other way in which the interview is to be held in a studio, then arrangements should be made accordingly in the studio. For the radio studio interview, a good recording machine is required, a lip microphone is used which prevents extraneous sound from getting injected into the microphone.

How to Get an Interview: Getting an interview can often be difficult, because the interviewer is generally viewed with suspicion. The interviewer labours between two competing factors. One, the public has the right to know and you are the tool employed to gather the information. Two, from the legal point of view nobody can be forced into talking hence, the job can be tiresome and at times, very frustrating.

It is very important that one's own participation in the interview is secondary. One must let the interviewee do most of the talking.

To make this happen smoothly, a number of skills have to be deployed like:

(a) There is the direct approach-to telephone and tell the interviewee what you want.

(b) The end round: A secretary in a business or government office will generally try, and give you the 'brush off'. The attempt of the interviewer should be to try and make the secretary one's friend.

(c) When faced with repeated failure, find out the person's hide-out and with an overdose of apology, just barge in.

(d) Sit in: It pays to just 'sit and wait' till the subject of interview shows up in spite of secretaries saying that 'the boss has no time to see you'.

(e) The appeal: As soon as you get the glimpse of the reluctant interviewee, make your appeal as quickly and strongly as possible.

(f) Be courteous and polite: Tell the interviewee that there are two sides to every story, and we want to know yours. Thus, you arouse the interviewee's curiosity and attention. In many cases, it pays to tell the interviewee of the other side.

Do's and Dont's for an Interview

(a) Be operational on time for the interview. This is very important. It shows the importance of the interviewee and that he has not been taken for granted. In a nut shell, you must be ready right on time to start the interview.

(b) Outline your reasons for being there, unless you are working on something very sensitive.

(c) Start the interview with a broad question. This helps you to size up the person and also collect your thoughts. It also helps to receive information you may not have anticipated.

(d) Do not interrupt until the interviewee has relaxed. Avoid making the interviewee uncomfortable at the outset. It would be of little value.

(e) Let him speak at length on his favourite topic/ achievement/feat. You will get nuggets of information. The irrelevant facts can always be edited out.

(f) Grunt and chuckle occasionally.

(g) Stick to your subject.

(h) Avoid commenting except to egg him on to top more. Let the interviewee do most of the talking.

(i) Do not end the interview till you have the basics-how does he spell his name, official title, age, etc. Preferably get the details in advance from his staff and then get it confirmed by him.

(j) Be understanding. Do not be insensitive. Make the interviewee feel important. Keep the interviewee at ease.

Interviewing Skills: Advance preparation for the interview by way of well-thought out questions and a thorough consideration of approach is very helpful. One need not fear that the final outcome will sound stilted with no natural spontaneity. Usually the reverse is true.

Taking Notes: Taking notes is an essential part of interviewing. Some take down everything, even irrelevant and redundant remarks. Take down only what is important. People sometimes stop talking when you start writing and so taking down only the important remarks may not be possible. And you don't always know what is relevant until you have written it all down and reviewed it.

(i) Write as fast as you can.

(ii) Keep hand and mind together, listen to key phrases. A tape recorder helps you to review the interview *in toto*. It is a must for a question and answer story.

Conducting An Interview: Know your subject. Read the person's eyes and mannerisms since these offer a reliable clue on how an interview is to be handled. Since the interview rarely goes as planned, therefore the interviewer requires a lot of instinct.

How to Establish Rapport with the Interviewee

(a) In many small and big ways, try to make your interviewee feel nice, cheerful and important.

(b) Outline your reasons for being there. Bring the interviewee up-to-date on what you are looking for.

(c) Start with a broad question. This helps you to see the person and collect your thoughts. It also gives you an opportunity to receive information which you may not have anticipated.

(d) Stick to the subject. Do not ramble or chit-chat. Neither is it advisable to beat around the bush. So go ahead and simply ask your questions straight-away.

(e) Doodling or writing down a lot of useless matter in your notebook can be helpful. Those who have important information to transmit, like to feel they are being recorded. You might be asked to show what you have taken down. For all that, jotting down points helps you to prepare the transcription of the interview-session for publication.

(f) Listen. Listen. Listen. Not only does this make the interviewee feel good and wise, but it also helps you to control the interview. An interviewer might start speaking with good intentions and slowly digress. You can bring him back to point. "You were saying something about the time you were in college, prison, etc. When was that?" And you are back on the track.

(g) Be understanding. Nobody likes insensibility. The interviewee is often quite nervous while discussing his/her wrong doings, sin or tragedy. Help him/her to relax. If your mind goes blank, just say, "Excuse me. I forgot where we were and what I need to ask".

Other Tasks

The reporting profession is unlike any other profession. At times, some slight carelessness in doing one's duty, can cause incalculable harmful repercussions, both for the news organisation and society. A slight laziness in cross checking certain facts could endanger the credibility of the news organisation.

Responsibility towards the News Organisation: As a reporter, you have to follow the character, style and policy of your newspaper or magazine or news agency. There are conservative papers which may prefer to stick to routine coverage, not bothering about investigation of scandals. In such papers, you have to stick to their policy even if it cramps your style. But in a news organisation with a more dynamic approach to news, you must develop the skills of an investigator. Whatever you do as a reporter will affect the newspaper and its reputation. So you must take pains to ensure accuracy and objectivity in your stories.

Responsibility towards the Sources: Your sources are sacred. Your credibility in their eyes could be a major factor in your performance as a newsperson. There are sources with whom you will have to take great pains to establish your credibility to make them open up towards you. You will have to assure them that no harm will come to them, and if they so desire, you must keep their identity a secret.

Responsibility towards the Reader and Society: As a news reporter, you have a duty to provide accurate, unbiased and objective information to the reader. Every effort must be made to ensure that the news is accurate, free from prejudices and that all sides of the news event are presented fairly.

To maintain your credibility with the reader you have a duty not to accept things or favours or pursue any activity that might compromise your integrity.

However, in these days, publicity seekers including those in private business, organise press conferences and conduct tours with attractive gifts and other incentives. While private firms depend mainly on advertising for publicity, they sometimes want their activities to be carried as news items since news carries greater credibility than advertisements. News reports are written by newspapers who are supposed to be independent and objective.

2

News Selection

The news items that appear in newspapers are also called news stories. In literature stories may not have their basis in actual events, but a news story is always based on facts. History is also based on facts but it deals with things of the past while news stories are on current events. Further, a news story is normally written in inverted pyramid style, that is, the most important facts come first followed by other facts in order of significance.

The inverted pyramid style has developed in journalism over the years. It helps the readers who don't have enough time to read the whole story. It also helps sub-editors who can easily discard as much of the story from the tail without affecting its readability.

News Story Structure: Let us have a look at a typical news story.

Plea Rejected: London, May 1 (PTI)—The British Government today rejected the plea of Sikh separatists for recognition of 'Khalistan', which they had proclaimed in Amritsar three days ago.

A foreign office spokesman said the unity and territorial integrity of India were central to peace and to the well-being of the whole region, when asked about reports that the separatists had appealed to Britain and certain other countries to recognise 'Khalistan'.

Past elections in Punjab had demonstrated that the people did not support secession. Therefore, the question of recognising 'Khalistan' did not arise, he added.

(*The Tribune*, Chandigarh, May 2, 1986)

No UK Recognition for Khalistan which appears in bold type is the head line. It is put at the head of the story and gives an idea to the newspaper reader about the subject of the story.

London, May I is the date line. It tells the reader the place and the date of the news story.

(PTI) is credit line. The newspaper has published this story which was supplied by news agency Press Trust of India and by putting (PTI) the paper acknowledges the source of the story and this gives the credit to the news agency.

Sometimes the name of the reporter or correspondent appears below the headline with a By or From. For example, "From V.S. Karnic" or "By Kanwar Sandhu". It is termed *byline.*

The first paragraph of the story is called *intro* or *lead.* In the above example, "The British Government today rejected the plea of Sikh separatists for recognition of `Khalistan', which they had proclaimed in Amritsar three days ago," is the intro.

The rest of the story is called *body* of the story. Intro gives the most important information which is contained in the story and therefore it is the most crucial part. It should contain highest quantum of news value. A good intro is prerequisite of a good story. The proverb—'Well begun is half-done'—goes very well in this case; you really do half of the work on a news story if you write a good intro. The body of the story will automatically follow in the inverted pyramid style.

News Covered

News is not always unexpected and therefore news coverage of expected events can be planned. Of course we cannot plan an accident or crime coverage before it happens or is committed. But we can plan follow up coverage of the accident or crime.

For the purpose of planning every newspaper or news agency maintains a diary and it is kept up to date. Depending on the nature or duration of an event the necessary staff is organised and concerned members given time to prepare if possible. Necessary telegraphic, telephone or telex facilities should be provided to the correspondent if he is sent out of town or abroad to make sure that he is able to file news.

There is a daily meeting of reporters presided over by the chief reporter and of special correspondents presided over by a' bureau chief to finalise this kind of planning and to tie up loose ends. The chiefs before this meeting confer with the news editor and the editor.

In some newspaper offices, the editor presides over the meeting of the entire reporting staff. This may happen in any newspaper if the situation warrants for the purpose of proper planning.

Coverage of state legislatures and Parliament is also planned. Similarly, election coverage and coverage of budget needs extensive planning where all available hands are used and everybody is given some job or the other depending on special qualifications or capabilities or shortcomings.

Follow-up of reports that have already appeared in the newspaper or other newspapers is also planned together with special investigative stories.

Basically, news gathering is a planned exercise but the plan has to be flexible so as to account for the uncertainty of events.

Oral Press Briefing: Information and publicity personnel in government departments, public and private sector, and in other organisations constantly feed the press with publicity and information material in written form, such as press releases, features, articles, backgrounders, letters to the editor and also advertisements.

The Purpose: The purpose of oral briefing is to supplement and reinforce the conventional written publicity material. It is an opportunity to highlight certain events, and also to clarify the complicated issues to press representatives through questions and answers. Sometimes, better results are achieved by face-to-face discussion with the correspondents, rather than giving information to them through written publicity material.

To get the best results, out of the oral briefings, it is necessary that these should be organised in a methodical manner. Every care has to be taken as to when and how to give oral briefing. Oral briefing is of different types.

Queries from Press Representatives: An accredited press correspondent may put a query on any aspect of working of the government department or other organisation. Such queries are treated as confidential and the replies are to be given only to the press representative concerned on exclusive basis. It should not be shared with other press representatives. The confidence of correspondent should be respected. The decision to treat the query exclusive or otherwise rests with the information personnel. He should exercise his discretion with care, so that he is not charged with discrimination by other correspondents. At the same time, his action should not discourage the individual initiative of a correspondent and induce him to explore other sources of information for a scoop or an exclusive story.

Generally, queries from only accredited representatives are answered. City reporters' query may also be attended to, if the matter is of local interest such as University, Zoo, Delhi Milk Supply, etc.

The query should be noted down and the official concerned should be approached for relevant and correct answer. The press correspondent should be replied without much delay, and with as much details as possible.

The answering of queries from press representatives helps in checking correspondents relying on unofficial and unreliable sources, or on gossips. Also, in the garb of query the information personnel can plant a story on exclusive basis in a paper. However, stories of general public interest should not be given to one correspondent only.

Special Press Briefing: Press briefing is specially arranged for accredited correspondents taking interest in a particular subject-field. The purpose is to explain the background of a happening, not necessarily for its being used as a news story. In these briefings, all accredited correspondents are not invited. These briefings are in the nature of special briefings on a particular subject.

Besides the ministers and secretaries, these briefings are also organised by senior officials for giving detailed information and elucidation on complicated matters. The officials should not be too much reticent and tight-lipped in replying to inconvenient questions as that will defeat the very purpose of such briefings.

Separate press briefings are sometimes conducted for foreign correspondents on important aspects of national development, since foreign correspondents may not be interested in minute details or subjects which are of interest to Indian correspondents.

Press Meet: Press conference provides an opportunity to communicate directly with the representatives of the press. They, in turn, present the news to the public. The press conference should be held only if the government or the organisation has to give out some important news. It is wrong to hold a press conference when there is no worthwhile news to give. The press conferences are usually held when actual news is to be given out. The purpose is to explain to the press correspondents and selected editors the scope and purpose of an important report or statement which is likely to be of public interest. It is also held to give a general view of the policy and activities of the government or other organisations. Sometimes press conferences are also held to explain to the press a specific important development of sufficient public interest.

The press conference should never be held on a routine affair or a trivial matter. On the other hand, the government press conferences may be utilised to announce all major policy decisions and important announcements when Parliament or Assembly is not in session. The conference should be conducted by those who are competent to explain the rationale and implication of the issues. Only in this way, the press conference acquires meaning and content and helps developing better relationship between the government and the press.

Press conferences are generally arranged for ministers or secretaries. For other officers also, press conferences may be arranged on specific subjects if they are authorised to communicate with the press. In the case of public sector and private sector organisations, the chairman and managing directors and also other senior officers may hold press conferences on specific subjects.

The invitees to the government press conference are normally all accredited correspondents including foreign correspondents, editors of local newspapers, accredited cameramen and representatives from AIR, Doordarshan, Photo and Films Division depending on the importance of the subject and the dignitary holding the press conference. An uptodate list is kept in the Press Information Bureau of the Government of India, and also in the State Public Relations/ Information Directorates for this purpose.

In the case of private organisations, all correspondents who normally cover the organisation should be invited to the press conference. For this purpose, a standard list of invitees should be kept and updated from time to time. Where the name of the special or concerned correspondent is not correctly known, it is better to extend a blanket invitation to the news editor or the chief reporter who would assign a representative whom he considers best qualified to handle the story.

Official invitees to the press conference should be reduced to the minimum. Information or public relations officer should be present at the time of the press conference. This holds good for non-official press conferences also. The chief executive and head of the concerned department should, however, be present at the conference.

Invitations to the press conference are sent well in advance indicating the date, day, time, subject and venue of the conference. Also, the name of the person who is to hold the press conference and his designation or status should be indicated.

In regard to the timing of the press conference, it is advisable to hold it in the forenoon or early afternoon so that reports of the press conference may get into the Dak edition of papers. The holding of press conferences late in the evening on unimportant subjects is of little use. If a press conference is held over a cocktail party in the evening, or over dinner on a subject not of immediate interest, it is advisable to request the invitees to write the story next day for publication on the day after. Generally, correspondents agree to this suggestion, as in that case they have not to rush to the office to file the story in the night. It will also be too late to get good display of the story in the newspapers.

The duration of the press conference is, generally, from thirty minutes to one hour.

Tea, coffee, soft drinks and snacks may be served at the press conference. It is better to serve refreshments at the end of the conference at a separate counter. It will interfere with the work if refreshments are mixed up with the business session. In any case, it should not be made too lavish an affair.

Before the press conference, the information officer or the public relations officer should brief the speaker in advance about the correspondents and the nature of questions likely to be asked. Where business houses have public relations officers, they should fully brief the top executive and suggest the line of approach for the presentation of the subject-matter, so that the executive can speak with certain amount of informality and ease, before the press conference begins. They should also give a proper but brief introduction of the speaker and the subject. This will help in making proper impression and impact on the representatives of the press.

The speaker, holding the press conference, should see to it that unrelated questions are not entertained, and that no correspondent or group of correspondents monopolise the conference. Also, disproportionate time should not be given to any single question. Discussion on individual and personal cases should be avoided. Generally, not more than half a dozen questions are to be allowed on one aspect of the subject.

It is necessary to prepare a comprehensive note on the subject of the press conference. This note should be distributed a little before the press conference is to start. This helps in many ways, particularly in checking facts and statistics. Also through this note the department or organisation can project its point of view. Such a prepared note also helps absentee correspondents. The background note is not released to the newspapers but only given to the correspondents who attend the press conference. If the press conference is conducted by the business concern in regard to a new product, the prepared note on the subject is a 'must'. But if the press conference relates to the general policy, it is not absolutely necessary.

The press conference should be held at a centrally located and easily accessible place. There should be adequate space for the correspondents, and all necessary facilities such as mike, light points and writing desks should be provided, if possible. The press conference should be held, in case of an urgent matter, in the conference room of the business house or organisation. If the accommodation is not suitable, it can be held at a centrally located place. If the conference is not in regard to an urgent matter, it can be held in a leading club or hotel. In any case, the surroundings of a press conference should be congenial.

The arrangements for the press conference should be well thought out. The transport may be provided both ways, if the press conference is held at some distant or out-of-the-way place. If the press conference relates to an urgent matter, for instance, about a strike or labour trouble there will not be any time for social niceties. However, if the conference is called for the introduction of some new product, etc. it may be over a lunch, dinner, or cocktail.

The person, conducting the press conference, should be advised to avoid 'off the record' remarks as far as possible. It is better to say at the press conference 'I cannot comment', rather than making some observation and requesting the press to treat it as confidential.

It is not necessary to have a verbatim record of the press conference, unless it is on a very important subject and attended by a very important dignitary. No press release is to be issued on the press conference.

It is a wrong policy not to give equal treatment to all newspaper representatives, even though some of them may have been unfair in the interpretation of news or embarrassed the organisation in the past. Despite this, the publicist should treat them on an equal basis. Under no circumstances, should any press representative be excluded from the press conference on this account. In fact, it should be a matter of policy to invite a dissenting or critical correspondent. This may disabuse him of the wrong facts in his mind, or false information planted in his mind by a rival.

The public relations officer should prepare himself for the follow-up of the press conference. There may be questions on which full answers could not be given at the press conference. He should immediately get the information, and make it available to the person who asks for it.

VVIP Press Conference: A press conference by the Prime Minister or a VVIP, particularly a foreign dignitary, is somewhat different from the normal press conference discussed in the preceding paragraphs. The following are important points to remember:

1. The invitation to such conferences, in the case of Government of India, is normally sent under the signature of the Principal Information Officer. In the case of State governments it is issued by the Director of Public Relations. The head of the organisation in public or private sector should send such invitations.

   The invitation should give a clear indication of the day, date, time and venue, but unlike other conferences, it is not necessary to mention the subject. The name and designation or status of the dignitary should be mentioned. In the case of press conference by chief ministers, the subject of the press conference may also be given.

   Invitations should be extended to all accredited press correspondents including those provisionally accredited, editors of local newspapers, accredited cameramen, including foreign news agency and foreign newspapers. The invitation should also be extended to AIR, Doordarshan, Films Division, Photo Division, accredited photographers, and Doordarshan newsreel cameramen including those representing foreign agencies, and also to foreign broadcasting and television organisations.

   For such conferences, invitation to other officials should be given on specific request after duly considering the request on its merit. Information personnel, who are not directly concerned, are generally not expected to attend the conference. In any case, their number should be reduced to the minimum.

   The invitation to the press should be marked 'Not For Publication', and it should be indicated that the invitees should be seated fifteen minutes before the start of the conference. Invitation should be made non-transferable, and correspondents should be requested to bring the invitation letter or card with them.

2. In the case of such press conferences, it is also necessary to inform the Superintendent of Police (Security), Superintendent of Police (Traffic), Secretary to VVIP, External Publicity Division, and Foreign Regional Regulation Officer and other concerned officials.
3. The timings of such press conferences should be preferably in the forenoon or early afternoon, so as to cover the Dak edition of the newspapers. The timings would, however, depend on the VVIP's convenience.
4. The venue of the conference should be at a place which has necessary facilities. The press representatives should be able to use mike without difficulty. In Delhi, the venue of such press conferences is Vigyan Bhawan. Outside Delhi, it may be at Raj Bhawan, or PIB office, or at some other central place where adequate facilities are available. The venue should be got cleared from the security point of view.
5. The duration of such press conference is, normally, confined to forty-five minutes.
6. Cameramen should operate from fixed positions without obstructing the view. They should not move from one position to another during the press conference. They should use noiseless or ruffled cameras. Cameramen are not expected to occupy seats which are meant for correspondents. Only accredited cameramen should be permitted for the coverage. They are given a few minutes to adjust themselves before the beginning of the conference. There should not be click-off throughout the conference.
7. The correspondents should be requested to use microphone, if there is such facility, while asking questions to facilitate recording. Before asking a question the correspondent should mention his name and the name of the newspaper and agency he represents. They should be advised that not more than two or three questions should be asked by one correspondent. Monopolisation of the proceedings by a few correspondents should not be

allowed, and time should not be lost over minor and irrelevant questions or personal grievances.

8. The correspondents should not leave the press conference till it is over. The filing of the stories in between puts the other correspondents at a disadvantage.
9. The full text of the press conference should be released, on the same day, to all accredited correspondents and newspapers, for their use and also for reference and record purposes. If the conference is organised by the PIB their regional and branch offices are also provided with the text. For preparing the full text it is necessary to deploy an adequate number of reporters/ stenographers to take down verbatim record. Also, the transcript should be checked with the tape-recorder, which should be used in such conferences.
10. The Overseas Communication Service and the Central Telegraph Office should be intimated in advance, so that they make necessary arrangements to cope up with the rush of foreign press traffic on the day of the conference.
11. It is not necessary to give any background material, unless it is on a speck subject.
12. No snacks or tea or coffee, as served in other conferences, should be given in VVIP conferences. Only drinking water is to be served. This is done to make the conference a functional affair.

Get-together: The purpose of informal meetings and press get-togethers is to develop and strengthen the relationship between the organisation and the press. This gives an occasion to intimately know the correspondents at personal level. These social gatherings are held over lunch, dinner, or cocktail parties. Since these are not business sessions, no news is normally disseminated to the correspondents on such occasions. It is not possible to invite all the accredited correspondents at a time for such informal meetings. It is advisable to invite them in small groups by rotation. Care, however, has to be taken to ensure that all correspondents, who are covering a particular subject-field, are invited during a reasonable period of time.

The Functions: Press correspondents are also invited to functions. If the function is of a local nature, reporters are invited, otherwise invitation is extended to all correspondents covering the subject-field. If the function is held at any out-of-the-way place, the reporters should be provided transport both ways. The transport may start from some pre-determined central place. At the venue of the function, there should be proper press enclosure, so that the press correspondents have frontal view and can also easily listen to the speakers. No person other than press representatives should be given entry in the press enclosure.

Background material should be prepared in advance. The same can be handed over to the press representatives at the time of function. If there are prepared speeches, the text should be kept ready and given to press representatives. The programme and other details of the function should also be given to them. At such functions, refreshments, etc., are also provided to the correspondents. If audio-visual coverage of the function is required, AIR, Doordarshan and newsreel cameramen should be invited. Light points and other facilities, required by them, should be checked in advance.

When the press representatives are invited to the function, the organisers should not insist that the press should come in a particular dress. The dress may have been prescribed for others, but to insist on the press to conform to a particular dress is not a correct practice. They have been invited to project the work of the organisation, and it is not fair to impose any unnecessary restrictions on them. It is unfair to expect correspondents to keep a large set of clothes to suit a particular occasion.

If desired, the press representatives should be allowed to leave the function before it is formally over. The press correspondents sometimes have to leave earlier, either for providing timely coverage to the function, or they may have other engagements or assignments. Their leaving the function early should not be considered as a discourtesy.

Conducted tours of groups of correspondents are also organised to major development projects or other manufacturing concerns. These should not be rush visits and degenerate into holiday excursions. Such visits are of great benefit to small and medium newspapers. They should be invited on regional basis. The correspondents of medium and large newspapers may also be conducted to such projects. They should also be given facilities to cover the projects on their own. In such visits, sufficient time should be allowed to the press representatives to go round the project, meet concerned officials and see for themselves the progress.

The conducted tours should be organised with a great deal of care. This requires considerable expertise. The selection of correspondents, air/rail/road reservations, hotel bookings, messing and transport arrangements, recreational facilities, proper background material and other details should be properly worked out before such tours are undertaken. These should not become counter-productive. They should result in greater harmony between the organisers and the press.

It is difficult to lay down any rigid rules or guidelines for conducted tours for journalists organised by the government, public sector undertakings, or other agencies.

The size of the party and the duration of tour vary depending on a number of factors-resources, projects to be covered and their importance in national context. However, the upper limit of 20 persons and 15 days is generally not to be exceeded. The selection of the newspapers, national and regional, is to be finalised by the organisation sponsoring the tour. Newspapers in Indian languages should get adequate representation. The nomination of particular persons, to be included in the party, should be left to the editors. The organisation may suggest a name indicating the reason, if any, but the final decision should be that of the editor. Also, the selection of newspapers, should be rotated for different tours, so as not to give any impression of patronage. This policy achieves wider and varied coverage.

Normally, travel of the party is by rail, road, or steamer. Travel by air, where considered necessary, is also to be undertaken. Expenses during the journey, and on boarding and lodging vary depending on places to be visited, but they should be kept within reasonable limits so as to make maximum use of the resources.

For instance, members of the party, who normally reside outside the place of commencement of the tour, should be requested to join the party *en route,* if the programme permits of such an arrangement. Also, where any concession is admissible to an individual or party under the rules of airlines, railways, or shipping services, this should be availed of. No liquor should be served while these tours.

The organisations, sponsoring the tour, should prepare in advance background material about the projects to be visited by the party. Some knowledgeable person or persons should be earmarked to brief the party at the spot. It helps the conducting officer, accompanying the party, to have assistance of a liaison officer from the organisation conducting the tour.

The programme should be drawn up in such a manner that the members of the party have some time for leisure and also for sight-seeing, for which suitable arrangements should be made. It is not necessary for the conducting officer or others to vet the story filed by newspaper representatives, except in case of defence and on a few other subjects. However, all assistance is to be given to them to check facts and figures and to clarify doubts, and misgivings.

Except in case of spot news coverage, it is advisable to fix a future date on which the story would appear simultaneously in all the papers. This gives time to the members of the party to prepare the story. In the absence of such an arrangement, it will be rush work and would defeat the very purpose of the visit.

Important Things

Basic elements of a news story can be found by asking and trying to find answers to six basic questions popularly known as the five Ws and one *H.* The five Ws are—What? When? Where? Who? and Why? and the *H* is How?

There was a time when journalists were supposed to answer all the questions in the intro. But slowly it was discovered that it resulted in overcrowding of the opening para, loss of clarity which at times confused and irritated the reader.

The style book of News Agencies Pool of Non-aligned Countries has this to say on this subject, "Basically a news story must answer the three Ws: What? Where? and When? As a rule the answers to these should find place in the opening paragraph. Three other questions could be Who, Why and How? But they do not necessarily arise in all stories. Except where they themselves form the cardinal point of a story, answers to them can usually be accommodated in the later paragraphs."

Thus, there is no hard and fast rule about these Ws and H and their inclusion in the intro or lead. A story may not have answers to all of them but all these questions should be asked to identify the basic elements of a news story. Then, according to news value, the most important element should come in the intro.

An intro may be in reply to one or more or all of these questions, but there should be no compromise on clarity of expression. If a reader has to look over a sentence a second time to understand it, then it cannot make a good intro or lead.

A test for elements of news and their proper order could be provided with four letters from 'news' as keys:

N for newsworthiness—does the story contain news values?

E for emphasis—does the intro contain the most important and interesting fact?

W for the five Ws and the H—do their answers exist in the story?

S for sources of information—does the story identity or imply the source where it is necessary?

Types of Intros or Leads: Newsmen deal with a very wide range of subjects and everybody has his own way of presenting things. Therefore, there are innumerable ways of writing intros and leads.

This variety is obvious to everybody who reads newspapers carefully as the same news story is presented in different ways in different newspapers, while the same paper presents different stories in different ways. Any two reporters, doing the same story, will write it differently and this explains the variety.

There are various ways to classify intros or leads depending on different criteria. Based on the number of incidents involved, the intro could be simple or complex.

(i) *Simple lead* involves a single incident. Even if the event has several different incidents, the intro takes account of a single incident. Simple lead is very common in newspapers and should normally be favoured as it is easy to write it clearly. For a complex event like police action in the Golden Temple, *Indian Express,* Chandigarh, gave a simple lead:

TOI News Service: Chandigarh, Aug. 19. The Punjab Police and para-military forces entered the Golden Temple complex at Amritsar this afternoon to clear it of "terrorists, separatists and anti-national elements."

(ii) *Complex lead* involves more than one incident in the intro. It is normally used when similar or related incidents are clubbed together in one story. One has to be careful with this kind of intro as it is normally long, and at times confusing. Various incidents of violence in Punjab have been clubbed in this complex lead *(Indian Express,* Chandigarh):

Chandigarh, April 30. Three persons were killed and two others injured by suspected terrorists during the last 24 hours while a petrol pump and two liquor vends were looted in Faridkot district. Among the killed is a brother of a Deputy Superintendent of Punjab Police.

Two armed terrorists gunned down Rajiv Kumar, a dispenser at Pakhoke village near Taran Taran and seriously injured Daljit Kumar. Both were travelling in a tonga. They were made to get down and shot at. Jaspal Singh, a brother of Mr. Sukhdev Singh, a DSP posted at Batala, was also killed by the terrorists.

According to a report from Moga, four car-borne armed persons today looted a petrol pump, and two liquor vends at three different places in Faridkot.

It appears from the intro (the first paragraph) that all the incidents took place in Faridkot district while the second and third paragraphs make it clear that three different districts were involved.

Taran Taran is in Amritsar district while Batala is in Gurdaspur district. A little more care was needed to avoid this mistake. In the following example care has been taken to avoid a similar mistake:

Chandigarh, April 28. Mr. Sant Singh Gill, Congress (I) MLA from Beas, and Mr. Pradeep Kumar, a security guard of Mr. Surinder Kumar Billa, Rashtriya Hindu Sangathan Leader, were today gunned down in a fresh spurt of terrorist violence in Punjab.

Based on the grammar of the sentence, intros can be classified into several categories.

Substantive Clause Intro: New Delhi, May, 6 (UNI). Despite adverse agro-climate factors, foodgrains production in 1985–86 was likely to touch 150 million tonnes, the Agriculture Minister, Mr. Buta Singh, disclosed today.

Conditional Clause Intro: New Delhi, Aug. 2 (UNI). The Minister of State for Agriculture, Mr. Yogendra Makwana, has assured the Rajya Sabha that the government would take prompt action if charges of bungling against any of the NAFED officials were found to be true.

Present Participial Intro: United National, Sept. 9, (PTI). Calling the United Nations' current financial crisis "Yet another" challenge to multilateralism India has asked members to defeat those trying to weaken the world body.

Past Participial Intro: Cherrapunjee, July, 30, (PTI). A large number of people here were disappointed today as President Zail Singh cancelled his Cherrapunjee visit due to inclement weather.

Prepositional Phrase Intro: Dhaka, Jan. 9, (PTI). In the backdrop of the political imbroglio in Bangladesh, the leaders of the two major Opposition alliances held an unexpected parley last Sunday at an undisclosed venue to discuss the launching of a movement to make the government of President H.M. Ershad concede to Opposition demands to ensure free and fair elections.

Infinitive Phrase Intro: Jayaprakash Pattan (Pune), June 5, (UNI). Fifteen Muslim members of the Janata Party including the former UP unit chief, Mr. Abbas Ali, on Thursday resigned from the primary membership of the party to protest against the resolution on the Muslim Women's (Protection of Rights of Divorce) Bill adopted at the fourth national convention here.

Intros or leads can also be classified according to the elements of the news (five Ws and H) that dominate in the lead:

Who Lead: Hoshiarpur, March 5, (PTI). The Punjab police chief, Mr. J.F. Ribeiro on Saturday said maintenance of law and order in the state was not an easy task.

What Lead: Bombay, Aug. 9, (PTI). M.V. Jhansi Ki Rani, a 76,600 dwt bulk carrier, owned by the Shipping Corporation of India (SCI), ran around at Fredric Reef, some 500 km off the Australian east coast around 2 p.m. yesterday, a delayed report reaching the SCI's headquarters in Bombay said. No casualties were reported.

Where Lead: Sonepat, Jan. 5, (UNI). Rail traffic on Sonepat-Delhi junction of Northern Railway remained disrupted for about five hours following the derailment of two bogies of a goods train near Ganara railway station, about 16 km from here early this morning.

When Lead: Ahmedabad, July 10 (UNI). Since Vedic times, ancient Indian astronomers observed and carefully studied rare celestial phenomena, including comets, according to Mr. Parmanand Desai, executive director of the Vedhshala (astronomical observatory) in suburban Naranpura here.

A close study of some of the not so well-known Sanskrit works cast new light on comets, the "old faithful visitors" to the solar system, he said.

Why Lead: New Delhi, Oct. 2 (UNI). Delhi police have put their men and machines to "Highest alert" following reports of intelligence agencies that the recent developments in Punjab might force terrorists to seek sanctuary in Delhi.

How Lead: Jayaprakash Pattan (Pune) Nov. 6 (PTI). Janata Party's national council meeting plunged into turmoil this afternoon when Swami Agnivesh staked his claim for party presidentship after Mr. Chandra Shekhar was unanimously re-elected.

As the confusion in the Ashoka Mehta Shamiana—the venue of the meet—came to an end, election returning officer, Bapu Kaldate, owned up his mistake in declaring that he had received only the nomination of Mr. Chandra Shekhar and announced that the election would now take place tomorrow morning.

Another classification is possible on the basis of the variety of presentation in the intro.

Astonisher: This intro is of moderate length, from twenty-five to thirty-five words and tries to arrest the reader's attention by presenting the unexpected, but not of earth-shaking importance.

Ludhiana, Sept. 15. As many as 27 persons were killed and another 26 were injured when two Punjab Roadways buses collided head on the Ludhiana-Malerkotla road near Gopalpura village this morning.

Cartridge or Capsule: This lead is brief and goes right to the point and presents news with high concentration of news value.

New Delhi, Sept. 5. Six cases of AIDS disease (Acquired Immuno Deficiency Syndrome) have been detected in Tamil Nadu.

Punch: Milder than the astonisher or cartridge, its length is somewhere between cartridge lead and the astonisher lead. It is useful for presentation of news that is not inherently exciting or sensational.

Lusaka, Nov. 19, (AFP). Women are under-represented in and misused by the mass media, a study on women in the media has shown.

Historical or Literary-allusion Lead: It draws some character or event in history or literature in relation to an event or person in the news.

London, Jan. 5, (AP). Britain's royal family faces yet another embarrassment from the abdication crisis of 1936, with a London newspaper announcing it had secured for publication the love letters of the Duke and Duchess of Windsor.

Question Lead: It fits with unusual or routine stories that need an informal tone as well as with those that deal with matters of universal interest.

New Delhi, Sept. 29 (PTI). What accounts for the phenomenal rise of the marwaris in the industrial field?

Working Factors

Geographical factors and the social set up have been responsible for drawing the best from the community, says a recent study. The study on Industrial Entrepreneurship of the Shekhawati Marwaris, was made by Dr. D.K. Tanket, of the department of business administration, in the University of Rajasthan. Marwaris, particularly those from the Shekhawati region of Rajasthan, are "unsurpassed by any other community in the world," Dr. Tanket says. The region at one time accounted for 60 per cent of investment in the private sector.

The dry climate of the region compels the people to wage a continuous struggle against the vagaries of nature. Entrepreneurship springs out of adversity, the study says.

Direct Quotation: When the lead is using a direct quotation it should be short and eye-catching.

Mumbai, June, 5, "1 have no other friends except those that are strictly political," said Mr. Pranab Mukherjee to Mr. Pritish Nandy in an interview in the *Illustrated Weekly of India* April 27–May 3).

Indirect Quotation: Instead of using the speaker's actual words, the reporter can say what the speaker said in his own words. Credit must be given to the speaker in the intro. Compared to direct quotation more information can be given in this variety of intro.

New Delhi, Aug. 15 (PTI). Prime Minister Rajiv Gandhi spoke to Punjab Chief Minister S.S. Barnala over the telephone this morning and congratulated him for the prompt action taken in flushing out terrorists and other anti-national elements from the Golden Temple complex in Amritsar.

Contrast Lead: It attracts readers' attention by comparing extremes. Here is an interesting example:

Jammu, January 22. The "darbar move" of the secretariat and other government offices has been in vogue in Jammu and Kashmir from the times of the Maharajas. Mr. G.M. Shah has now introduced the "darbar move" of the detenus as well. That is how a state government employee at Kud put it to ENS on Tuesday.

He was referring to the winter "move" of the detenus from the tourist bungalow at Kud to some warmer place.

Direct Address Lead: It speaks directly to the reader or an interesting subject or one with a universal appeal.

Dallas, May, 9 (AP). Living in Dallas may be hazardous to your marriage. A new book of statistics carrying data from about 785 international cities, reveals that Dallas is the divorce capital of the world with 84 divorces per 1,000 people.

Descriptive Lead: Also known as situation or picture lead, it tries to paint a word picture of an interesting person, place or thing to help create mood for the story.

Lucknow, May 5 (UNI). One could hardly see any crossing or eye catching spot or an electric or telegraph pole in "Kumbh Mela" area at Hardwar, where something or the other was not written in the form of a banner or a hoarding or a poster concerning what one could do to improve prospects of child survival and development, as part of a campaign launched by UNICEF.

Parody Lead: It attempts to play on words, using widely known proverbs, quotations, song titles, currently popular sayings book titles and other expressions to help establish immediate identity with the reader and to bring a bit of sparkle to what otherwise might have been a routine story.

Bangalore, Sept. 1 (PTI). Comet Halley has said 'au revoir' after more than eight months of its tryst with the solar system.

Prof. K.R. Sivaraman of the Indian Institute of Astrophysics (IIA), coordinator for the country's Halley observation programme, told UNI that the comet was now moving away from the solar system.

One-two-three/one-two-three four Lead: This kind of intro is rarely used now. But it is useful in giving the salient points of an important programme or putting important budget provisions. In this kind of intro a general statement is followed by various important points with numbers (1), (2), (3), (4) or letters (a), (b), (c), (d) and so on.

Staccato Intro: It consists ot short clipped words, phrases, sentences, sometimes separated by dots or dashes. It is casually disruptive and should not be used if the facts of the story do not justify it.

Midnight an old Yamuna Bridge... a scream... a shot... a splash... a second shot... a splash.

This morning Delhi police recovered bodies of a couple.

Miscellaneous Freak Lead: This type of intro has a novel approach in sentence structure and presentation, in order to catch the reader's attention.

Nagpur, Nov. 28. It's Kapil Dev, of course. All the idle speculation on the choice of a captain for next month's visits to Sharjah and Australia after the setbacks in Sri Lanka were set at rest by the selectors, here, this afternoon. And it took them only five minutes to decide to retain Kapil Dev for the job.

The formal announcement of the unanimous choice of Chandu Borde (chairman), Hanumant Singh, Kripal Singh, Amber Roy and Manmohan Sood was made by the Indian board secretary, Ranbir Singh Mahindra. And it surprised nobody. Chairman Borde said that no other name was discussed. "There was no difference of opinion, any rumours of dissensions on the issue are false."

Many of the above leads actually summarise the story and therefore they can be described as *summary leads.*

With interpretative news stories becoming more and more prominent in journalism, *interpretative leads* are also becoming common in newspapers. Interpretative leads normally do not quote anybody and begin with a statement from the writer of the story. The interpretative lead gives the assessment of the reporter or special correspondent based on facts of the situation. Here is an example:

By Ramesh Kumar

Washington, April 5. The future of India's entire national television network and its two-way telephone system is under enormous strain. For the launch of Insat I-C the only back up satellite for insat I-B (itself the only satellite to handle this enormous Indian workload for the last 30 months) is now postponed indefinitely.

India has abandoned all plans to launch insat I-C through the US space programme following the unexpected explosion of the US space rocket Delta over the Atlantic on Sunday night...

Thus, we see that all sorts of composition can be used in an intro. Its contents must have highest news value in the story. It must be easy to read and understand.

The Body: After the intro is written, the body of the story will follow in the logical order of inverted pyramid style.

Mention of the source in the lead is inescapable, when the news point is controversial or, in any case, not indisputable. But where the fact is unchallengeable, the opening paragraph may give the straight news, bearing the source for mention in the next.

In such cases, one should avoid starting the next paragraph with: "This was announced (or stated) here today by...." Such a sentence just after lead arrests the momentum of the story. The second paragraph can go straight to the next important point of the story, bringing in the source in an easy manner, so that the story is kept moving smoothly.

In the body of the story, choice of apt words is essential to ensure precision and better readability. The body should be concise and shorn of all verbiage. It should take notice of all material points concerning the news event, elaborate or background them where necessary, but should not be burdened with dispensable details.

The Facts

Adjectives and epithets (descriptive terms) retain their significance only when used in proper context and sparingly, chosen carefully and used aptly. They add colour to a news story and improve its quality. On the other hand, they can mar a story when used needlessly. Further, in view of objectivity, no adjective or any other expression that smacks of bias or involves a value judgement should be used. Language should be used carefully to avoid any value judgement when it is not intended. For example, while reporting a police firing one can say. "The police had to open fire,.. " or ".. was forced to open fire". The correct way to give a factual narration is, "The police opened fire". But when a minister or an official states that the police had to open fire, it may be reported as such with attribution.

Quotations should not be over used and must be restricted to more telling portions. Sometimes a couple of words within quotation marks are more effective than a whole sentence. It should be remembered that excessive use of quotations can spoil a copy. In reporting statements or speeches the safest verb is "said". There is no harm if it appears repeatedly in a copy. In appropriate circumstances, an occasional change from "said" should be considered.

Verbs that substitute "said" are: observed, remarked, stated, averred, declared, affirmed, pointed out, told, informed, opined, confirmed, admitted, accepted, conferred, alleged, denied, rejected, repudiated, refuted, argued, contended, disclosed, revealed.

"Remarked" may be used with any ordinary statement, but "observed" and "stated" may be used only where there is really an observation or a statement. They are not to be treated as normal variants of "said."

"Averred" is legalistic in use and it is better to steer clear of it. "Declared" is acceptable subject to the condition that the person making the concerned declaration is competent to do so. "Declared" must be backed by the strength of authority, not in an absolute sense but in relation to the concerned statement.

"Affirmed" has an element of "firmness" in it and is stronger than "said". "Asserted" is stronger still. The use of these verbs, if at all, should be restricted.

"Opined" sounds pedantic and therefore should not be used except as part of a quoted passage.

"Told" and "informed" cannot stand by themselves. "Told" or "informed" whom? "Told newsmen or a conference or informed Parliament would be correct, but not, "Mr.. told that..."

"Pointed out" may be used only in relation to a universally accepted proposition or an incontrovertible fact, and not in relation to a matter on which views differ, or are likely to differ. Since it is not always easy to determine what is a universally accepted proposition, the use of "pointed out" is best avoided.

"Accepted," "refuted" and "confessed" should too be avoided. "Admitted" is admissible in the coverage of court proceedings.

The words "denied", "rejected", and "repudiated" may be selected on the basis of how strong a denial or contradiction is. "Argued" and "contended" should be used when a serious contention is involved and not when a mere opinion is expressed.

"Alleged" can be used with reference to a statement which contains an allegation or a charge. "Revealed" should be avoided altogether. "Disclosed" can be used when the person has the competence to make the disclosure.

Sentences should assert. The reader does not want to be told *what is not,* he should be told *what* is. As a general rule newsmen should strive to express even a negative thing in a positive form. For example, "The project was not successful", should be written as "the project failed". Likewise, "They did not pay attention to the complaint", should be written as, "They ignored the complaint".

No sentence should contain unnecessary words and no paragraph should have any superfluous sentence. There should be the right words in the right order. Adjectives and adverbs should be used only when they add to precision and economy of a sentence.

Redundancies or meaningless modifiers should find no place in news copy. No word should have a parasite consuming space and debasing language. An accident is either unique or it is not. It cannot be "rather unique". It is like being "rather pregnant". In "widow of the late Mr..." words "the late" are redundant since "widow" presupposes that the husband is no more. One should not write "at 9 a.m. in the morning". It should be either "a.m." or "morning".

Repetition is always needless, at times it becomes irritating. A peculiar journalistic problem is repetition of source. It has crept into Indian journalism through Associated Press (AP) news agency copy. Once the report has identified the source of the information there is no need to keep parading it. Only if identity is in doubt should it be repeated.

The grammar of the language applies to newsmen as it applies to others. On finer points of usage the style book of the newspaper or news agency should be adhered to. Many newspapers have not developed style books. They can make use of the Press Trust of India Style Book with modifications to suit their specific requirements.

Matter of Selection

Reporting the news is a very important function in the journalistic profession. In the modern age, the responsibilities of a journalist have increased manifold for informing the people about the day to day happenings. A good newsman must know that simply recording of happenings is not enough. Today, the citizens are being controlled by multiple authorities like Local Government, State Government and the Central Government. Not only this, the citizens depend on so many non-governmental institutions also. The survival of man is today much dependant on how his neighbours behave. In the ever increasing pressure on the day to day life of man, his demands have also increased manifold. As a consequence of these, the responsibilities of the press have also increased.

Special Things

Today, the newspapers and magazines devote more and more space for backgrounding the news. The total flow of news today has increased immensely. Dependence of the people on the information supplied by the newspapers has increased. With this, the need for accurate reporting has also increased. The surperficial inaccurate treatment of news is full of dangers. Firstly, such a shabby treatment can shake man's faith in the press and secondly, misguided and misled by the inaccurate news reports, man may become a dangerous citizen.

Thus, it is obvious that getting the facts is the key to news reporting. Since the facts are so many, therefore, good reporting is the discovery of right facts. It not only involves the discovery of as many important facts as possible, but their selection as well as their presentation in such a way so as to make a comprehensible story. Since a reporter's duty is to report, therefore he must carry his tools with him, *i. e.*, a notebook and at least two pens for writing. He should also keep a few coins for telephoning at the time of need and his press card to identify himself.

In the beginning, reporters might begin their career in a local newspaper. Here, they might have to do the rounds of police stations, fire stations, hospitals and town halls to collect some stories. These chores which seem boring can teach a lot of basic things regarding his profession to a reporter. A budding junior reporter should try to learn everything about his job. He should try to know about every nook and corner of his town, its past history and future planning. He should also try to meet the important persons of his town like the clergy, political leaders, industrialists, teachers, doctors, etc. Sometimes, a junior reporter may have to cover many events in his town like a film show, an exhibition a political meeting, a cricket match, an annual flower show, etc. He should not hate to attend these meetings, on the other hand, he should always be on the look out for a good news. Sometimes, even a casual conversation may lead to some very good human story. In fact, at such social events when people meet one another and exchange gossips, these gossips may yield some very good news for a reporter.

The reporter should try to possess a good knowledge of shorthand so that he can take down notes and report the accurate stories. The importance of accuracy can well be realised, when we know that today's newspaper reader not only reads the newspaper but also listens to the radio and watches the TV. He will lose his faith in the newspaper as a media of information, if he reads inaccurate reports.

As far as the art of interviewing is concerned, you can best learn it by your experiences. In this regard, you must remember the following points:

(i) You should never go to take an interview without any preparation.

(ii) Try to find out as much background information as possible regarding the interviewee and his profession.

(iii) After knowing the background information of your interviewee you must plan the questions that you want to ask. Of course, during the interview you may not follow the script exactly, as one question might lead to some other question.

(iv) Before ending the interview, you must check up your list of questions to see if any important question has been left out.

(v) You should not follow the tough questioning technique of television interview. You must remember that a television interviewer has a very little time at his disposal.

(vi) A journalist must decide his approach regarding the putting of questions within the first minute of the meeting, whether it is going to be a direct or indirect approach.

(vii) You should always try to interview the man at the top.

(viii) You should not be afraid of talking to important or influential persons. You should remember that their need for good newspaper publicity is as much as your need for an interview with them.

(ix) When you are going to interview some very important person, try to know at the beginning itself as to how much time he can give you, so that you are able to ask all important questions before the interview ends.

(x) It is better if you carry a small notebook than a very large one, which you can safely balance on your knee without distracting the attention of the interviewee. Sometimes, even the use of a tape recorder can inhibit a free atmosphere in the interview.

(xi) Of course, if the interviewee gives you some detailed figures and statistics, then take down these slowly and carefully. Even you can recheck them with the interviewee.

(xii) Whenever an interviewee makes some startling statement, it is always a good thing if you check up, whether you can quote his statement, so that later on he may not complain.

(xiii) A reporter should always identify himself by telling his name, profession and the paper for which he works, so that the interviewee should know that whatever he speaks is going to be printed in such and such paper.

(xiv) If an interviewee has spoken certain things after telling the reporter that these are off the record then the reporter must preserve this confidence.

(xv) Sometimes, an interviewee may make some statement by saying that his name may not be mentioned, so that he may deny having said any such thing later on. Such non-attributable statements are published at the reporter's or paper's own risk.

After a reporter has brought his information he has to write it properly. He has to write something which is readable. Therefore, after obtaining the facts a reporter should put them in order, to make a good story. If the news is very urgent, the reporter can tell it to his office over the telephone. In fact, a good reporter should always keep in touch with his office.

As far as the writing of a story is concerned, it should always be short and must contain the main facts of the interview. The opening sentence of a news story should be catchy, interesting and captivating. You must remember the fact that a news story should never be started in the fashion of an academic essay. While writing a news story you should write the most important facts, in the first few paragraphs. After writing a news story you must check-up the following things:

(i) That you have mentioned the facts and figures correctly.

(ii) That you have mentioned the names with their correct spellings.

(iii) That you have quoted your interviewee accurately.

(iv) That you have explained the technical terms properly.

(v) That no important link in the story has been left out.

First of all, the collection of facts:

Fact Collection: According to a foreign editor, a newspaper must have the courage, fairness and a sense of duty to the readers and the community. Its primary duty is gathering of news, even at the peril of its soul. It must see that the news is not tainted. A journalist is free in making his comments, but he must stick to the facts and realise that the facts are sacred. Therefore, he should not try to change or misquote the facts. All journalistic stories are supposed to begin with facts and develop from there. Of course, they also begin with a journalist's point of view. Now-a-days, a lot of information is received by a journalist by telephone, telex, radio and television so that news has to be selected.

Everyday, there is a long list of events to be covered by a newspaper or a news agency. If the Parliament is in session, its proceedings have to be covered. There may be important cases going on in the courts which may have to be covered. Then, there may be some government functions like an inauguration of a project or a meeting, etc. that need press coverage. Similarly, there may be some workers' demonstration, agitation or strike. Sometimes, there might be a communal riot, an accident or a natural calamity which are news-worthy and need coverage in the press.

A journalist must have the quality of persistence in collecting his facts. However, the approach of a journalist should not be tough. The journalist has to collect and assemble his facts intelligently. A good journalist should try to collect as many facts as he can before he sets out on a story or to interview some person. He can dig many of these relevant facts from reference books or from past newspaper cuttings. These reference books and the newspaper clippings will provide very useful information to a journalist regarding the preliminary facts of a subject. Many big newspapers have their own library containing the important reference books and also newspaper cuttings about important people and subjects filed in a systematic manner. There are so many reference books like Who's Who, year books, dictionaries, various World Gazetteers, encyclopaedias, guides, Guinness Book of Records, Fowler's Modern English Usage, etc. which can prove very useful at the time of need.

Some journalists combine the deductive and the investigative methods. For investigative journalism a journalist first of all checks with his reference books. He reads what has been written previously on the subject. Then he analyses the problem and starts investigating the true facts of the case. In fact, there are three kinds of writers of news. First of all, there is the reporter who writes what he sees. Secondly, there is the interpretative reporter who writes what he sees and what he construes to be its meaning. Thirdly, there is the expert who writes what he construes to be the meaning of what he hasn't seen.

A journalist should never go very far from the basic facts that he cannot grasp at something solid, if he feels that his deductions are slipping. Sometimes, a journalist may be driven to guess work; which he may think is his intelligent deduction, in order to maintain his own reputation for expertise. But a good journalist should try to avoid this pitfall, because nobody wants to know what he thinks. People want to know the facts and the good skill of a journalist lies in selecting the right facts. Of course, facts may be a mixture of what he can discover and what he deduces. But it should not be his invention. Sometimes, it so happens that a journalist tends to get the story which he asks for. Many individuals may give him the answers, which they think the journalist would like, due to their gentlemanliness or because they want to be nice to him.

The Communicator: The communicator is not just the sender of a message. Whether he be a reporter, special correspondent or an outside informant, the communication worker has grown up with certain impressions and value judgements about the socio-economic, cultural and political significance of an occurrence. His impressions are not substantially different from those of his compeers and colleagues in the media organisation and ultimately, they are the same as those of the top management personnel who control the medium. There are some exceptions to this general rule. Some newsmen have left their organisations precisely because of the incompatibility of their views with those of their organisations. By and large, however, the selectors in all stages have certain common bonds of selection philosophy which is unwritten, yet visible in actual operation. Communication is part of the total socio-economic and political structure prevailing in a country. Culture is again manipulable by those who control the ingredients of its social structure: means of production (technology), marketing, finance capital and employment capabilities.

In the first step of selection, therefore, the selector leaves out certain aspects of reality (which is one, holistic, and integrated, although consisting of several aspects). He does this either intentionally or unintentionally, probably because of a set pattern of selection in his mind conditioned by his past education, cultural upbringing, his country's national and foreign policies, his social class, or his corporation's economic objectives. The modern newspaper organisation being a huge, capital intensive, highly centralised and high technology oriented corporation, stays in business to make profits. Therefore, those who work for it will have to select a story that will sell. Is there any coercion on the selector at this stage? Perhaps not. Journalists are by nature free spirits who wish to do their job unhindered by their own bosses or by pressure groups or by government. However, as Gans says, journalists, despite their resentment of bureaucracy and toeing the hierarchical or organisational executive line, are in fact, part of a well-formed bureaucratic set-up that 'suggests' rather than 'orders' specific tasks.

Senior executives in a news organisation exert a certain amount of pressure on the newsmen because like any other business or social organisation, the press is hierarchical in its structure. But the whole hierarchy is conditioned by the socio-economic and political climate prevailing in the country. It is relevant to quote Gans again as he studied newsroom decisions by participant observation. He writes:

> Because news organisations are assembly lines on which people must work together to manufacture a product against a deadline, they almost always generate conformity. Few top editors are either sufficiently powerful or Machiavellian to manipulate the pressures for conformity...Yet they resolve uncertainty, decide which selection considerations have priority, set tones and some precedents, which then require conformity. Senior editors do much the same in their sections (1979-98).

Informal methods failing, formal authority is used to bring the 'deviant' reporter back to the organisational policy track. In fact, 'deviations are discouraged or prevented by six factors', according to Warren Breed.

They are: the use of formal authority and sanction, with the possibility of giving controversial stories to 'safe' men to handle desire of newsmen to get on in their careers, the lack of any alternative group allegiance to support deviance; the gratifications of remaining in the in-group and finally handling news according to policy becoming a value in itself corporations which have direct or indirect control over several media in many countries. This is the age of monopolistic communication practices.

The policy, according to Breed who studied the role of news selectors or 'gatekeeper' in detail, is usually to protect property and class interest.

The communicator in the first step is, therefore, under the influence of the organisation he works for, whether or not he admits it. If he is a person outside the news organisation, he is still under the influence of the business or government organisation he is working for. This factor of corporate influence over selection is of vital significance in modern media organisations because of the trend towards concentration and centralisation of mass communication technology, production, and ownership; and the interlinkage between news organisations and out side organisations including some government agencies. As mentioned earlier, communication industries in both rich and poor countries are under the tight control of huge conglomerates.

The Message: In the second stage of selection, that is preparation of the report, words or pictures are selected in such a way that those aspects of reality selected in the first step are presented effectively. Again, the reporter's subjective decisions play a significant role at this stage.

News Evolution

Development news category comprises 12 sub-themes: Health, education, literacy, transport and communication, agriculture, industry, housing, population planning, energy, ecology, human rights and national integration. This chapter focuses on the coverage of these issues on the front page and inside pages in the sample dailies. The chapter also analyses the direction of treatment given to these issues by the sample dailies.

Frequency of News Items and Space: On the whole, *Eenadu* (436) published the highest number of developmental news items, followed by *The Hindu* (246), *Indian Express* (209), and *Andhra Jyothi* (195).

Table shows that the coverage of developmental news in the four newspapers differed widely in terms of priority given to the 12 sub-themes. *The Hindu* gave first rank to agriculture with 47 (19.9%) news items whereas *Indian Express* accorded first place to health and human rights each 44 (21%) news items, The two Telugu newspapers—*Andhra Jyothi* and *Eenadu,* on the other hand, gave first place to health and second place to transport and communication.

Percentage Distribution of Frequency of News Items on Development News by Themes

	Dailies											
Sub theme	*The Hindu*			*Indian Express*			*Andhra Jyothi*			*Eenadu*		
	fr	*%*	*Rank Order*	*fr*	*%*	*Rank Order*	*fr*	*%*	*Rank Order*	*fr*	*%*	*Rank Order*
Health	47	19.1	2	44	21.0	1	52	26.7	1	81	18.6	1
Education	10	4.1	8	18	8.6	4	8	4.1	7	49	11.2	4
Literacy	9	3.6	9	4	1.9	9	3	1.5	10	19	4.3	9
Transport & Communication	22	8.9	5	17	8.2	5	34	17.4	2	79	18.1	2
Agriculture	49	19.9	1	18	8.6	4	27	13.8	3	48	11.0	5
Industry	14	5.7	7	20	9.6	2	15	7.7	6	36	8.3	6
Housing	1	0.4	12	6	2.9	8	5	2.5	8	20	4.6	8
Population Planning	8	3.3	10	4	1.9	9	2	1.0	11	2	0.6	12
Energy	29	11.8	4	19	9.2	3	20	10.3	4	50	11.5	3
Ecology	33	13.4	3	12	5.7	6	8	4.3	7	15	3.4	10
Human rights	17	6.9	6	44	21.0	1	17	8.7	5	23	5.2	7
National integration	7	2.9	11	3	1.4	10	4	2.0	9	14	3.2	11
N =	246	100		209	100		195	100		436	100	

Note: Figures in parenthesis are totals.

Next, the four newspapers showed remarkable differences in the coverage of the remaining themes. *The Hindu* gave second place to health (19.1%) while *Indian Express* ranked industry second. *Eenadu* and *Andhra Jyothi* gave second place to transport and communication with 79 (18.1%) and 34 (17.4%) news items respectively.

The Hindu reported only one news item on housing and eight news items on population planning. *Indian Express* reported only four news items on population planning. But, *Andhra Jyothi* and *Eenadu* had two news items each on population planning.

The least covered sub-theme in all the dailies was national integration. The correlation of coverage given to the different sub-themes by the four newspapers that *Andhra Jyothi* and *Eenadu* had greater similarity of coverage. The Hindu is less correlated with *Indian Express.*

Correlation Coefficients of Frequencies of Developmental News Items by Themes among Four Sample Dailies

	The Hindu	*Indian Express*	*Andhra Jyothi*	*Eenadu*
1. The Hindu				
2. Indian Express	.52			
3. Andhra Jyothi	.76"	.72*		
4. Eenadu	.58	.55	.88*	

* P = <.01

Moreover, the four dailies show a significant differences in the average number of news items they carried on developmental themes. *The Hindu* carried a mean of 5.85 news items per issue while *Indian Express* carried 4.9 news items, *Andhra Jyothi* 4.6 items and *Eenadu* 10.4 items. Evidently the dailies differed in their coverage of developmental news. *Eenadu* gave more attention to developmental themes and *Andhra Jyothi,* the least. The differences among the newspapers were highly significant (P <.01) as evident from the analysis of variance results shown in table.

Analysis of Variance of Frequencies of Developmental News Items in Four Newspapers

Source	*SS*	*df*	*MS*	*F*
Between groups	892.11	3	297.37	21.9*
Within groups	2225.66	164	13.57	
Total	3117.78	167		

* P <.01

On the allocation of space to developmental news, the data show that *Eenadu* gave a larger share of space to developmental issues than the other three. *Eenadu* gave 5690.5 column centimetres of space to developmental news, the highest among the four newspapers. *The Hindu, Indian Express* and *Andhra Jyothi* followed in the order in terms of frequency of news items.

In the allocation of space to developmental issues, in the frequency of news items, the four newspapers differed significantly in terms of space given to different sub-themes. *Indian Express* gave first place to human rights (20.2%) in terms of space. Although, *Andhra Jyothi* and *Eenadu* gave first place to health in respect of frequency of news items. In terms of allocation of space, *Andhra Jyothi* (21.9%) and *Eenadu* (19.2%) gave first place to transport and communication. Health, on the other hand, took second place in *Indian Express* (16.9%), *Andhra Jyothi* (19.6%) and *Eenadu* (14.2%) while *The Hindu* (11.4%) ranked the three fourth Interestingly, *The Hindu* put the issue of ecology (13.4%) in the second place.

Percentage Distribution of Space by Development Themes in the Sample Dailies

Categories	Dailies											
	The Hindu			Indian Express			Andhra Jyothi			Eenadu		
	Space	%	Rank Order	Space	%	Rank Order	Space	%	Rank Order	Space	%	Rank Order
Health	547.5	11.4	4	633.3	16.9	2	536.8	19.6	2	809.5	14.2	2
Education	168.5	3.6	8	242.4	6.4	7	173.2	6.3	6	609.5	10.7	5
Literacy	168.2	3.5	9	94.9	2.6	10	43.2	1.6	11	262.9	4.6	8
Transport & Communication	525.8	11.0	5	232.3	6.2	8	597.9	21.9	1	1091.7	19.2	1
Agriculture	1289.2	26.9	1	418.4	11.1	4	447.6	16.3	3	785.2	13.9	3
Industry	301.6	6.3	6	309.1	8.2	5	187.6	6.8	5	541.3	9.5	6
Housing	28.1	0.6	12	107.5	2.9	9	130.7	4.8	8	331.6	5.8	7
Population planning	160.9	3.3	10	61.6	1.6	12	11.7	0.4	12	12.4	0.2	12
Energy	620.4	13.0	3	550.3	14.8	3	267.9	9.8	4	735.3	12.9	4
Ecology	640.5	13.4	2	274.4	7.3	6	118.4	4.3	9	196.3	3.4	9
Human rights	226.9	4.9	7	760.2	20.2	1	163.6	6.2	7	104.9	2.9	10
National integration	98.4	2.0	11	68.2	1.8	11	55.3	2.0	10	149.9	2.6	11
N=	4776.0	100		3751.6	100		2753.8	100		5690.5	100	

Ecology received a consensus rank order of three in the two English dailies and a consensus rank order of four in the two Telugu dailies. The other two themes — population planning and national integration received lowest coverage by the sample dailies.

Population planning took the last place in *Indian Express, Andhra Jyothi* and *Eenadu* gave it tenth place. The other issue, national integration, received 11th rank in *The Hindu, Indian Express* and *Eenadu* and tenth rank in *Andhra Jyothi.* The four dailies differed significantly in terms of space devoted to developmental news.

Analysis of Variance Results on Space Devoted to Developmental Themes in the Four Newspapers

Source	*SS*	*df*	*MS*	*F*
Between Groups	116621.47	3	38873.82	9.6*
Within Groups	663601.49	164	4046.25	
Total	780222.97	167		

* P <.O1

Eenadu, on the average, devoted more space (135.48 col. cms) to developmental themes compared to the other three. *The Hindu* (11371 col. cms), *Indian Express* (89.32 col. cms) and *Andhra Jyothi* (65.09 col. cms) followed. The analysis of variance test showed a statistically significant difference among the four newspapers at P <.01 level.

Front Page: Because the front page is very significant in newspapers, the study analyses developmental news content on the front page in terms of frequencies and space.

Frequency of News Items and Space: Table provides the details of this analysis. Not even one news item figured on the front page of the sample dailies on the following sub-themes: national integration, health, housing and population planning.

Eenadu carried the highest number of news items (18) on developmental themes on the front page. *Indian Express* had 12 news items while *Andhra Jyothi* and *The Hindu* had nine and three news items respectively. Even in terms of space, *Eenadu* gave more space (430.5 col. cms) to these sub-themes while *The Hindu* came last with 59.7 col. cms. The Hindu carried only one news item on the theme, transport and communication and two news items on energy on the front page. *Indian Express* allocated only four news items with a total of 51.1 col. cms to human rights and one news item on agriculture with a column length of 6.4 cms.

As many as four news items were allocated to agriculture in *Andhra Jyothi. Eenadu* carried 10 news items with a total column centimetres of 241.9 to energy while the other themes received insignificant coverage.

Inside Pages

Frequency of News Items and Space: The four newspapers revealed interesting differences in the allocation of frequency of news items and the extent of space in the inside pages to different sub-themes or development.

Table shows that two sub-themes in each daily dominated across the four dailies. In *The Hindu,* health (19.3%) and agriculture (20.2%) issues dominated in terms of the number of news items while in *Indian Express,* health (22.3%) and human rights (20,2%) dominated. But, *Andhra Jyothi* and *Eenadu* focussed on the two sub-themes health and transport and communication. *Andhra Jyothi* allocated 28 per cent of news items to health and 17.7 per cent to transport and communication. *Eenadu* allocated 19.4 per cent of news items to health and 18.7 to transport and communication.

Distribution of Frequency of News Items and Allocation of Development Themes on Front Page in the Sample Dailies

	Dailies							
Categories	*The Hindu*		*Indian Express*		*Andhra Jyothi*		*Eenadu*	
	fr	*Space*	*fr*	*Space*	*fr*	*Space*	*fr*	*Space*
Health	—	—	—	—	—	—	—	—
Education	—	—	1	12.3	—	—	—	—
Literacy	—	—	1	30.6	—	—	1	23.9
Transport and	1	12.9	2	27.1	1	69.4	1	18.4
Agriculture	—	—	1	6.4	4	214.8	4	84.7
Industry	—	—	—	—	1	34.7	2	61.6
Housing	—	—	—	—	—	—	—	—
Population planning	—	—	—	—	—	—	—	—
Energy	2	46.8	1	20.2	2	45.5	10	241.9
Ecology	—	—	2	63.6	—	—	—	—
Human rights	—	—	4	51.1	1	22.2	—	—
National integration	—	—	—	—	—	—	—	—
N =	3 (1.2%)	59.7 (1.3%)	12 (5.7%)	241.3 (6.4%)	9 (4.6%)	386.6 (14.0%)	18 (4.1%)	430.5 (7.6%)

Percentage Distribution of Frequency of News Items and Space by Development Themes in Inside Pages

Categories	*Dailies*							
	The Hindu		*Indian Express*		*Andhra Jyothi*		*Eenadu*	
	fr	*Space*	*fr*	*Space*	*fr*	*Space*	*fr*	*Space*
Health	19.3	11.6	22.3	18.0	28.0	22.9	19.4	15.4
Education	4.1	3.6	8.6	6.6	4.3	7.4	11.7	11.6
Literacy	3.7	3.6	1.6	1.8	1.6	1.8	4.3	4.5
Transport and Communication	8.6	10.9	7.6	5.8	17.7	22.5	18.7	20.4
Agriculture	20.2	27.3	8.6	11.7	12.4	9.9	10.5	13.3
Industry	5.8	6.4	10.1	8.8	7.5	6.5	8.1	9.1
Housing	0.4	0.6	3.0	3.1	2.7	5.6	4.8	6.3
Population planning	3.3	3.4	2.0	1.7	1.1	0.6	0.5	0.2
Energy	11.9	13.1	9.2	15.2	9.7	9.5	9.6	9.6
Ecology	12.8	12.6	5.2	5.2	4.3	5.0	3.6	3.7
Human rights	7.0	4.8	20.2	20.2	8.6	6.0	5.5	3.1
National integration	2.9	2.1	1.6	1.9	2.1	2.3	3.3	2.9
N=	(243)	(4716.3)	(197)	(3510.2)	(186)	(2347.3)	(418)	5260.1)

Note: Figure in parentheses are column totals.

In the allocation of space, *The Hindu* gave more space to agriculture (27.3%), followed by ecology (13.1%). *Indian Express* allocated more space (20.2%) to human rights while *Andhra Jyothi* gave more space (22.9%) to health. *Eenadu* gave more space (20.4%) to transport and communication. Three sub-themes—literacy, population planning and national integration received less than 5 per cent in terms of number of news items and allocated space.

The Location: We have also analysed news coverage by geographical category *(i.e.,* local, state, national and foreign) to determine the significance assigned by the sample dailies to these 12 sub-themes.

Local Nexus: Table provides date about the coverage of local news on development in the inside pages. The data reveal that *Eenadu* carried the highest number of news items (24*), followed by *Andhra Jyothi* (108). However, *The Hindu* and *Indian Express* carried 38 and 46 news items respectively.

Three newspapers, *The Hindu, Indian Express* and *Andhra Jyothi,* gave prominence to health theme in the inside newspaper columns by carrying the highest number of news items. But, *Eenadu* gave transport and communication the first place. Between the two Telugu dailies, *Andhra Jyothi* gave prominence to the sub-theme health followed by transport and communication whereas the reverse was the case in *Eenadu.*

Population planning received less coverage in all the newspapers. *The Hindu* published only one news item with 8.4 col. cms whereas *Indian Express* gave one news item with a length of 4.4 col. cms. *Andhra Jyothi* carried one news item with 5.4 col. cms on the sub-theme. *Eenadu* did not allocate even news item to the theme although the paper carried the highest number of developmental news items in the local news category as compared to other dailies.

Distribution of Frequency of News Items and Allocation of Space to Local News by Development Themes in Inside Pages

Categories	*The Hindu*		*Indian Express*		*Andhra Jyothi*		*Eenadu*	
	fr	*Space*	*fr*	*Space*	*fr*	*Space*	*fr*	*Space*
Health	18	159.9	16	109.3	37	393.3	59	571.9
Education	2	38.2	9	46.8	4	135.0	34	4.6.3
Literacy	1	18.1	2	34.3	3	43.2	15	197.2
Transport and	4	55.4	6	80.2	26	428.6	65	907.7
Agriculture	3	38.1	2	22.6	10	108.6	20	243.2
Industry	1	24.6	3	23.9	4	41.0	8	103.9
Housing	—	—	2	21.4	5	130.7	14	244.1
Population planning	1	8.4	1	4.4	1	5.4	—	—
Energy	2	29.3	1	32.2	3	22.5	6	77.9
Ecology	2	13.6	1	25.7	5	95.6	7	121.6
Human rights	1	6.2	2	10.7	8	84.2	9	58.0
National integration	3	40.2	1	8.1	2	18.3	11	120.1
N=	38	432.0 (15.4%)	46	419.6 (22%)	108	1506.4 (55.4%)	248	3051.9 (56.9%)

State News: Table provides data on the coverage of state news under the developmental theme in the inside pages. *Eenadu* topped by publishing 101 state news items in the inside pages, followed by *The Hindu* (84), *Andhra Jyothi* (46) and *Indian Express* (36).

But, in terms of allocation of space, *The Hindu* devoted the highest area of space (2078.4 col. cms) among the four newspapers, followed by *Eenadu* (1738.9 col. cms).

In terms of coverage given to the sub-themes on developmental themes, *The Hindu* published the highest number of news items (26) on agriculture while *Indian Express* gave prominence to three sub-themes—health, transport and communication and human rights by reporting 6 news items each. Unlike the English newspapers, two Telugu dailies *Andhra Jyothi* and *Eenadu* carried 11 and 23 news items respectively on the sub-theme, energy. Another sub-theme, literacy had 4 news items in *The Hindu,* news items in *Indian Express* and 3 news items in *Eenadu* while *Andhra Jyothi* did not publish a single news item on the theme.

National News: Table provides the coverage of national news on development in terms of frequency of news items and space. Table shows that *The Hindu* carried the highest percentage of news items (18.6%) on agriculture, followed by two sub-themes health (13.8%) and energy (13.8%). In terms of space also, agriculture received the highest percentage (23.2%) in *The Hindu. Indian Express* gave prominence to human rights both in terms of frequency of news items (20.2%) and space (19.2%). Health received second place in *Indian Express* in terms of frequency of news items (17.3%).

Health received greater coverage in *Andhra Jyothi* both in terms of frequency of news items (22.2%) and space (18.4). Agriculture came second in *Andhra Jyothi* with 19.4% of news items and 16 per cent of space. Quite contrary to other three papers, *Eenadu* give first place to energy by allocating 31.3 per cent of news items and 37.3 per cent of space.

Distribution of Frequency of News Items and Allocation of Space to Static News by Development Themes in Inside Pages

Categories	*Dailies*							
	The Hindu		*Indian Express*		*Andhra Jyothi*		*Eenadu*	
	fr	*Space*	*fr*	*Space*	*fr*	*Space*	*fr*	*Space*
Health	12	176.1	6	49.6	6	58.7	8	120.1
Education	3	35.5	3	29.7	4	38.0	13	186.9
Literacy	4	113.5	1	16.6	—	—	3	62.4
Transport & Communication	10	267.2	6	94.1	6	110.7	9	131.2
Agriculture	26	786.2	5	126.4	1 0	277.8	20	459.9
Industry	4	124.8	4	26.6	—	—	1	13.1
Human rights	2	24.0	6	77.9	3	35.0	4	29.7
National integration	—	—	—	—	—	—	—	—
N =	(34.1%) 84	(43.5%) 2078.4	(17.2%) 36	(13.6%) 510.5	(23.6%) 46	(29.3%) 800.0	(23.2%) 101	(30.5%) 1738.9

Percentage Distribution of Frequency of News Items and Space to National News by Development Themes in Inside Pages

Categories	*Dailies*							
	The Hindu		*Indian Express*		*Andhra Jyothi*		*Eenadu*	
	fr	*Space*	*fr*	*Space*	*fr*	*Space*	*fr*	*Space*
Health	13.8	10.6	17.3	17.6	22.2	18.4	14.9	11.3
Education	4.9	4.9	5.8	6.6	—	—	3.0	2.2
Literacy	3.9	1.9	0.9	1.7	—	—	1.5	0.4
Transport & Communication	6.8	7.6	4.8	2.5	5.6	15.3	5.9	6.9
Agriculture	18.6	23.2	8.7	8.9	19.4	16.0	8.9	7.9
Industry	8.8	8.0	12.6	10.3	13.9	14.9	17.9	20.2
Housing	0.9	1.4	1.9	1.6	—	—	1.5	0.9
Population planning	5.9	6.4	1.9	1.6	2.8	1.7	—	—
Energy	13.8	15.3	14.4	18.0	16.6	14.4	31.3	7.3
Ecology	11.8	12.3	9.6	9.6	5.6	4.3	5.9	5.6
Human rights	6.9	5.3	20.2	19.2	8.3	5.3	4.6	3.4
National integration	3.9	3.0	1.9	2.4	5.6	9.7	4.6	4.1
N =	(102)	(1908.9)	(104)	(2503.8)	(36)	(382.7)	(67)	(743.0)

Note: Figure in parentheses are column totals.

Distribution of Frequency of News Items and Allocation of Space to Foreign News by Development Themes in Inside Pages

Categories	*Dailies*							
	The Hindu		*Indian Express*		*Andhra Jyothi*		*Eenadu*	
	fr	*Space*	*fr*	*Space*	*fr*	*Space*	*fr*	*Space*
Health	3	9.8	4	33.2	1	14.5	4	33.3
Education	—	—	—	—	—	—	—	—
Literacy	—	—	—	—	—	—	—	—
Transport & Communication	10	59.2	—	—	—	—	1	2.5
Agriculture	1	22.6	2	44.5	—	—	2	22.6
Industry	—	—	—	—	—	—	1	13.6
Housing	—	—	2	49.3	—	—	—	
Population planning	1	30.0 —	—	—	—		2	12.4
Energy	—	—	—	—	—	—	—	—
Ecology	9	139.8	—	—	1	6.0	3	20.6
Human rights	7	94.5	15	190.8	3	24.2	7	51.6
National integration	—	—	—	—	—	—	—	—
N =	22	355.9	23	317.8	5	44.8	20	156.6

Eenadu placed industry in the second place by allocating 17.9 per cent of news items and 20.2 per cent of area of space.

Foreign News: Table shows the nature of developmental news coverage under the foreign news coverage.

Indian Express carried more news items (23), followed by *The Hindu* (22), *Eenadu* (20), and *Andhra Jyothi* (5). But in terms of space, *The Hindu* allocated more column centimetres of space (355.9), followed by *Indian Express* (317.8), *Eenadu* (156.6) and *Andhra Jyothi* (44.8). Health and human rights figured prominently in foreign news in the four newspapers.

Health had received three news items in *The Hindu* for in *Eenadu* and one in *Andhra Jyothi.*

Human rights had more news items in *Indian Express* (15), followed by *The Hindu* (7), *Eenadu* (7) and *Andhra Jyothi* (3).

The Assessment: We have attempted to assess the direction of treatment given to the 12 sub-themes on development. The coefficient of imbalance was used to find the degree of treatment given to 12 sub-themes by the sample dailies.

For this purpose, a three-point scale—favourable, unfavourable and neutral— was adopted.

The aim was to capture the aspects of developmental processes made explicit by the newspapers. For instance, a news item highlighting the strength, growth and positive was adjudged as favourable.

A story showing explicit delay, lapses and conflicts was adjudged unfavourable.

Table shows *The Hindu* reported favourably a larger number of development-related stories whereas *Indian Express* and *Eenadu* published more unfavourable stories. Similarly, *Andhra Jyothi* also focussed more on unfavourable stones (72) in a total of 195.

As Table shows between the two English dailies, *The Hindu* put more emphasis on the positive coverage of development news (+.023).

Of the two Telugu dailies, *Eenadu* gave critical treatment to majority of development news items.

Directional Analysis of Coverage of the Total Developmental News Items in All the Sample Dailies

Dailies	*Direction of coverage*				*Coefficient*
	n	*F*	*UF*	*Ne*	*of imbalance*
The Hindu	246	88	7	86	+.023
Indian Express	209	75	78	56	-.005
Andhra Jyothi	195	68	72	55	-.007
Eenadu	436	110	181	145	-.067

n = number of news items.

F = Favourable UF = Unfavourable; Ne = Neutral

X^2 = 18.7 P <:01 (df=6)

Stories by emphasising negative references (-.067). Although, *Andhra Jyothi* covered fewer development stories, the emphasis was on negative aspects (-.007). *Indian Express* was critical in its coverage (-.005). The four dailies significantly differed in terms of the coverage of developmental news items *(X2* =- 18.7 P <.01 df~6).

Tables show the direction of treatment in the coverage of the sub-themes under development. *The Hindu* carried a larger number of stories on health (12) and agriculture (16) favourably compared to *Indian Express. Indian Express* had a larger number of favourable stories on health (13) and industry (11). *Andhra Jyothi* carried considerable number of favourable stories on agriculture (lb) and industry (10). *Eenadu* carried news items more critically on transport and communication (39) and energy (26).

Direction of Analysis of the Development News Items by Newspaper

	Dailies											
Sub theme	*The Hindu*			*Indian Express*			*Andhra Jyothi*			*Eenadu*		
	F	*UF*	*Neu*	*F*	*UF*	*Neu*	*F*	*UF*	*Neu*	*F*	*UF*	*Neu*
Health	12	8	27	13	1	19	10	18	24	19	22	40
Education	3	3	4	9	1	8	—	4	4	15	18	16
Literacy	5	3	1	3	2	—	—	2	1	4	12	3
Transport & Communication	7	7	8	8	4	5	15	12	7	18	39	22
Agriculture	16	15	18	3	10	5	16	7	4	15	24	9
Industry	6	6	2	11	7	2	10	3	2	13	10	13

Contd...

Sub theme	*The Hindu*			*Indian Express*			*Andhra Jyothi*			*Eenadu*		
	F	UF	Neu	F	UF	Neu	F	UF	Neu	F	UF	Neu
Housing	—	—	1	4	—	2	2	2	1	2	2	6
Population planning	5	2	1	3	1	—	—	1	1	—	—	2
Energy	10	8	11	8	6	5	7	7	6	9	26	15
Ecology	11	15	7	4	7	1	1	6	1	3	5	7
Human rights	8	5	4	8	28	8	4	10	3	3	13	7
National integration	5	—	2	1	—	1	3	—	1	9	—	5
N =	88	72	86	75	78	56	68	72	55	110	181	145

(Dailies)

F = Favourable;

UF = Unfavourable,

Neu = Neutrak

Theme-wise Coefficients of Imbalance of Development News Items in the Sample Dailies

Sub theme	*The Hindu*	*Indian Express*	*Andhra Jyothi*	*Eenadu*
	Dailies			
Health	+ 0.021	+ 0.006	— 0.053	— 0.010
Education	—	0.222	— 0.25	— 0.022
Literacy	0.123	0.120	— 0.444	— 0.265
Transport & Communication	—	0.110	0.038	— 0.131
Agriculture	0.006	— 0.216	0.197	— 0.093
Industry	—	0.11	0.311	0.030
Housing	—	0.444	—	— 0.30
Population planning	0.234	0.375	— 0.25	—
Energy	0.023	0.044	—	—0.176
Ecology	— 0.05	— 0.145	— 0.531	— 0.044
Human rights	— 0.083	0.289	— 0.207	— 0.245
National Integration	0.510	0.444	0.562	0.413

Overall, *The Hindu* gave more positive coverage to health (0.021) than *Andhra Jyothi* and *Eenadu*. Table gives the coefficients of imbalance pertaining to coverage of development sub-themes. The sub-theme health received a positive coverage in *The Hindu* and *Indian Express*. All four dailies placed emphasis on the unfavourable aspects relating to ecology and human rights. The coverage in *Eenadu* was negative on all but two sub-themes. With the integration the emphasis was on negative aspects of all other sub-themes.

News Characteristics: Our objective is to provide a profile of news covered under different subject categories in terms of frequency and space and location of news.

Units of Analysis: All in all, a total of 18,457 news items, 252 editorials and 693 letters to the editor came up for analysis in four newspapers, viz. *The Hindu, Indian Express, Andhra Jyothi* and *Eenadu* during the study period. Of the total news items, *Eenadu* published the highest number of news items, followed by *The Hindu, Andhra Jyothi* and *Indian Express.*

Out of the total 252 editorials, the highest number appeared in *Indian Express* (102) followed by *The Hindu* (71), *Eenadu* (40) and *Andhra Jyothi* (37) in descending.

Out of the total of 693 letters to the editor, *The Hindu* (266) published the majority with *Indian Express* (210) corning second. In the two Telugu papers, maximum number of letters appeared in *Eenadu* (141) with *Andhra Jyothi* (79) in two.

Distribution of Units of Analysis by Frequencies and Space in the Sample Dailies

	The Hindu		*Indian Express*		*Andhra Jyothi*		*Eenadu*		*Total*	
Unit of Analysis	*fr*	*space*	*fr*	*space*	*fr*	*space*	*fr*	*space*	*fr*	*space*
News item	5448	78931.3	3615	54998.7	3928	43669.0	5466	51848.7	18457	229447.9
Editorial	71	1911.4	102	2161.8	37	1206.4	42	1529.3	252	6808.9
Letter to the Editor	266	2054.8	210	1488.6	76	425.7	141	605.0	693	4574.1

n = 42 editions for each daily; Space in column centimetres

Developmental vs other themes: Table shows the distribution of developmental vs other themes in terms of frequency. On the developmental theme, *Eenadu* (436) published the highest number of news items out of a total of 1086 news items in the total sample. *The Hindu* (246) came second with *Indian Express* (209) and *Andhra Jyothi* (195) in two.

In terms of percentages, only 5.8 per cent of the total number of stories in all papers consisted developmental category. Similarly, of the total of 252 editorials, only 20 editorials reflected development themes. *The Hindu* devoted 9.8 per cent of its editorials to developmental themes in comparison to other dailies. Of the two regional dailies, *Eenadu* devoted more editorials to development. In the category of letters to the editor, a total of 86 letters (13.5%) appeared on development. The highest number of letters appeared in *The Hindu* (38), followed by *Indian Express* (17), *Andhra Jyothi* (16) and *Eenadu* (15).

Distribution of Units of Analysis for Development Vs other Themes in Terms of Frequency of News Items in the Sample Dailies

	Dailies				
Unit of Analysis	***The Hindu***	***Indian Express***	***Andhra Jyoti***	***Eenadu***	***Total***
News items					
Other	5202	3406	3733	5030	17371
Development	246	209	195	436	1086
Development (%)	4.5	5.8	4.9	7.9	5.8
Editorials					
Other	6.4	95	34	38	230
Development	7	7	3	4	21
Development {%)	9.8	6.8	8.1	9.5	8.7
Letters to the editor					
Other	228	193	60	126	607
Development	38	17	16	15	86
Development (%)	14.2	8.1	21	10.6	13.5

Allocation of Space to Development News: Table presents data on allocation of space to the developmental theme by the sample newspapers. In terms of the newshole (*i.e.* total print area of news in all the four newspapers) only *7.5 per cent* of the composite space occupied the developmental theme.

Taken individually, *Eenadu* allocated 10.9 per cent of space to developmental category. Other newspapers gave almost equal space to the developmental category: *The Hindu* (6%), *Indian Express* (6.8%) and *Andhra Jyothi* (6.3%).

Regional Focus: Table shows that *The Hindu* and *Indian Express* allocated more than 50 per cent of news items and space tc national news. Nearly half of the news items (49.3%), *Eenadu* comprised local news.

But, *Andhra Jyothi* placed more emphasis on local news in terms of news items and space. However, *The Hindu* and the *Indian Express* allocated only 7.2 per cent and 11.6 per cent of space respectively to local news in terms of frequency.

In the coverage of state news, *Andhra Jyothi* dominated all the other dailies both in terms of frequency and space. It devoted 21.5 per cent of news items and 27.1 per cent of the newshole to state news. *The Hindu* and *Indian Express* allocated a higher percentage (53%) to national news than the two Telugu dailies, both in terms of frequency and space.

Although, foreign news received significant coverage in the two English dailies, little coverage received in the Telugu papers both in terms of news items and space.

Location of News: Table presents the distribution of news between the front page and inside pages in the sample dailies.

Indian Express published the highest number of news items (464) on the front page, followed by *Andhra Jyothi* (416), *Eenadu* (391) and *The Hindu* (380).

Andhra Jyothi ranked number one in space allocated to news on the front page. *The Indian Express* came next with 13.2 per cent followed by *Eenadu* (12.4%) and *The Hindu* (6.9%).

Distribution of Space between Development and other Subject Categories in the Sample Dailies

Unit of Analysis	*Dailies*				
	The Hindu	*Indian Express*	*Andhra Jyothi*	*Eenadu*	*Total*
News items					
Other	74155.3	51247.1	40935.1	46158.2	212495.7
Development	4776.0	3751.6	2733.9	5690.5	16952.0
Development (%)	6.0	6.8	6.3	10.9	7.5

Space in column centimetres

Percentage Distribution of Frequencies of News Items and Space by Regional Focus in the Sample Dailies

	Dailies															
Region	The Hindu				Indian Express				Andhra Jyothi				Eenadu			
	fr	%	space	%	ft	%	space	%	ft	%	space	%	fr	%	space	%
Local	391	7.2	3593.0	4.6	421	11.6	36605	6.7	1553	39.5	17554.5	40.2	2696	49.3	22750.8	43.9
State	896	16.5	12643.2	16.0	575	15.9	7512.0	13.6	846	21.5	11859.8	27.1	1143	20.9	13536.6	26.1
Nation	2889	53.0	45836-4	58.0	1918	53.1	34340.9	62.5	1181	30.1	10942.0	25,1	1235	22.6	12003.9	23.1
Foreign	1272	23.3	16858.6	21.4	701	19.4	9485.5	17.2	348	8.9	3312.7	7.6	392	7.2	3557.5	6.9
N =	5448	100	78931	100	3651	100	54998.9	100	3928	100	43669.0	100	5466	100	51848.7	100

Percentage Distribution of News Items between Front Page and Inside Pages in the Sample Dailies

	Dailies																	
Location	The Hindu				Indian Express				Andhra Jyothi				Eenadu				Total	
	fr	%	space	%	fr	%	space	%	fr	%	space	%	fr	%	space	%	fr	space
Front page	380	6.9	7258.8	9.2	464	12.8	7255.4	3.2	416	10.6	8646.8	19.8	391	7.2	6424.5	12.4	1651	29585.50
Inside page	5068	93.1	71672.5	90.8	3151	87.2	47743.5	86.8	3512	89.4	35022.2	80.2	5075	92.8	45424.2	87.6	16806	199862.4
N =	5448	100	78931.3	100	3615	100	54998.9	100	3928	100	43669.0	100	5466	100	51848.7	100	18457	229447.9

Percentage Distribution of Frequencies of News Items by Subject Categories in the Sample Dailies

Categories	The Hindu			Indian Express			Andhra Jyothi			Eenadu		
	fr	% Order	Rank	fr	% Order	Rank	fr	% Order	Rank	fr	% Order	Rank
Development	246	4.5	7	209	5.8	6	195	4.9	6	436	7.9	6
Politics & Govt. acts	1668	30.6	1	1031	28.5	1	1366	34.8	1	1688	30.8	1
War, Defence protests	300	5.5	5	198	5.5	7	181	4.6	7	253	4.6	7
Economic activity travel & transport	540	9.9	4	363	10.0	4	271	6.9	5	443	8.3	5
Crimes, moral problems, conflicts, etc.	722	13.3	3	524	14.5	3	681	17.3	2	682	12.4	3
Accidents & disasters	109	1.8	8	117	3.2	8	139	3.6	8	125	2.3	9
Science & invention	27	0.5	10	17	0.4	10	5	0.1	12	12	0.3	12
Public welfare	41	0.8	9	28	0.8	9	76	1.9	9	252	4.6	8
Arts & popular amusement	1499	27.5	2	816	22.7	2	661	16.8	3	963	17.6	2
General human interest	278	5,1	6	286	7.9	5	320	8.2	4	559	10.2	4
SC/ST	11	0.2	12	7	0.2	12	12	0.3	11	21	0.4	11
Women	16	0.3	11	19	0.5	11	21	0.6	10	32	0.6	10
N =	5448	100		3615	100		3928	100		5466	100	

In the inside pages, *The Hindu* published the largest number of news items (93.1%) followed by *Eenadu* (92.8%).

In terms of space, *The Hindu* (90.8%) ranked first followed by *Eenadu* (87.6%), *Indian Express* (86.8%) and *Andhra Jyothi* (80.2%).

Analysis of Subject Categories: Table shows how the sample dailies covered news under the twelve different subject categories.

Politics and government category ranked first in terms of the number of items, followed by arts and popular amusements and crimes, moral problems.

Each of the four newspapers allocated 60 per cent or more to these three categories put together.

Correlation Coefficients of Frequencies of News Items by Subject Categories among Four Sample Dailies

			The Hindu	*Indian Express*	*Andhra Jyothi*	*Eenadu*
1.	The Hindu					
2.	Indian Express	98				
3.	Andhra Jyothi	66*				
4.	Eenadu	.49	.5	.75*		

*P < .01

As can be seen, development subject category ranked sixth in three newspapers which *The Hindu* ranked in seventh place in terms of coverage.

Science and invention took 10th place in English dailies, it ranked 12th in *Andhra Jyothi* and *Eenadu.*

Table shows the two English dailies—*The Hindu* and *Indian Express*—closely correlated (r - .98 p < .01) in terms of frequency of news items on the 12 subject categories which *Andhra Jyothi* and *Eenadu* also showed close correlation.

Percentage Distribution of Space by Subject Categories in the Sample Dailies

Categories	Dailies											
	The Hindu			Indian Express			Andhra Jyothi			Eenadu		
	Space	%	Rank Order	space	%	Rank Order	space	%	Rank Order	space	%	Rank Order
Development	4776.0	6.0	4	3751.6	6.8	5	2733.9	6.3	4	5690.5	10.9	4
Politics & Govt. acts	28334.4	35.9	1	16114.8	29.3	1	18825.1	43.1	1	17114.0	33.0	1
War, Defence protests	4456.3	5.6	5	2742.1	4.9	7	1815.5	4.1	7	1958.7	3.8	8
Economic activity, travel & transport	7393.2	9.3	3	5812.9	10.6	4	2037.9	4.6	6	244.7	8.2	5
Crimes, moral problems, conflicts, etc.	7333.5	9.3	3	6269.5	11.4	3	6631.9	15.2	2	6357.0	12.7	1
Accidents & disasters	736.7	0.9	7	1041.6	1.9	8	1200.1	2.8	8	835.5	1.6	9
Science & invention	374.7	0.6	9	291.2	0.6	11	63.4	0.2	12	94.2	0.2	12
Public welfare	671.2	0.9	8	532.9	0.9	9	1040.7	2.4	9	2765.2	5.3	7
Arts & Popular amusements	22032.62	7.9	2	14254.1	25.9	2	6404.03	14.7	3	8430.5	16.3	2
General human interest	2396.8	3.1	6	3658.3	6.7	6	2399.5	5.5	5	3559.3	6.9	6
SC/ST	173.5	0.2	11	120.3	0.2	12	205.4	0.5	11	282.4	0.6	10
Women	252.6	0.3	10	409.4	0.8	10	311.3	0.7	10	233.7	0.6	11
N =	78931.3	100		54998.7	100		43669.0	100		51848.7	100	

Allocation of Space to Subject Categories: Table shows in allocation of space to different themes in the sample newspapers.

Politics and government acts again ranked first in all the newspapers in terms of space. Two other categories—arts and popular amusements and crime, moral problems, etc., received second and third places across the four dailies.

These three subject categories put together received more than 60 per cent of the newshole in all four newspapers. *The Hindu* gave 73.1 per cent to these three subject categories put together while *Indian Express* gave 66.6 per cent. *Andhra Jyothi* devoted 73 per cent of the total newshole to these three categories combined, while *Eenadu* devoted 62 per cent.

On space given to development subject category, *Eenadu* with 10.9 per cent dominated the other three newspapers.

The Hindu, Indian Express and *Andhra Jyothi* allocated 6 per cent, 6.8 per cent and 6.3 per cent respectively. However, in terms of space, development received fourth rank in three of the dailies.

Public welfare subject category received negligible space followed by other categories, e.g., women, science and invention issues.

As seen from Table even in terms of space the two national dailies and the two Telugu newspapers showed high correlations (r - .98 and r = 0-96) respectively.

Correlation Coefficients of Space by Subject Categories among Four Sample Dailies

	The Hindu	*Indian Express*	*Andhra Jyothi*	*Eenadu*
1. The Hindu				
2. Indian Express	.98			
3. Andhra Jyothi	.90	.87		
4. Eenadu	.93	.92	.96	

P < .01

Developmental Themes by Regional Focus: Table shows the frequency of news items and extent of space devoted to development subject category by regional focus.

Overall, the two Telugu dailies carried more news items on local issues relating to development subject category while the English dailies allocated more news items to national news under development subject category.

Table shows that *Eenadu* (56.9%) followed by *Andhra Jyothi* (55.4%) allocated the highest percentage of news items to local issues in the development category.

Among the two English dailies, *Indian Express* devoted 22.1 per cent of news items to local issues in the development category.

On the other hand, *The Hindu* published more news items (34%) and devoted more space (43.5%) to state issues under the development category as compared to other dailies.

But, under the national issues in development category, *Indian Express* carried more news items (49.7%) and space (66.7%) compared to other three dailies. *The Hindu* allocated 41.5 per cent of news items and 39.9 per cent of space to national issues under the development subject category.

Front Page: The front page in a newspaper displays the most important news stories to capture the attention of the readers.

Therefore, the present study provides an analysis of how the selected newspapers cover the 12 subject categories on the front page.

The Analysis

Frequencies: Table shows the percentage distribution of the number of stories on the 12 themes that appeared on the front page. *The Hindu, Indian Express, Andhra Jyothi* and *Eenadu* gave the first rank to politics and government acts.

Andhra Jyothi carried the highest percentage of news items (65.4%) followed by *Eenadu* (62.6%), *The Hindu* (55%) and *Indian Express* (513%).

Crimes, moral problems, etc., received second rank in all the four newspapers: The *Hindu* (22.4%), *Indian Express* (18.6%), *Andhra Jyothi* (13.6%), and *Eenadu* (13.3%).

Percentage Distribution of Frequency of News Items and Space, to Development Themes by Regional Relevance in the Sample Dailies

	Dailies							
Region	***The Hindu***		***Indian Express***		***Andhra Jyothi***		***Eenadu***	
	fr	***Space***	***fr***	***Space***	***fr***	***Space***	***fr***	***Space***
Local	15.5	9.1	22.1	11.2	55.4	55.1	56.9	53.6
State	34.0	43.5	17.2	13.6	23.5	29.3	23.2	30.6
National	41.5	39.9	49.7	66.7	18.5	14.0	15.3	13.0
Foreign	9.0	7.5	11.1	8.5	2.5	1.6	4.6	2.8
N =	(246)	(4775.2)	(209)	(3751.7)	(195)	(2733.9)	(436)	(5690.4)

Note: Figures in parentheses are column totals.

Development received insignificant coverage in terms of frequency of news items in all the four newspapers.

While *The Hindu* gave 0.8 per cent to the theme, *Indian Express* allocated slightly higher percentage (2.6%).

Andhra Jyothi and *Eenadu* dedicated 2.7 per cent and 4.6 per cent respectively. The three newspapers *The Hindu, Indian Express* and *Andhra Jyothi* ranked development in the seventh place while *Eenadu* gave it fifth rank.

Human interest received sixth rank consistently in all the four papers within the range of 2.3 per cent to 3.6 per cent.

Space: Table shows the percentage of space to the 12 themes on the front page. Again, politics and government acts ranked first in all four newspapers.

The Hindu, Andhra Jyothi and *Eenadu* allocated 62.5 per cent to 65.7 per cent while *Indian Express* gave 55.2 per cent crimes, moral problems, etc., received second place across the four dailies within the range of 14.3 per cent to 17.2 per cent.

The Hindu gave only 0.8 per cent of front page space to development, while the other three newspapers gave a slightly higher percentage: *Indian Express* (3.3%), *Andhra Jyothi* (4.6%), and *Eenadu* (6.7%).

Percentage Distribution of Frequency of News Items by Subject Categories on Front Page in the Sample Dailies

Categories	Dailies							
	The Hindu		Indian Express		Andhra Jyothi		Eenadu	
	fr	Rank Order	fr	Rank Order	fr	Rank Order	fr	Rank Order
Development	0.8	7	2.6	7	2.7	7	4.6	5
Politics & Govt.	55.0	1	51.3	1	65.4	1	62.6	1
War, Defence & protests	10.5	3	9.9	3	5.0	3	6.9	3
Economic activity, travel & transport	4.2	4	3.9	5	2.9	5	2.3	7
Crimes, moral problems, conflicts, etc.	22.4	2	18.6	2	13.6	2	13.3	2
Accidents & disasters	3.4	5	6.9	4	4.8	4	5.6	4
Science & invention	0.8	7	0.4	9	—	—	—	
Public welfare	—		0.4	9	0.2	9	—	
Arts & popular amusements	0.3	8	1.9	8	2.1	7	1.6	8
General human interest	2.3	6	3.6	6	2.6	6	2.8	6
SC/ST	0.3	8		–	0.2	9	0.3	9
Women	—	—	0.4	9	0.5	8	—	—
N=	(380)		(464)		(416)		(319)	

Percentage Distribution of Space by Subject Categories on Front Page in the Sample Dailies

	Dailies							
Categories	*The Hindu*		*Indian Express*		*Andhra Jyothi*		*Eenadu*	
	Space	*Rank Order*	*Space*	*Rank Order*	*Space*	*Rank Order*	*Space*	*Rank Order*
Development	0.8	7	3.3	6	4.6	3	6.7	3
Politics & government acts	62.5	1	55.2	1	65.7	1	62.6	1
War, defence & protests	10.8	3	10-9	3	3.0	5	5.1	4
Economic activity, travel & transport	4.3	4	4.6	4	2.6	6	4.8	5
Crimes, moral problems, conflicts, etc.	17.2	2	16.6	2	15.0	2	14.3	2
Accidents & disasters	1.9	5	4.1	5	4.3	4	3.6	6
Science and invention	0.2	9	0.7	9	—	—	—	—
Public welfare	—	—	0.4	11	0.5	10	—	—
Arts and popular amusements	0.6	8	0.7	8	1.4	8	0.6	8
General human interests	1.6	6	3.0	7	2.1	7	1.9	8
SC/ST	0.1	10	—	—	0.2	11	0.4	9
Women	—	—	0.5	10	0.6	9	—	—
N =	(7258.8)		(7255.3)		(8646.8)		(6424.6)	

Percentage Distribution of Frequency of News Items by Subject Categories in the Inside Pages of the Sample Dailies

Categories	Dailies											
	The Hindu			Indian Express			Andhra Jyothi			Eenadu		
	fr	%	Rank Order	fr	%	Rank Order	fr	%	Rank Order	fr	%	Rank Order
Development	243	4.8	7	197	6.2	6	186	5.3	6	418	8.2	6
Politics & government acts	1459	28.8	2	793	25.3	2	1094	31.2	1	1443	28.5	1
War, defence & protests	260	5.1	6	152	4.8	7	160	4.6	7	226	4.6	8
Economic activity, travel & transport	524	10.3	4	345	10.9	4	259	7.4	5	434	8.6	5
Crimes, moral problems,	6.37	12.5	3	438	13.9	3	623	17.9	3	630	12.4	3
Accidents & disasters	87	1.7	8	85	2.7	8	119	3.3	8	103	2.0	9
Science and invention	24	0.4	10	15	0.4	11	5	0.1	12	12	0.2	12
Public welfare	41	0.8	9	26	0.8	9	75	2.1	9	252	4.9	7
Arts and popular amusements	1498	29.8	1	807	25.6	1	652	18.5	2	957	18.8	2
General human interests	269	5.3	5	269	8.6	5	309	8.8	4	548	10.8	4
SC/ST	10	0.2	12	7	0.2	12	11	0.3	11	20	0.4	11
Women	16	0.3	11	17	0.6	10	19	0.5	10	32	0.6	10
N =		5068	100		3151	100		3512	100		5075	100

Percentage Distribution of Space by Subject Categories in Inside Pages of the Sample Dailies

Categories	Dailies											
	The Hindu			Indian Express			Andhra Jyothi			Eenadu		
	Space	%	Rank Order	Space	%	Rank Order	Space	%	Rank Order	Space	%	Rank Order
Development Politics &	4716.3	6.6	5	3510.3	73	5	2347.3	6.7	4	5260.1	11.6	4
government acts	23792.8	33.0	1	12115.2	25.4	2	13142.4	37.6	1	13091.1	28.8	1
War, defence & protests	3672.6	5.1	6	1950.1	4.0	7	1556.6	4.5	7	1656.0	3.7	8
Economic activity, travel & transport	7081.4	9.9	3	5480.0	11.4	3	1819.9	5.2	6	3935.4	8.7	5
Crimes, moral problems, conflicts, etc.	6098.0	8.5	4	5070.7	10.6	4	5330.8	15.2	3	5662.9	12.4	3
Accidents & disasters	597.6	0.8	9	740.3	1.5	8	825.2	2.3	9	608.4	1.3	9
Science and invention	356.3	0.5	10	242.2	0.5	11	63.4	0.2	12	94.2	0.2	11
Public welfare	671.2	0.9	8	503.8	1.0	9	997.9	2.9	8	2765.2	6.1	7
Arts and popular amusements	21985.8	30.7	2	14198.8	29.7	1	6283.9	17.9	2	8395.6	18.4	2
General human interests	2280.1	3.2	7	3435.3	7.2	6	2209.0	6.3	5	3479.0	7.6	6
SC/ST	168.0	0.2	12	120.3	0.3	12	185.0	0.5	11	252.6	0.6	10
Women	252.4	0.3	11	376.3	0.8	10	259.9	0.7	10	233.7	0.6	10
N =	71672.5	100		47743.3	100		35022.2	100		45424.2	100	

Note: Figure:, in parenthesis are totals.

Inside Pages: In the inside pages, newspapers place all types of news depending on their importance. These stories are displayed with a view to capturing the attention of the readers.

The sample dailies follow this predictable pattern. Usually, to help the reader in locating the categories of news such as local, state, national and foreign.

The newspapers place these stories in pre-determined pages. This apart, newspapers also place news relating to business and commerce, sports, etc., in the specific pages allocated to them in the inside pages. The present study has analysed news on different subject categories in terms of frequency and space.

Frequencies: Table shows the nature of coverage of themes in the inside pages in terms of frequencies.

One notable feature of the news in the inside pages is that both the English and the Telugu dailies show significant differences in their coverage in terms of frequencies.

The Hindu and *Indian Express* gave first place to arts and popular amusements category while *Andhra Jyothi* and *Eenadu* gave first place to politics and government acts, followed by arts and popular amusements. Politics and government acts category constituted more than one-fourth of the number of news items in all four dailies.

Crime, moral problems, etc., ranked third in all four newspapers with different proportions of frequencies.

Table further shows that even in the inside pages, the development subject category received significant coverage in all four newspapers. *The Hindu* (4.8%), *Indian Express (6.2%) Andhra Jyothi* (9.3%), and *Eenadu* (8.2%).

Space: Table focuses on the space allocated to different themes in the inside pages. Table shows the priorities the newspapers gave to different subject categories in the inside pages in terms of space. *The Hindu, Andhra Jyothi* and *Eenadu* gave first place to politics and government acts category while *Indian Express* assigned first place to arts and popular amusements. The two English newspapers *The Hindu* and *Indian Express* assigned third place to economic activity, travel and transport whereas the two Telugu papers *Andhra Jyothi* and *Eenadu* assigned sixth and fifth rank respectively to the same theme. The development subject category ranked fourth in the two Telugu newspapers and a rank of five in the two English dailies in terms of space in the inside pages.

What are the sources of news, from where do newsmen get news, is a question that a layman generally asks. Sources of news are innumerable, if one has a nose for news he can get it while walking on the road or even casually talking to people. At times news comes to the newspaper office without any effort just because it is a newspaper. But a lot of effort also goes into gathering news.

Press Meet

It is different from press conference or press briefing in several respects. The latter is organised by the ministries, departments, business houses and other institutions to project their activities. All arrangements for press conferences such as issue of invitations, background material, decision in regard to the venue, timings, subject, etc., are made by the organisations concerned. In 'Meet the Press' programme, however, it is the other way round, i.e., the press clubs or press associations or press organisations invite the VIP to meet them. All arrangements for such 'Meet' are done by the press organisations. In such meetings, there is no fixed subject and no background material is given. The arrangements, such as refreshments, etc., are all made by the press organisation itself which is inviting the VIP to meet them.

Press Handouts: Press release, press note, press statement or press handout mean the same thing. It is a statement on behalf of government, political party, institution or even an individual given to the press. Normally it is signed or on official stationery or cyclostyled or Xerox copy issued by an office which is competent to issue it.

It is an important source of news for journalists. Joint communiques issued by the two governments, memoranda given to authorities and dignitaries, messages of dignitaries are also normally given to the press in this form. Sometimes it carries the words 'Press Release', 'Press Note', etc. on the top but at times such words are not mentioned at all. The first step to deal with a handout or press release is to read it carefully and understand it. Then the reporter has to find out the important newspoints and evaluate there in the order of importance. Then comes his skill at news writing. He has to write the intro covering the most important point and then proceed to the body of the story in logical order.

Let us consider the following government handout:

Press Information Bureau
Government of India

(46/86)

I.S.D. Service to Belgium and Netherlands Introduced

New Delhi

May, 27, 1995

International Subscriber Dial (ISD) Service to Belgium and Netherlands was inaugurated here today by the Minister of Communications, Shri Ram Niwas Mirdha. Shri Mirdha made the inaugural call to the Netherlands and spoke' to Dr. J.F. Scherpenhuizen, Secretary of State, Telecommunications. The Minister also inaugurated the service to Belgium by speaking to Shri Eric Gonsalves, Ambassador of India in Belgium.

Speaking on the occasion, Shri Mirdha said that with the above introduction, there are now eleven countries to which subscribers in the metropolitan areas of Bombay, New Delhi, Madras and Calcutta and cities connected with ISD network could dial their telephone calls directly. The above direct subscriber-to-subscriber facilities will not only lead to quicker telephone service between India and the two countries for trade and commerce, but will also lead to better understanding and cooperation between the people of India and the people of Belgium and the Netherlands.

The Minister further said that a decision has been taken by the Cabinet to convert Overseas Communications Service into a Corporation. The new Company will come into existence on 1 April 1986 and will take over all the responsibilities of the Overseas Communications Service. This conversion is being done to provide scope for faster growth of international telecommunication facilities and services. The Minister was confident that the new Company will not only maintain/operate the present services but will spare no efforts to plan and provide expansion of present services, new services and also further improve the quality of services provided to the Indian customers.

Overseas Communications Services provides international telecommunication services to many countries through the medium of INTELSAT Satellites and IOCOM Submarine Cable through four gateway centres at Bombay, New Delhi, Madras and Calcutta.

The Seventh Five Year Plan of OCS includes expansion and improvement of existing services, providing a submarine cable system, which will be India's second such system, between India and United Arab Emirates, introducing small dish satellite earth stations for telematics services, a full-fledged international gateway at Calcutta and establishment of satellite communications with ships at sea through INMARSAT coast earth station in New Bombay.

VN/BKA/PM

365/2 25-2-86 11-45hrs"

This is a typical example of a government handout. Many state governments also follow the same or similar pattern with some variations.

There are two major news points in this press release. One is the opening of ISD service to Belgium and the Netherlands and the other is the decision to convert Overseas Communication Service into a Corporation. Any one of the two can be taken as the lead point in the intro. If the decision about the corporation has not been announced earlier that should be the lead point for it is a major decision and the story should refer to the opening of the ISD service as the occasion when that decision was disclosed by the minister.

There is a large variety of such government handouts. These may be about a minister's speech, text of banquet speeches, announcement of government decision through a press note, summary of official reports, text of messages on behalf of ministers, or the content of agreement signed with different countries or firms. Programmes of dignitaries issued in the following form can also be used as a source of information but the story is written giving just the highlights of the programme in the general inverted pyramid style of writing. Here is an example of a programme handout:

Press Information Bureau
Government of India

'4'

Tentative Programme for the State Visit of H.E. Mr. Shinyong Lho, Prime Minister of the Republic of Korea.

New Delhi

August 28, 1996

Sept. 3, 1990

2230 Arrival by AF 181 (Delhi Airport-Civil side)

Sept. 4, 1996

0930 Visit Rajghat, wreath laying and planting of sapling 0945 Visit Shantivana and lay wreath

0952 Visit Shakti Sthal and lay wreath

1315 Lunch by the Prime Minister and Smt. Sonia Gandhi in honour of the distinguished guests (Hyderabad House) 1630 Call on President (President's study)

1700 Call on Prime Minister followed by talks (Parliament House)

2000 Dinner by FICCI (Maurya Sheraton) *Tuesday, March 4, 1986*

0955 Call on Vice-President and Smt. Venkataraman (6, Maulana Azad Road)

1100 Call by Minister of External Affairs (Rashtrapati Bhavan)

1300 Lunch by the President in honour of the distinguished guests

1655 Address Press Conference (Vigyan Bhavan)

1920 Reception by the Ambassador of the Republic of Korea *Wednesday, March 5, 1986*

1055 Reach Delhi Airport (Civil-Ceremonial Lounge) 1105 Final Departure (LH-664)

Separate programme for Mrs. Lho

(When not accompanying H.E. Mr. Shinyong Lho, Prime Minister)

Sept. 5, 1996

1540 Visit S.O.S. Children's Village. *Composition of Party*

1. His Excellency Mr. Shinyong Lho, Prime Minister of the Republic of Korea
2. Mrs Shinyong Lho
3. Mr. Sang Ock Lee, Vice-Minister of Foreign Affairs
4. Mr. Soon Ben Ha, Secretary General to the Prime Minister

BKB: SLK 368/1 (25-2-86) 12-15hrs.

The above examples of government handouts mention the facts clearly though one can argue about the presentation. However, a reporter often has to deal with handouts which do not make much sense and has to write the story by doing some extra work so that it makes some sense for the readers.

The following is an example:

Press Note

New Delhi, Dec. 30, 1983

The Chief Minister of Andhra Pradesh, Shri N.T. Rama Rao, had a busy schedule today on his one-day visit to Delhi. The Chief Minister, who arrived from Hyderabad this morning met the Union Ministers for Commerce, Irrigation, Industries, Shipping and Transport, and Finance. He discussed with them various problems relating to the State.

He had a luncheon meeting with the Union Minister for Petroleum and Chemicals, Sri Shiv Shankar, at the latter's residence. Shri P.V. Narasimha Rao, Union Minister for External Affairs, and Shri K. Vijaya Bhaskar Reddy, Union Minister for Shipping and Transport were also present at the meeting.

In the evening, the Chief Minister met Members of Parliament from Andhra Pradesh belonging to different parties and apprised them of the developments in the State, as well as of the issues referred by the State of the Union Government. Sri P.V. Narasimha

Rao, Minister for External Affairs, and Sri P. Shiv Shankar Minister for Petroleum and Chemicals were also among those present. The Chief Minister later hosted a dinner for the Members of Parliament.

Apart from these official engagements, Sri Rama Rao also met leaders of various political parties during the day. In the morning, he went to the residence of Sri H.N. Bahuguna, President of the Democratic Socialist Party, who has just returned from the United States after a heart operation, and enquired about his health. Sri K.P. Unnikrishnan, Secretary, Congress (Socialist) Party, called on the Chief Minister in the afternoon, followed by Sri Atal Behari Vajpayee, President of the Bharatiya Janta Party. They discussed the general political situation in the country, with particular reference to the events in Punjab. Sri Rama Rao had a telephonic conversation with Sri C. Rajeswara Rao, General Secretary of the Communist Party of India. In the evening, Sri Rama Rao called on Smt. Tarkeshwari Sinha, Secretary, Democratic Socialist Party, at her residence to bless her newly-married daughter and son-in-law. The Janata Party President, Shri Chandrashekhar, is scheduled to have a meeting with Sri Rama Rao late this, evening. Sri Rama Rao will leave for Gwalior tomorrow morning, accompanied by Shri Atal Behari Vajpayee, to address the National Council Meeting of the Lokdal and a public meeting there in the evening. He will return to Hyderabad on Monday afternoon via Bombay.

Just hectic activity does not make news. The reporter should find out what happened in various meetings and get some important news peg on which he could tag the story. Further, there were two kinds of meetings: one with central ministers and the other with Opposition leaders. There could be different stories on that. A reporter is supposed to do a lot of leg work on it, then only a good story would be possible. The handout only says, whom the chief minister met and where he is going. The reporter should use this information to get other facts from different sources. While dealing with press releases, the reporter must give background information wherever necessary. Sometimes major announcements are made by the government through press notes with only a few sentences. In such cases the reporter has to add a lot of information and background while writing the story and give it the importance that it deserves.

The following two paragraphs were handed over to newsmen by Principal Information Officer of the Government of India to announce army Rule in Punjab.

"In view of the escalating violence by terrorists in Punjab, the Governor of Punjab has asked the Central Government for the assistance of the Army to help in restoring law and order. Government has accepted the Governor's recommendation. The Army has been called in aid of the civil authority and Lt. Gen. Ranjit Singh Dayal, Chief of Staff, Western Command, has taken over as Adviser (Security) to the Governor of Punjab. The paramilitary forces deployed in Punjab will continue their work but under the overall command of the Army.

'In order to ensure coordinated action against terrorist activities, which in recent days have extended to the Union Territory of Chandigarh, the Governor of Punjab has been appointed Administrator of the Union Territory of Chandigarh also, as a temporary arrangement for two months.'

This announcement made the first lead story in almost all Indian newspapers and some had banner headline. Background details of related activity were also incorporated into the story. The announcement did not mention Press Information Bureau or Government of India on it, did not have even date or place on it. But this was handed out to newsmen by the Chief of P.I.B., the Principal Information Officer so it carried all the authority of the government. There is another similar example but this time the handout at least gave the place and date.

'Army action in the Golden Temple and various hide-outs of terrorists which started on the 3rd June marked the first phase of restoring law and order in Punjab. The next phase is restoring complete normalcy with special thrust on developmental work. Government have decided that at this stage they should accept the resignation of the Governor of Punjab, Shri B.D. Pande, and of Shri P.S. Bhinder IGP (Law and Order) and induct a new team at the top administrative levels in the State. Government propose to make a thorough overhaul of the civil and police set up in the whole State and revamp administrative machinery in order to make it an effective instrument for development and maintenance of law and order. A high level Committee of experts in civil and police administration is being set up to submit recommendations on this.'

Announcement regarding the new Governor, new Heads of police administration and other senior officials is being made separately.

New Delhi

Jan. 19, 1994

Such handouts are very informal and short, and they need all the skills of a reporter. On such occasions the efficiency and contacts of the reporter are on test.

Similar situations can arise in political reporting also. On April 6, 1982 Chaudhary Charan Singh called just two news agency reporters and handed over the following two paragraphs with his signatures and date:

> "I have been thinking of retiring from active political life for the last two years or so, but my friends would not release me. I have, however, now taken a decision to the above effect without taking my colleagues into confidence so that I may be enabled to live the rest of my days in peace. While so retiring, I carry one regret, however; namely, that although nearly 35 years have elapsed since political independence was achieved, hardly any of the dreams or ambitions, which men of my generation who had the good fortune of participating in the struggle for national emancipation under Mahatma Gandhi's leadership, used to entertain in regard to the resurgence of our Motherland, has materialised. On the contrary, serious ailments—moral, social, political and economic—are afflicting our body politic particularly since the early part of 1980—ailments that are eating into its very vitals."

Charan Singh

6-4-82

Reporters asked from Chaudhary Charan Singh some questions but he did not say anything beyond what was in the handout. The story appeared in newspapers the next day with a lot of background amounting to his political obituary. Related political activity also formed part of the story and there was some attempt at interpretation also. In some interpretative stories doubts about the finality of this decision were expressed and events proved that the interpretation was correct.

Many a time memoranda or representations from various bodies or groups to dignitaries are also given as handouts. When Prime Minister Charan Singh could not prove his majority in the Lok Sabha, President N. Sanjeeva Reddi dissolved the House. In protest against this decision the members of Parliament belonging to the Janata Party went in procession to Rashtrapati Bhavan and their representatives led by party President Chandrashekhar gave him a memorandum which they called 'Protest'. Copies of the protest were handed out to newsmen:

Protest

We have come here to register our strong protest against your decision to dissolve the Lok Sabha. The nation is stunned by your decision. Your decision is unconstitutional, arbitrary and grossly discriminatory to the prejudice of the Janata Party and its leader, Babu Jagjivan Ram.

Moreover your decision is an unwarranted burden on the people of India who had given a clear mandate to the Janata Party for a period of five years and who after the fall of the Charan Singh Government were eagerly looking forward to a period of sound and purposeful administration under Babu Jagjivan Ram and the Janata Party, purged of elements which had made the healthy functioning of Government and Party impossible. Legal and constitutional opinion has been unanimous that, after the fall of Charan Singh Government, Babu Jagjivan Ram, Leader of the Opposition, should have been invited to form the Government and demonstrate his majority in the Lok Sabha.

Political opinion, too, has been unanimous that if Babu Jagjivan Ram is invited to form the Government, that government would be a stable and unshakable government and would last its full term upto 1982. Significantly the political opposition to his leadership stems from sections who have a vested interest in instability.

This morning when Shri Jagjivan Ram, accompanied by Janata Party President, Shri Chandrashekhar, met you at your instance, you informed them that you had still not finally made up your mind. Shri Jagjivan Ram then categorically informed you that the Janata Party is in a position to form a stable and viable government which shall prove its majority in the Lok Sabha at any time that you suggest.

They also offered to submit to you a list of majority of the members of the House supporting the government whenever you desired. Your only response was "I am in no hurry". It is astounding that within an hour of this assurance you proceeded to dissolve the House.

You have thus misled our party and the nation. You have flouted overwhelming legal expert opinion. You have exposed the nation to risk of instability and chaos. You have prevented an undisputed leader of the backward and weaker sections of our society from occupying the exalted office of Prime Minister. You have installed instead an immoral defector in the place which legally belonged to the former. You have frustrated the dreams of Gandhiji when they were about to be realised.

The nation cannot but conclude that you have allowed your self to be influenced by considerations extraneous to your duty and unworthy of your high office. You have obviously aligned yourself with forces and people that are anathema to the people of this country. We will now leave you to the judgement of the nation and of future generations.

We have accepted your challenge and are confident that the people will ratify our judgement of you.'

The reporter has to use his judgement and skills while dealing with such cases. He must read it carefully and then work on it to give it the shape of a news story it deserves. He should look for the gaps of information and try to fill them going beyond the handout. He should also add necessary background whenever required and should also take care of other related activities before finalising the story. All this depends on the judgement and the skill of the reporter. He can make or mar the story. He must try to make it.

Different Classes

The innumerable sources of news can be classified into various categories depending on the criteria applied. Similarly, there is no fixed source that is proper for all kinds of stories. A particular source, however highly placed, may be relevant for one kind of story but totally irrelevant for another. This makes it necessary to determine in each case the appropriate source or sources. The source should always be named in the stories except in special circumstances.

A source is hard when the facts of a report come from the horse's mouth, where they are ascribed to the concerned person or persons by name. On the government policies, for example, the Prime Minister or other ministers, top officials of the concerned ministries or departments, etc., are the hard sources. But they are not hard enough with regard to matters that do not fall within the purview of their own functioning. Equally hard are official press releases and briefing by "spokesmen" even if not identified by name. If the name of the source is not given because of certain reasons but the same is authentic enough to be considered as hard source, the following phrases are used to indicate authenticity.

It is authoritatively learnt means that the source is as good as official.

According to *knowledgeable* or *informed sources* means that the source is not official but has access to official information. *According to a source* (or *quarter) close to* X would mean that information may be taken as if it is coming from X.

Often, especially in diplomatic matters, an official spokesman discloses an authentic piece of information on the understanding that it is released without attribution, that is, on what is called *understood basis.* The press publishes it with, "it is understood" or "... is understood to be," etc.

When a general opinion within a particular group with a wide base is to be given, the practice is to quote "circles" for example, political circles, trade circles. Such sourcing can relate to reactions, comments, etc., but not to any hard news. These are considered weak sources.

There are other phrases that constitute weak sourcing: "It is learnt", "it is believed", "it is stated", "it is gathered", "it is reliably learnt", or "according to reliable sources", "according to political observers" or "according to political circles".

Sources can also be classified as government sources and non-government sources. Government sources include legislative, executive and judiciary, and institutions attached to them. Non-government sources include political parties, voluntary and other non-government institutions and members of the public.

Role of News Agencies: Though, news gathering is the job of the reporters, all the news that is printed in a newspaper is not gathered by its reporters, correspondents and special correspondents. Some comes from them and some from retainers or stringers who are not on the regular staff but send news to the paper as and when they get it.

The main source of news for a newspaper is news agencies or wire services. We find their credit lines—PTI, UNI, Reuters, AP, AFP, TASS, etc., with the dateline of the story or in some papers after intro such as 'reports PTI'.

The wire services have large network of teleprinter circuits connecting hundreds of cities and towns from where their reporters gather news and after processing it deliver to newspaper subscribers in their news room at a teleprinter receiver set.

India now has two news agencies or wire services—PTI (Press Trust of India) and UNI (United News of India). Both have a language wing Univarta (of UNI) and BHASHA (of PTI). There were two multilingual wire services with Hindi as base language—Hindustan Samachar and Samachar Bharti. During the internal emergency declared in 1975 all the four were merged by government into Samachar. But the status quo ante was restored and the four agencies again revived by the Janata Government. Because of poor management and inadequate support from the press, the two language agencies—Hindustan Samachar and Samachar Bharti have collapsed. Though, not yet liquidated they are dead for all practical purposes.

News agencies should not be confused with newspaper agents also called news agents. A news agent sells newspapers and periodicals. Similarly, a name such as Central News Agency, can also be confusing. It may not be a news agency but a news agent supplying newspapers and magazines to homes or at their show room.

News agencies or wire services do not sell newspapers but they collect and sell news to newspapers. They also have reporters, sub-editors, news editors, special correspondents and foreign correspondents. News agency desk processes copy from reporters and foreign news agencies not for printing but for creeding to newspapers on their teleprinter network. News agency copy is also called *creed* in the newspaper news room.

From Electronic Media: Besides these sources, namely reporting staff and the wire services, monitoring of radio and television stations also serves as source of news. Almost all newspapers have a provision for monitoring to check whether they have all important news items. Radio and television are regularly monitored by news agencies also and sometimes prove of great help.

Then, there are press releases that directly reach newspaper offices. They are either passed on to the reporters or handled by he desk depending on the discretion of the news editor.

The telephone also at times serves as a news source as somebody from the site of an accident may ring up a newspaper office and give a tip which would be later followed by reporters.

Besides these sources that are normally reflected in the byline or credit line, there are other classifications of news sources which find mention in the intro or body of the story and indicate from where or how the news has come to the reporter. These include:

Press Release or Handout: Signed or unsigned statement issued by a government department, civic body, political party, institution or organisation released to the press is called press release, press note, or press handout.

Press Conference or Briefing: A formal conference of pressmen invited by a dignitary in which after initial announcement he answers questions of newsmen. It is also called news conference.

Press briefing is similar to press conference in that newsmen are told something and they can ask questions. The difference is that briefing is done by a spokesman who is authorised to make a statement and answer questions on behalf of a dignitary, department or party.

A Prime Minister holds a press conference, while a spokesman of the Prime Minister's secretariat or a spokesman of the external affairs ministry briefs the press. A party president addresses a press conference while a party general secretary briefs the press. But the president of the party may brief the press on the proceedings of national convention of the party. Similarly, the Prime Minister may brief newsmen on proceedings of a summit conference or he may brief Indian newsmen travelling with him about what transpired between him and the head of the host state.

Formal Aspects: There is a very thin dividing line between them, press conference sounds more formal while briefing is less formal.

Interview: Interview is also growing in importance these days. More and more news items are based on interviews of dignitaries. Sometimes even news agencies creed stories based on interviews which are to be published by some paper or magazine.

Legislatures: Legislatures and civic bodies when in session become major sources of news. When Parliament is in session all government decisions are announced in Parliament. Similar is the case of state legislatures and civic bodies.

Courts: All courts serve as sources of news. Proceedings of various courts on important cases and important judgements by High Courts and the Supreme Court come in the news.

Conferences, Seminars and Symposia: These are also sources of news depending on the subject and organisation involved.

Speeches: Speeches in legislatures, in seminars and conferences, public meetings, diplomatic dinners and bodies like UN form a major source of news.

Reports: Official reports published by government and sometimes by other institutions also serve as source of news. Besides, eye witnesses at the site of a crime or accident, police, hospital staff and district authorities also serve as sources of news. In international coverage UN and related bodies are also important news sources, along with other countries' government, political and non-government sources.

There is division of labour in the reporting staff. The units allotted to reporters and special correspondents are called beats. A reporter may be in-charge of police, crime news or hospital news so the police, crime or hospitals will be his beat. Reporters can have more than one beat. In fact all the government departments, political parties and institutions where news is expected are listed and distributed as beats among the reporting staff.

The allotted beat is the responsibility of the concerned reporter and he should make arrangements to get all the news from his beat. If activity is such that he cannot cope with it alone he has to ask the news editor or chief reporter for additional hands, but if he misses something and if it is carried by the rival paper he will come under fire from his superiors.

In his beat, the reporter will have to look for his own sources which could be relied on. He cannot be present all the time but he has to be in touch with key persons who inform the press and those who have information and also those who are in a decision-making capacity. Regular contact with these people ensures routine coverage of the beat and may at times help in getting something exclusive which may not appear in any other newspaper. Big news which is broken by a reporter is called scoop. A reporter cannot have scoops everyday but if he is regular at his beat he will not miss a scoop when it is possible to get one.

3

Elements of News

In common parlance of news is what is new. News is what everyone wants to know about. A newspaper office's main concern is to gather and report news-local, state, regional, national, and international. The basic understanding about news is essential for any editorial work in a newspaper/news agency or a news magazine. In this chapter, we shall define news and try to understand all the elements which make news.

We shall also discuss at length the significance of "news values" for a reporter. The sources of news are very important for a journalist. Therefore, we shall discuss the characteristics of various news sources in this chapter.

Before you proceed further, try to find out what you mean by news. Have you ever though about the nature of news? You must be listening to radio to update yourself with the happening of the country and the World. You must also be reading newspapers. Why do you read them? Your answer may be "to get information". And without the information you may feel that you are lost to the World. You would not be able to relate yourself with the society-politically, socially and economically.

You would not like to read Monday's newspaper on Thursday to update yourself. Do you? Of course, we go back to the old newspapers to confirm certain information, but definitely, in general, we do not do that everyday.

There are several definitions of news. News may be defined as "anything timely that interests a large number of persons, and the best news is that which has the greatest interest for the greatest number". In other words, the news is the timely report of events, facts, and opinions and interests a significant number of people. The news is a new piece of information about a significant and recent events that affects the audience and is of interest to them.

Having situated ourselves in the world of the 'news', let us now try to put all our ideas and understanding of the news and see if we can have a definition of the news.

Now, we shall present to you some definitions, of the news. But a world of caution. You will surely find them almost comprehensive and almost all encompassing-but not complete. Therefore, we must remember that the news is relative. It changes with the changes in other factors related or connected to it. The definition of a news item is dependent on: the size of the community; the periodicity of the publication; the social character and economic base of the Community; the focus of attention or emphasis of the Community.

You must be aware of the famous definition of news developed by Jhon B. Bogart, City editor of the New York 'Sun'. He defined the news like this, "when a dog bites a man, that is not news; but when a man bites a dog, that is news". Jhon Bogart pointed out very correctly that unusual events fall under the purview of the news.

Later, another famous editor of the Sun, defined the news as, "...everything that occurs, everything which is of sufficient importance to arrest and absorb the attention of the public or of any considerable part of it". You must be familiar with the name of Joseph Pulitzer, the publisher of the New York World. He defined news as, "original, distinctive, dramatic, romantic, thrilling, unique, curious, quaint, humorous, odd, and apt-to-be-talked-about".

The founder of the first School of Journalism, Walter William, defined the news as, "...News, in its broadest sense, is that which is of interest to the readers-the public...". The former managing editor of the New York Times said that the news was "...anything you can find out today that you didn't know before". We may provide you with some more definitions but we may do so at the risk of repeating ourselves or padding up this section unnecessarily.

Let us recapitulate the salient points of the news. The News is perishable-when the event is understood and the tension is eased off-the news gets less informative and more of history; of interest to a large number of people; of unusual events and happenings; what is new to the public; an event put forward by a reporter-without a reporter, a news item does not exist.

However, you should remember that the general notion of the news varies with people and situations. Generally, though some of the points about news, may vary, but essential ingredients of the news are universally recognised.

Values of News Items

Importance and interest are often described as news values but in fact these represent the sum total of news values or intrinsic characteristics that distinguish news from non-news. Identifying and measuring these values is usually called news sense. It is commonly believed that reporters identify news by intuition. But this intuition, which should be called' news sense, develops in news men who sub-consciously, learn how to measure news values.

Change: It is a basic news value. If nothing happens there will be no change. But the world is not static. Every moment things are different from the moment before. The bigger the change and the more the people affected by this change the more important it is from the news point of view.

Conflict: Actual conflicts and even the danger of conflicts make news as they tend to bring about major change. All wars and threats leading to wars have proven record of newsworthiness. But conflicts of smaller dimensions like group or personal conflicts resulting in crimes, strike and demonstrations, etc., also make news.

Even conflicting ideas and resulting debates make up news. Tension and suspense often associated with conflicts are also regarded a news values.

Disaster: Be it a result of natural calamity like an earthquake or a volcano eruption or be it a man made event like the Bhopal gas tragedy or the Kanishka crash-disasters always make news. It is also true of disasters of lesser dimensions like boat tragedies, small acts of sabotage resulting in loss of life or property or both.

Progress: Progress is also a news value as it is the positive result of efforts made by society. It improves quality of life. Through routine struggles of life frequently emerge shining successes. From laboratories after years of work emerge new devices, new inventions, new remedies. All this and its various dimensions make news.

Consequence: The immediate and long-term consequence of an event also makes news. The more people it affects the greater the consequence. Fear of consequences of an event also makes news. Thus, possible consequences of a nuclear war makes news and all efforts to avert it and failures or successes in that direction make news.

Consequence also serves as measure of conflicts, disaster and progress. The greater the consequence, the more the news value.

Cause: Like consequence, the cause of a newsworthy event also makes news. Every event has consequences so has it causes also. The cause of a hotel fire may be known immediately, it will make news, but if it is not known all efforts to find out the cause and possible interpretations will make news.

Similarly, various theories and interpretations of Punjab crisis will keep on making news from time to time.

Eminence and Prominence: Involvement of eminent personalities in an event adds to its news value and it is directly proportional to the prominence of the person. Thus, if an eminent scholar says something on a problem it will have news value while the same remarks made by an ordinary person may go unnoticed. When Mulk Raj Anand fainted while speaking at Lucknow it became national news. If this would have happened to a less known figure the importance of that event would have been reduced to that order.

Prominence is many a time built up by media. Media had a major role in bringing Jarnail Singh Bindranwale, Charles Shobhraj, Billa and Ranga and Rajnarain into prominence. And then whatever they said or did, even if it did not have any other news value, got into newspapers just because of their prominence. People were interested in them because they were familiar. A big chunk of news in media is about those who are known.

Timeliness: It is also a basic news value as old news is no news. In a highly competitive world of journalism every medium tries to be first with news. News is a highly perishable commodity and therefore every medium tries to give the latest available to score a point over the other.

Proximity: News is meant for human beings. The prime concern of a man is himself then he is interested in his neighbourhood. If other things are equal, proximity becomes key news value. A traffic jam in Bombay will be more inwortant for a newspaper published from Bombay but may not find a place in a Delhi newspaper. If the Prime Ministers visiting Madras his activities will get more space in the Madras edition of Indian Express as compared to the Chandigarh edition of the same newspaper.

Novelty: If a dog bites a man, it is not news, but if a man bites a dog, it is news. This old newspaper saying recognises the news value of the unusual novelty.

Human Interest: Almost everything in news concerns human beings, but this particular news value is the emotional context of the news event. Anything that appeals to everybody not because of interest in the subject but because everybody shares human experience has news value. Human interest is the element with which the reader identifies anything familiar that stirs his feelings. Crime stories often have a human interest angle that makes them readable.

Human interest content of stories is higher when ordinary persons are involved in extraordinary situations-an adventure, a disaster, a tragedy or a triumph. Human interest is also evolved when it depicts extraordinary persons in ordinary situations.

Hard and Soft News

The news is mainly divided into two main categories-Hart and Soft News.

The Hard news is mostly event-centred. It is a narration of an event. The Hard news items are centred on, "What, when, where and why". Consider the following news item taken from the front page of "The Hindustan Times", Delhi Tuesday, May 20, 1997.

500 Killed in Bangla Cyclone

At least 500 people were killed and several hundreds missing when a powerful cyclone hit Bangladesh's southeastern coastal disctricts today, report agencies.

Official sources said that at least 400 people have been killed in Cox's Bazar and 100 others in Patuakhali. Storm, tidal surge and house collapse were responsible for the killings, the sources said.

The cyclonic storm with a speed of 200 kph pounded the coastal belt this afternoon. Thousands of houses were flattened and trees and electric poles uprooted by the storm. The Chittagong district control room sources said that the storm started hitting almost all the coastal areas of the district with light rainfall accompanied by gusty wind.

Officials said about 3,00,000 coastal dwellers were evacuated to makeshift shelters.

No doubt, the major thrust of a daily newspaper is the hard news. The main task of the dailies is to provide information to the readers. But, another type of news-more of analysis, reasons, background and interpretation-is becoming a very important segment of the daily newspaper. Mere accounts of events do not satisfy the readers. They would like to enter beneath the upper crust of hard news. This type of news is called Soft news. Consider the following news item.

This is taken from the edition of the Hindu as of the Hard news.

Conferences Without Travel

Video-conferencing equipment is playing a major role in a worldwide communications revolution. Time and travel costs have been saved by providing people with the facility to talk face-to-face with colleagues and customers anywhere in the world by operating video-conferencing equipment from their desks.

The system, which over a keypad giving easy control over the audio visual link. Groups of people can be brought into a conversation by the system which also allows slides and illustrations to be displayed and common documents produced.

Video-conferencing technology will bring more efficient management control, quicker response time and better use of a company's resources.

It is bringing benefits in many different fields, including medicine and education. In California, for instance, it is being used for remote consultation and diagnosis between far flung medical establishments, meaning less travel for patients and rapid access to specialist advice for surgeons.

Best Product

News is one of the best known commodities in today's world. Everybody who understands a language and has access to mass media recognises it. The concept of news must have existed even before the beginning of the era of mass media. One may find relics of a primitive system in remote tribal areas where people exchange local news during weekly markets just by talking to one another.

When two friends meet after sometime they exchange information which can be called personal news. Letters written to friends and relatives carry what can be described as news by them. This kind of information exchange is continuing since early days of human society in one form or the other.

Everybody will agree that death makes news. If a person dies of a disease or an accident it makes news. The importance of this news is related to the importance of the person and/or deadliness of the disease.

Mrs. Indira Gandhi was assassinated. It was a big news. If she had died of a heart attack or in an accident, even then it would have been big news. That news was important because of the importance of Mrs Gandhi-other factors were there, but the biggest news value of that event was the person involved.

If a person dies in a road accident in madras it will be news in Madras; but if he dies of AIDS in a Madras hospital it will become news of not only national but of international significance. In this case the importance of news is because of the disease.

But even ordinary death of an ordinary old man will make news at least for those who know him and are related to him. It may not appear in a newspaper but it will be news to some people. Thus, we can say that the concept of news in human society is as old as recognition of death as an event and its communication by any means to those whom the event would affect. Revolutions in transport and communication have led to various changes in significance and reach of the news but the basic concept is the same.

In this sense the concept of news may even be older than the concept of God. But as even today we do not have a universally agreed definition of God, there is no definition of news on which everybody agrees.

Before the era of newspapers and electronic media, news was communicated by word of mouth.' Public announcements by those in power were communicated to the people by various kinds of drummers. Such announcements even now dominate the news coverage in the newspapers, radio and television in almost all countries respective of ideology. Radio and television stations become first targets in coups and those who snatch power from the old regime use these electronic drummers for their first announcements.

Though, the concept is very old the word 'news' is relatively recent in origin. In English it appeared as "news" in 1423, "news is" in 1485 and evolved to "news" in 1523. It was only after 1550 that it became "news" and even in 1622 there was Butler's Weekly News in London while in 1685 we had such sentences as: "The amazing news of Charles at once were spread".

The four letters of the word news have been described as representing the four directions-North, East, West and South. News can come from any of these directions. But as we see every day all events do not make news. Only important and interesting events make news. Further, an event itself is not news-it becomes news when its account is available. Thus, Bhagalpur Jail blindings made news several weeks after the event. Similarly, activities of Coomar Narain and Ram Swaroop were going on for quite some time before they made news 'when' the account became available.

History is alsc an account of important events. Bu: it relates mainly to the past. News is in a way current history. Today's newspapers will be source. Material for historians of tomorrow as today historians consult newspapers of yester years in the archives. What is happening today may go down in history, but its account which media gives now is news.

But if new facts about an event of historical significance are brought out today then it will make news. What Richard Nixon wrote about the Indo-Pak war of 1971 made news more than a decade later.

Not only events but opinions also make news. Opinion of former Prime Minister Rajiv Gandhi about arms race in the world makes news. The opinion of the man in the street about the budget makes news. Editorial comments by important newspapers can also make news for other newspapers.

Coverage of the Indian Prime Minister's visit in the media of the country visited will make news in India. What the Pakistani press is publishing about an event in India may be news for the Indian press. What the US press wrote about the Bhopal gas tragedy was news for Indian newspapers.

With these varying situations in mind we can attempt a definition of news: "News is an account of a recent event or opinion which is important or interesting".

Importance and interest are two factors that present unlimited variety and thus explain why an event is newsworthy for one newspaper or broadcasting station and not for many other newspapers and radio or TV networks; why one news item becomes world news while another may be fit for only a local daily.

Identification and Review

You know intuitively what a story is. Ever 'since you were old enough to speak, you have been telling stories and listening to stories. As soon as you could, you began reading them-mostly children's fiction at first, then factual stories as you grew older and began to read school books, magazines, and newspapers.

So you've been conditioned all your life to recognise stories. But when it comes to analysing the components or putting together a story yourself, how well do you fare? Can you dash it off as quickly as you can tell it to a friend? Or do you freeze when you sit down at the typewriter?

If you are or would-be writer who freezes, chances are you have one or more of these problems:

1. You don't have all the necessary facts. You can't supply the specific who, what, where, when, why, and how that are the essential ingredients of every story.
2. You're a poor typist, and you're thinking less about the story than about where to put your fingers.
3. You have no clear picture of the person you are addressing. You can't identify his interests.
4. You don't understand fully enough the concept of "story."

Each point is important. Reporters always should have more information than they think necessary. They also must know what is important to the audience and have enough typing skill that manual awkwardness won't interfere with clear thinking. But above all reporters must have a good idea of what constitutes a story.

It is true that all the news doesn't appears in story form. Every newspaper publishes a lot of information as statistics of his stock market reports, weather readings, football and baseball standings, lists of births and divorces. News broadcasters, having less time than the newspaper has space, devote less attention to lists of names and numbers, but they too deal with a certain amount of non-story material. News of this kind, however, can be gathered and recorded by anyone, regardless of talent or training. The reporter who expects to be more than a clerk must learn to put news in story form.

Imaginary and Real Stories

The beginning reporter, exercising caution, can learn something about "story" from fiction. News stories and works of fiction differ, of course. News consists only of actual persons and events, with nothing invented, whereas fiction consists of imagined characters and scenes. The reporter's goals, too, usually differ from the fiction writer's. Most news stories are designed to inform or explain, whereas fiction is written to entertain, evoke emotion, or stimulate thought.

But the essential elements of the "story" are the same people and action. Journalists can use the analogy to fiction as long as they remember that the people they deal with are real, and the actions they report are' only those that could be proved in court. Teachers of fiction define story as struggle. Call it conflict or merely action; the important thing is that something must happen. Without action, we have no story.

The simplest fiction plot involves one central character struggling to solve one basic problem. At the action progresses, the character encounters obstacles which require further action. In a good plot, the" protagonist may move two steps backward for each step forward. At any rate, he or she keeps moving, struggling against obstacles or opposing forces. Struggle is the essence, and the story ends when the protagonist wins, loses, or quits. The reader is interested as much in the struggle itself as in its outcome.

In fiction or drama, the conflict may be either internal or external. The central character may struggle against a personal foe, against the forces of nature, against society or some segment of it, or against his own selfish impulses. In sophisticated fiction, the opposing force is seldom personified. It is only a situation, with no heroes or villains, against which a fallible human being struggles. This is the brand of fiction that most closely resembles reality.

Fiction stories must include motivation and sequel-cases and effects. So should news stories. But perhaps the most important thing that reporters can learn from fiction is that all stories involve people individually or in groups in action.

Events never happen in a vacuum. People are always involved in them, and except for natural disasters-people usually cause them. The struggle may be anything but dramatic, the obstacles not even obvious, but struggles and obstacles are present in news as in fiction.

In its totality, news is the daily chronicle of mankind-people talking, arguing, fighting, trading, planning, building and destroying, winning and losing, making love and making war. It is the story of individuals and nations, humanity and inhumanity; and any definition that omits the human element misses the point entirely. All news concerns human beings. Even when a story is primarily about natural phenomena-storms, eclipses, toughts, floods, or earthquakes-we write about their effects on people or have people view them. We are human beings writing about human beings for human beings.

From all this, we can derive three rules for the beginning writer:

1. Put proper names into your story—names of individuals and organisations.
2. Use strong verbs—as strong as the action justifies.
3. Write mostly in the active voice, which stresses the actor. Most events don't just happen; people cause them.

Devoid of Overdramatisation

Before you charge off in a cloud of purple prose, bent on turning every story into a drama, a word of caution. No story is more, than an abstraction from reality. It is never life itself. Until it is written, it isn't even a story. It is merely an event, an idea, or a set of circumstances that becomes a story only through the reporter's perception and skill. And ethical reporters must always ask themselves whether they are seeing the "story" clearly and coolly or whether they are exaggerating the conflict and overdramatising.

Journalism has no place for the writer who "never lets facts stand in the way of a good story."

Life unlike fiction, is seldom melodramatic. It has few clearly defined heroes or villains, and even those can't be labelled as such. They can be characterised only through fair, objective reporting of their deeds and words. The "villain" in real life is seldom an individual or even an identifiable group. More often it is a situation that has developed over such a long period that the early causative factors-and the persons responsible for them-have been long forgotten. Society itself-the circumstances under which it exists, its customs, and its restrictions-is at the root of many evils. Thus, the reporters who look for a specific culprit usually are either wasting their time or distorting reality.

Nor should the reporter seek out controversy. Like violence, controversy usually will make itself known. It is true, without conflict no story exists. But conflict doesn't necessarily imply either violence or controversy. For example, a scientist searching for a cure to cancer is engaged in a conflict-against the forces of nature and the frustration of failures. This is by no means a controversy. Even when a controversy exists, the reporter must take pains to avoid portraying a simple difference of opinion as a confrontation.

The Constraints

As tellers of stories, journalists have several limitations. They have neither the time nor the space to develop a story as thoroughly and "realistically" as the fiction writer. Much of the minor action and physical description the fiction writer uses to make a scene vivid must be omitted as unimportant; the reader of news is more interested in the outcome than in the events leading up to it. Therefore, reporters seldom tell the story chronologically. Instead of keeping the audience in suspense, they being where fiction writers would end-with the climactic action and its net effect.

Nor do journalists have the fiction writer's freedom of expression. They can't comment on the action or enter the characters' minds. They writer only what is said or done, not what a person thinks or feels, which means that they often must present action without fully explaining its motivation.

In fiction, the story usually ends when the protagonist wins, loses, or quits. In news, it's not that easy. First, we have no protagonist in the fiction sense, because reporters don't take sides. Second, there are few winners and few losers (except in the sports report), and sometimes you can't tell one from the other. Further, the action refuses to stop at a convenient place. Some human struggles seem to continue without end, and the only way journalists can approach the fiction writer's "satisfactory ending" is by quitting when they have presented all the facts available at the moment.

More than a Story

To the writer of fiction, the story is in a sense its own end. But to the journalist, the story is only a container, a form in which news is presented. And it is easier to define the container than its contents. People generally agree on what constitutes a story, but they differ widely over what constitutes news.

News must be timely, factual information which has some value to the reader or listener. It may be enlightening, instructive, or only entertaining. It may be only in interesting tidbit to store away in the mind, something that adds to a person's general knowledge, or it may be information that can be put to use immediately, such as announcements of future events. Regardless of its nature, it can be considered news only if the reader sees some benefit in it.

Indirectly, or course, the public may benefit from almost any current, factual information. The more a person knows, the more he or she can talk about. People more a person knows, the more he or she can talk about.

People who gossip know this instinctively. And some people-salesmen, politicians, and others whose success depends partly on conversational ability-approach the news consciously with the goal of having something to talk about. (Reporters, too, can benefit from this approach. It they are well informed in several news areas in addition to their own, they seldom Jack an "ice-breaker" to open an interview.)

The Meaning

Anything You didn't Know Yesterday: If it doesn't somehow add to what your already know, it isn't news.

Whatever Interests the Reader: If it doesn't' interest somebody, it's not news. On the other hand, some highly interesting information-gossip, for example-may not be news because it lacks significance.

Tomorrow's History Today: This is a good definition of the outstanding stories and even of some less attention-getting stories that are laden with statistics. But it gives news more importance than the bulk of it deserves.

Any Change in the Status Quo: This approach is based on the notion that something must happen, or there's no story.

The Status Quo Itself: The prevailing situation, which the public may ignore or take for granted, can be important news when it is made visible and analysed.

A timely, factual report of events, ideas, and situations that interest the public-This may be the best definition of all. It combines timeliness and audience interest, and it is slightly less vague about subject matter. And, unlike the other definitions, it says that news isn't news until it is reporter. The list could go on for several pages. But perhaps the best advice to beginners is that if it's timely, something the general public hasn't heard or noticed before, if it interests you or an identifiable portion of your audience, then it's news.

Largely Regional

Telling a story implies an audience. Defining news-which is the content of the journalist's story-involves determining the relationship between events and the interests of your public. Thus, the concepts of story and news are inseparable from an awareness of audience or reader.

You may dream of writing the Big Story that will be read by everyone in the world, but it's only a dream. Even the most important international stories reach only a fraction of the world's population. And usually reporters write for a far more limited audience: the readers, listeners, or viewers in a precisely defined geographical area. The newspaper or broadcast station's first goal is to serve its own trade area. Most stories, therefore, are primarily of local or regional interest. The community-its economy, geography, history, traditions, and ethnic composition-plays a large role in determining what constitutes news.

For example, a story from Cuba presumably is more important to people in nearby Miami than it would be to Kansans. And a story from also or Stockholm will attract more readers in Minneapolis, with that city's large population of Scandinavian descent, than it would in Houston, New Orleans, or Santa Fe. Similarly, a change in the price of gold automatically is top priority news in Lead, South Dakota, whose only industry is the Homestake Gold Mine. And the price of corn means more in Iowa than in California.

No community, of course, is an entirely homogeneous group of people. Instead, it consists of many small publics within the general public. Each of these special groups is united by a common bond of interest. And to build and hold mass circulation, newspapers must recognise the particular interests of each group-blue-collar workers, fans, youth, housewives, parents of school children, the family and friends of the bride. Reporters soon learn to write for numerous publics with interests they may not share.

Sharing Interests

Regardless of their different interests, all our readers and listeners are human beings, and they are alike in all ways that one human being is like another. No study of the reporter's audience is complete, therefore, without some examination of what writers call "the human condition."

Lawrence Durrell wrote four novels, known collectively as The Alexandria Quartel, in which he attempted to demonstrate that in the final analysis all things will be shown to be true of all people. Perhaps Durrell's is an overstatement, but psychologists agree that all humans are much alike, that they are both rational and emotional, that they live in a constant state of conflict between self and society, that they are always struggling to reduce the tension of this conflict.

Humans are basically selfish, yearning for freedom yet realising that without social order no individual can be free. They know they are mortal, that someday they must die, a truth against which they constantly rebel. Since they can't attain physical immortality, their alternative goal is to live as long and as well as they can. Most people want love and affection, recognition for their achievements, and status among their peers. All want to be healthy and most want to prosper.

To summarise, all humans want a longer, healthier, and happier life both for themselves and their children, who may be their only ticket to immortality. And, perhaps unconsciously, they expect the media to supply information that will help them attain these goals. Primarily, people want stories that will:

1. Warn of imminent physical danger-an outbreak of war or local violence, an approaching storm, an epidemic, an unsafe product, or adulterated food.
2. Report developments that promise to extend life-a pace agreement, a medical discovery, improvements in hospital facilities, a new system of keeping physically fit.
3. Expose threats to individual freedom-political oppression, economic injustice, infringements of civil rights.
4. Help them improve their economic or political position-simple informative stories about business developments and the employment situation, or explanatory or even instructive stories about managing investments, preparing for retirement, juggling the family budget, or preparing the tax returns. A political or economic feature even may be a success story about a person the reader dreams of emulating.
5. Describe improvements or deterioration in the quality of living-urban decay, the crime rate, vanishing wildlife, advancements in housing and recreation, changing mores, improvements in clothing and cooking.
6. Tell what is happening or is expected to happen to their children readers want to know what kind of world their children will live in and how educators are preparing them for it.

Custodian's Role of a Reporter

To help protect their audience, many reporters view their role as that of a public watchdog. They stand ready to detect and report anything dangerous to the public's physical, economic, or political security-a hazardous drug, unsafe toys, business collapses, waste of public funds, political blunders, pollution of the environment, racial discrimination, violence and injustices of many kinds. They try to provide information that will "keep the establishment honest."

Because of this watchdog function, the press often is criticised as a purveyor of only bad news. Yet without this "bad" news, how would the public be warned? How could the average person acquire the information he needs to act with enlightened self-interest? The thoughtful editor realises that "bad" news is one of his more important commodities, that somehow he must keep the reader informed without becoming a chronic alarmist.

The first step towards balanced news judgement is to recognise that the press has a responsibility to report progress as well as threats. Arms limitations, cancer treatments, reduced taxes, and shorter work weeks are at least as important as the more depressing stories. Any event or situation that affects the reader's security in any manner, favourable or unfavourable, is top priority news.

Functioning Categorisation

Not all stories deal with life, death, taxes, food, clothing, and shelter. And of those that do, not all are concerned with immediate action. Reporters write many "idea" stories about religion and philosophy which deal with universal interests but which are hardly "cut, issues." In addition to such stories that appeal to the intellect, they write many that appeal largely to the readers' emotions-their vanity (they like to see their names in print), their curiosity about neighbours, their desire for a thrill, a shudder, or a laugh.

How can we classify such a wealth of subject matter with so many different goals? We could, perhaps, talk of "hard" news (that which is immediately useful) versus "soft" news (That which has delayed value). Or "spot" news (highly perishable because of the time element) versus "feature" copy (usable anytime this season). Or we could departmentalise news into sports, home and family, city, state, national, and international. Or we could distinguish between the investigative story, which can require weeks of digging, and the publicity story, which can require weeks of digging, and the publicity release which arrives without any effort on the reporter's part. We could even classify stories by whether they deal with events, ideas, or situations, or by whether they are informative, explanatory, or entertaining.

Perhaps the wise course would be to avoid categorisation completely. But to understand how professionals think, let's examine a classification system often used by working journalists. This divides stories into three categories: straight news, interpretation, and human interest. Like all classification, this system is arbitrary, artificial, and often difficult to apply. Indeed, it is a rare story of any length that is entirely "straight" with no interpretation or human interest. Nevertheless, these three categories are used so commonly that the beginner at least should be aware of them.

This often deals only with events. Straight news results from simple surveillance. Most routine stories-obituaries, meeting notices, traffic accidents, crime reports, and weather roundups-fall into this category. When city editors tells reporters to "play it straight," they mean to confine the story strictly to the facts and avoid any attempt to determine motivation or long range consequences or arouse any emotional response in the reader. On most simple stories, reporters encounter no problem; they play it straight automatically. But on some sensitive developments, editors may have to warn them against interpretation because motivation or consequence can't be determined immediately or because of the danger of arousing violent public response.

The Explanation

This is an effort to tell what the facts mean in terms of causes and effects. Even the world "interpretive" is enough to start a controversy in some newsrooms, where editors may argue long and inconclusively over the definition of objectivity. For this reason, many working journalists never speak of "Interpretive" pieces. They call them "backgrounders," "situationers" or "depth reports," if only to avoid arguments.

Interpretation, by whatever name it goes, deals more often with situations and ideas than with isolated events. It is explanatory writing, usually arising from analytical coverage of government, the economy, education, or social problems. It requires expect knowledge of the subject and an imposing array of facts, plus the ability to put a complex situation or idea into simple, understandable language. Reporters try to tell what the facts mean without resorting to speculation. Occasionally, when the meaning isn't clear, reporters may be forced to quote the speculation of other observers. If so, they must know the subject well enough to pick sources who can speculate with some authority.

Because the line between interpretation and editorialising is so fine, editors often discourage beginners from any attempt to "interpret." They' prefer to assign interpretive stories to reporters who already have demonstrated the necessary knowledge, judgement, and skill to present interpretation fairly and clearly.

Feature Type Article

Every reporter likes to write the story that is thoroughing, and interesting from beginning to end, the story that will still be usable next week or even next month because it has a semitimeless quality. Stories of this sort, which must rely on something other than immediacy for their appeal, are known as feature articles. The subject may be any thing—a person, an idea, a situation, a hobby, a process, or a historic anniversary. The purpose may be to inform, to explain, to instruct, or only to entertain. The only qualities that set the feature apart from other stories are its lack of immediacy and its depth treatment of an interesting or provocative subject. For good examples, see the inside pages of your Sunday newspaper.

A feature should have a 'news peg', that is, it should be related to a topic recently in the news. Sometimes the news peg is implicit; sometimes it is expressed clearly near the beginning. The "peg" is the writer's way of telling readers why the article is being published why they should bother reading it.

The rest of the story quotes businessmen, a banker, a lawyer, and several women on the divorcee's plight. At no point does it cite the date of any specific action. It appears, therefore, that it could have been written several weeks before publication.

Although, human interest is not an absolute requirement, most effective features contain a considerable amount. The reason is simple: human interest, expressed in colour, description, anecdote, and dialogue, is a proven means of keeping the reader's attention throughout a long story. This aspect of most features has caused some confusion in terminology. When editors tell reporters to "featurise" a spot news story, they usually mean to play up the human interest, to focus on whatever is amusing, odd, or unusual. They seldom mean to turn it into a genuine depth article.

Classic Criteria

All news judgements are relative. Whenever editors say "This is news," they mean for this newspaper in this community today. Tomorrow the story may be dead because it has lost its timeliness. Or it may be crowded out of the paper stories of greater significance. We can never judge a news story except in relation to other stories at the same moment. Even then, the evaluation of news is a highly subjective process.

One editor may view the events of the day in the broad context of world history while another views to the old-fashioned notion that "a dog fight on Main Street is worth more than a revolution in Latin America." The first accuses the other of provincialism; the second retorts that the first is guilty of Afghanistanism. Editors are no more agreed on news value than are readers.

Still, no matter how they apply them, all editors measure news values by the same yardsticks. These are:

Significance: whether the event promises or threatens to change the course of history. An event's significance is determined by how many persons it will affect, to what extent, and for how long. The reporter asks what will be the consequences.

Magnitude: how much, how much, how many, how big, how fast. Everything else being equal, a million is bigger news than a thousand. A plane crash that kills 120 is bigger news than one that kills five and a hurricane with 200-mile-an-hour winds is bigger news than one that barely qualifies. The reporter asks how many are dead and how much will it cost.

Timeliness: The reader wants information that's new. The reporter asks when did it happen, and ordinarily tries to work the day into the first sentence to let the reader know that it's new. Priority usually goes to the latest action, but even an action that happened long ago may still be spot news if it is only now being disclosed. For example, any new information about Noah's Ark would be news.

Proximity: A two-dollar word for the local angle. If all else is equal, here is greater than there. Readers are interested most in those events closest to them. The reporter asks where.

Prominence: Names make news, These are generally names of persons or institutions that already have aroused public interest. The name might be that of the president or a senator, a celebrity in sports or show business, or an institution such as Harvard, the US Marine Corps, or the Central Intelligence Agency. The reporter asks who.

Human Interest: A quality that every reader can relate to personal experience or recognise as a universal aspect of life. Does the story hit home? Here the reporter can examine only his or her own reaction.

Human Interest

In this kind of news, which usually focuses on an individual rather than a group, the actual subject is a feeling or an emotion. Writers however, don't editorialise or express subjective reaction. They achieve their effect best by "putting the reader there," by showing the event or situation that arouses emotions or a sense of humour. This is sensory writing, close kin to fiction, and reporters often use narrative organisation and other literary devices. They round out the story with colour, description, anecdote, dramatic quotes, or dialogue; but as in any other reporting, they never go beyond the provable facts.

A story of this sort, if it had been written without names, probably would have been rejected. Newsreporters tend to be extremely skeptical about "great human interest" stories. They more likely sound like good fiction, the more likely they are to be fiction.

4

Editing of News

A newspaper office or news agency receives a large assortment of news items. These originate from different sources. The news copy is written by experienced and inexperienced people and hence lack uniformity. In any newspapers, there is always a shortage of space for all news items, which are received in the office. A newspaper's success largely depends on the space and its most efficient, judicious and economic use. Hence, within the space set aside for news, as much news as possible needs to be packed to serve a divergent readership. Considering these factors, editing of the news copy becomes essential.

What is Editing?: All incoming news items, collectively called copy, is sifted, before being possessed, to achieve a balance of news between that originating within the organisation and that pouring in from outside. The unwanted matter gets weeded out and only the newsworthy stories are finally selected.

The Desk Management: The news room is headed by an editor or a chief editor or an editor-in-chief or a chief news editor. He plans and directs the day's news operations. He is supported by a team consisting of the news editors, chief sub-editors, senior sub-editors. In a news agency, news editors and chief subs looks after the smooth functioning of the news desk. They plan and write 'leads'.

What Makes News?: News has a number of characteristic elements:

Proximity: The nearer the origin of news, i.e., the closer it is to home, the more is its impact. For example, on a particular day, there may be 45 deaths in a boat tragedy in Bangladesh. But, on the same day, a local bomb blast that kills five people is sure to have more impact on the readers.

Timeliness: News grows old quickly. It decays and perishes fast. The more recent its occurrence, the more worthy it is. On the contrary, an event that happened six months back, but is discovered and reported now could grab the front page. For, e.g. the bank securities scam including Ketan Parekh.

Prominence: Names make news and the newspapers like to use as many local names as possible. For example, if the vice-chancellor of a university gets hurt while playing cricket, few people will take note of the incident. But, if a public figure like a minister is injured in a game, we have a more interesting story.

Consequence: A reader's interest is aroused in a large measure if an event or occurrence affects him, and more so, if he participates in the event. He is eager to know what will this mean to him in the long run. How will it affect him and his family. A steep hike in the prices of petrol, cooking gas, milk or an increase in water and electricity tariffs will have widespread consequences.

Human Interest: Any interesting story about people and their peculiarities, and their infinite variety, make for wider readership. The human interest stories are pure identification. These are the little things that have happened, or could happen to yourself or to your neighbours or friends. These stories are worth little or nothing as news in any strict sense. Yet these are worth telling.

How to Edit a Copy?: Ideally read a story, preferably thrice-once for familiarisation, once while you edit and third time to check your work. If the story has no glaring problems and if you fully understand it, you would be ready to edit it.

Format: A news story is divided into two parts-the lead and the body. The lead describes, simply and briefly, what happened and the body documents and elaborates the lead. Adequate attention should be paid to the lead. The intro should be concise and crisp. Details should be dispersed and blended in the subsequent paragraphs.

Opening Para: The most significant information is placed at the top and other details follow in their order of importance. Each succeeding para should add an essential detail without being dependent in content or style on what follows. Next, see if the second para supports the lead. The third para should continue the development implicit in the lead and in the second para.

Rewriting: While editing a story, the subeditor should look for errors in spelling, grammar and correct these. But an instant second look might sometimes compel him to rewrite it. Highlight the news point, taking care to avoid distortion and respect the facts produced by the reporter.

Headlines: When a reader looks for something interesting in a newspaper, it is the heading which catches, his eyes. A story, howsoever well-edited, would not attract him unless it is given a headline. The headline attracts the reader to go through the story. A headline sells the story. Writing a headline is like applying the finishing polish on a well-crafted piece of furniture.

Kicker: Kicker is another conventional headline, usually a one-line heading with a second line (kicker) above it in a different style and half the type size. It extends no more than midway above the main line.

Hammer: Hammer is the reverse of kicker, but, usually, in all capital letters. The big type is the kicker and the smaller type the main headline. One word, or two at the most, will suffice of the hammer. By virtue of their size, hammers impress the readers with their importance. But too many hammers on one page may dilute that significance, and destroy the look of the page.

Leads: This lead is different from the one already talked about. Suppose there is a train accident at a place 60 km from Punjab. Just an hour before the first edition of a newspaper goes to the press. But we cannot wait till the reporter telephones from the spot or comes back to file the story. We can give a short news about it and wait for further details. Many news items are bound to flow in on the same event, details will pour in once the reporter reaches the site, there shall also be eyewitness accounts. All these are tied together, highlighting the major facts and the lead is written for the newspaper's city edition.

A lead is a device, used mostly in the case of developing stories, for changing the story's emphasis in the light of new information of facts as these unfold.

Marks and Symbols of Editing

Slug: A news item or story may run into several paras, and also exceed one page. If running into pages, a news story has to be kept track of from amongst various stories, and chronologically arranged. Hence, these paras, in a page, are divided into two of three parts. Then, these parts are 'slugged' and numbered, i.e., given a label, which identifies that story for that particular day, and helps the editor on duty to bring different parts together. Related stories are slugged to make the relationship clear. Slug is an identification mark or tag. It is often the key word in a story and written on top left or right of a page.

Editing Symbols: As soon as you start editing a copy, the first symbol you use is for paragraph indentation. Even if your para is indented, you should mark this symbol on every para. This would help the typesetter in knowing that you want paragraph to begin at that spot. Always note that editing marks are large and clear.

Editing of Photographs

Pictures submitted for publication in the newspapers and magazines have to be edited to fit into the layout of the page, and also the unnecessary portions cut off, which the photographer might have added in the actual composition. The competent photo editor's job is to see to it that he does not waste space, and trims a picture keeping the main essence of the subject intact. This reduction process is called 'chopping'.

Only a Professional: It is the job of the photo editor to select the best photograph which tells the story on its own. The photo editor edits it to suit the space in the page without destroying or distorting the essence of the picture, and gives it a good display. It is the photo editor's duty to give the photographer ideas about the picture possibilities.

Qualities of a Good Photographer: A good photographer must be able to handle every assignment the editor gives him to his own satisfaction. One has to work with a great speed on a location. You should actually shoot a news event from several different angles, and let your photo editor decide which picture to use.

The newspaper photographs are based on factual situation. The photographs illustrates an event, bring depth into it, and probably comment on it. Usually, the photographer is given only an idea to work with, and is expected to create an appropriate photograph to illustrate it. This is where a good memory or a notebook will come in handy. The photographic techniques involved in shooting for magazines are not much different from those in newspapers. The technical skill is again taken for granted, and your primary concern is to illustrate the story clearly and completely.

Creative Cropping of Pictures: The intelligent photo editors adopt different creative cropping techniques to bring out the exact point of emphasis a 'pix'. They try to enlarge the main image, which will have a better visual impact. A photo editor studies the picture carefully, and decides about the cropping. First, he crops the picture mentally and then decides on the final edited photograph. A badly cropped pix can not be repaired. A good photo editor is one who can visualise how the picture will look like when it is cropped and printed in different sizes and shapes.

Choosing a Picture: In a professional organisation, the photographers leave contact sheets with the photo editors to enable them to choose the right frame, and mark the composition. Sometimes, the photographers send the exposed rolls, and leave the rest of the job to the photo editors. In most countries, where there is competition amongst the leading newspapers, the photo editor looks for pictures from the freelancers as well. He chooses the best picture, and places it in the newspaper. It leaves no bad feelings amongst the staffers, because they also know that their newspapers should have the best coverage. This system makes every photographer work very hard on the assignments, and be alert with the competitive spirit.

Captions: Even though the news picture is supposed to tell a story on its own, one should say where and when the incident took place. Caption writing is an art by itself, which conies with experience and aptitude. The picture and its caption are complementary to each other, and it is very essential to mention when and where the picture was taken, and who the persons seen in the picture are.

If the photograph is described in the body of the story, then there is no need for a separate caption and the pix could hang in between the paragraphs. Sometimes to box a powerful picture with just a detailed caption brightens the page.

Graphic Illustrations: In most coverages, photographer reaches the spot only after the incident takes place, and is able to take only the result of what had already happened. In such special cases the newspaper or magazine might have to depend upon graphic illustrations to detail the activities that had taken place on a particular spot earlier.

However, with the advancement of technology, photo editing is done by the computer, which eliminates all the unessential elements, and gives out only the section as per the commands. Photos can be stored and recalled on the computer as and when required.

Design and Layout

The newspaper composing and printing methods have gone through major changes during the past few decades. However, the basic function remains the same, to convert the printing matter into printable format. The composing methods used by newspaper industry range from hand composing to computer-guided operations. The major composing processes are:

Hand Setting: Hand setting is the original method of setting movable type. In this the compositor works with a composing stick, a type case and the metal type itself: letters, punctuation marks, figures, and spaces. The compositor adjusts the composing stick to the desired pica measure or line length. After taking out proofs and carrying out the necessary corrections, the next step is to make up the page. Since the composed matter consists of hundreds of individual pieces, it is essential that it is locked up, may be directly on the bed of the press.

Machine Setting: This method involves casting type from molten metal. There are four popular type casting machines:

Linotype and Intertype: These are mechanical methods of composing and casting type in the piece lines called 'slugs'. The name Linotype is derived from casting a line-of-type. In both systems, the operator sits at a keyboard.

The machine is adjusted to set type to the desired pica measure and leading. The upper front section of the machine carries a slotted metal container, which holds the matrices and when the operator strikes the keys, the matrices fall into positions to form a line-of-type. After the matter is composed the type is locked up. Any change within a line means that the entire line, or even all the succeeding lines in a paragraph have to be reset.

The basic difference between linotype and intertype is of the intertype of matrices. They can be used for casting headlines as well as body matter.

Monotype: As the name suggests 'monotype' casts the characters one by one rather than as a complete line. It is a combination of two machines, a keyboard and a typecaster. It is a two-machine method of casting individual type characters, mechanically.

To set type the machine is adjusted to the required pica measure and leading. As the copy is typed, it produces a perforated paper roll, which is used to drive the typecaster. A combination of holes dictates the letters, spaces and punctuation marks to be set.

To set type, the perforated roll is fitted on the typecaster, where it directs the casting mechanism by means of compressed air. The air passing through the perforations brings the matrix holder and the specific matrix ready to be filled with molten metal into proper position. Once the type has been cast, it is ejected onto a galley, one character at a time.

Ludlow: This is a combination of handsetting and machine casting operations. The operator sets the type matrices and leading in a composing stick by hand. The composed matrices are then locked up into a casting machine, where they are filled with molten lead to produce the slug.

Phototypesetting: It is also known as cold type-setting, as it does not involve metal casting. Its first phase resembles that of monotype setting. Unless the perforator or keyboard is attached to a video display unit, the operation is limited to conversion of copy matter into a coded perforated tape. This perforated tape is then fed into a programmed computerised unit, which projects the desired images of type characters onto photosensitive film. This film is then made up in mechanicals from which printing plates can be produced. Photo-composing provides a fast, flexible and reasonable economical method of setting type.

Daily Newspapers: Newspapers come in different shapes and sizes. There are newspapers that provide general public interest news to the readers, there are other which cater to the needs of the specialists. Every newspaper has its own way of presenting news, views and features.

The front page of a newspaper should be attractive, which will hold the attention of the readers. The front page is the "face" of a newspaper.

Newspaper Identity: Newspapers have a name and each newspaper tries to acquire a unique identity by observing different ways.

The Mast Head: On the front page, the masthead of a newspaper is much more than just the name of the newspaper. Some of its characteristics are:

— it is in distinctive bold print,

— it is in a big type size,

— it has a fixed place on the front page,

— it remains in the same form for years.

Headlines: Headlines are a means to attract the readers towards the news items. It is the responsibility of the page-designer to make each headline as distinctive as possible. Headlines are given generally by the sub-editors/copy editors.

Placement of Photographs and Cartoons: Picture is worth a thousand words. On the same basis, it can be extrapolated that a good cartoon is worth at least two thousand words. From a page designer's point of view, it is important to realise that photographs, cartoons and graphic have a special significance. Placing a picture or cartoon at wrong place may not only reduce its utility, but also reduce the design appeal of the total page.

A page designer has to examine whether the picture, cartoon, graphic, chart, has an independent value or it has to be juxtaposed with a particular news story. The size may have to be adjusted due to placement or space considerations.

Overall Page Design: There is a design in the page, a form and a structure. Each page designer has his own concept of beauty and page structure. To bring it out, he uses different type sizes, white spaces, placement of pictures, graphs, charts, cartoons, etc.

Pages Inside

Inside pages of a daily newspaper differ from the front page in their format, structure and presentation of contents. By grouping news items on specific pages we are able to give the newspaper a structure. The inside pages under one group often tend to cover as many news items as possible. Hence, often these pages may seem cluttered.

The Editorial Page: The format of this page looks similar in many newspapers in India and abroad. There is a section, on this page, where the editor(s) write their analysis of the major national and international news items. Along with that, there may be one or two articles written by prominent people on current topics. The design of the inside pages of a newspaper is relatively much more structured than the front page, which is dependent on the major happenings during the past few hours.

Advertisements: Advertisements have special significance for commercial publications. The very existence of newspapers and magazines depends on the revenue from advertisements. Hence, special care must be taken with regard to placement of advertisements along with the news stories on the pages. Advertisements are placed on these pages according to the product or service to be advertised. Large colour advertisements have special significance in page design.

Readability: Newspapers are meant to be read. As far as possible the news item should be contained in a neatly defined area. Each letter, each word and each story has special significance. Readability for a page-designer has a different meaning than that for a reporter, sub-editor or proof-reader. Readability from a page designer's point of view depends on placement of the news stories, typography and the overall page layout.

Copy Editor's Role

A copy editor is a bridge between a reporter and the reader. He has divergent roles to perform and docs one or more of these tasks while editing a copy. He need not execute all these functions simultaneously. A copy editor is a gatekeeper and image builder who protects a newspaper's reputation.

Duties of a Copy Editor: A Copy Editor:

(a) Removes rough edges from the copy and polishes it to make it presentable.

(b) Adjusts the copy to the style of his newspaper.

(c) Should carve out each story in a familiar language so that it runs smoothly through the average reader's mind. Smooth writing ensures smooth reading.

(d) Tailors story length to space requirements.

(e) Detects and corrects errors of fact.

(f) Simplifies, clarifies and verifies meanings.

(g) Adjusts stories to make them objective and fair.

(h) Adjusts stories to make these legally safe.

(i) Rewrites and restructures stories extensively, where necessary.

(j) Follow the policy of the newspaper.

(k) Corrects copy in the interest of good taste.

(l) Avoids sensation.

(m) Removes those points that could be called undue publicity.

(n) Deletes doubtful words and sentences.

Qualities: The production of a newspaper is a delicate and complex process. There is tension since a deadline is to be met. Amidst this tense atmosphere, the sub-editor has to perform his job meticulously. He should possess certain qualities to discharge his functions efficiently.

Calmness: Be calm and composed. You should not get excited when a big story breaks.

Decisive: Take quick and correct decisions. The editorial department has no place for indecisives.

Non-partisan: Never take sides.

Memory: Have a sharp memory for counter-checking facts.

Grasp: Size up the situation as it unfolds, and estimate its relevance.

Know your reader.

Self Confidence: Have confidence enough to correct a bad copy written by anyone.

Mature: Be mature enough to correct only bad copy, and not just make changes for the sake of changing.

Sceptical: Do not accept anything at face value. You should approach everything as a source of potential error.

Knowledge: Be a jack of all trades. A good editor should store most of the information as it comes across, and search for more.

Stability: Have enough stability to work under pressure.

Tools: The copy editor will require a set to tools, the lack of which may lead to loss of valuable time. These aids are indispensable. Often you may come across problems of spellings and facts. You should focus on the errors, and correct the name.

Language: The basic building blocks of journalism are words. You should respect the words, and follow the way these are arranged and strung together. Any misplacement of words could twist the meaning. Hence, you should pay attention to punctuation marks, grammar and syntax. All these are important in the sentence construction.

Punctuation Marks: Punctuation problems start and almost end with a comma. This little mark causes more trouble than the rest put together.

Punctuation marks brings in clarity and better readability. At the same time, too many of these clutter a story. There should be no comma after a verb unless it is immediately followed by a parenthesis.

Typographical Aspects

Today with the help of computers one can develop new type faces by incorporating variations in size, form and shape of each letter. It is the size, form and shape that determine and distinguish the type face of a letter. As page designers, we must select type by analysing its visual appearance as well as readability of its type face. While the choices may be many, editors of daily newspapers for the sake of economy, workability and convenience to its readers, make deliberate attempt to limit the variations of type faces used in their page make-up. Many newspapers adopt just one type face in different sizes throughout the newspaper.

Typography Enhancing Design: Each letter or alphabet has immense potential to be used as a piece of art.

Matching and Contrast: Because of economic and managerial reasons, newspapers use very limited type faces. Some newspapers may use only one. The only variation being the size. However, with the popularity of phototypesetting and offset printing, newspapers have a wider choice in matching and contrasting of type faces.

Emphasis and Highlights: In page layout, when we want to emphasise or highlight a word, an expression, a sentence, a paragraph or even a portion of the news item, we have many options before us. Some of them are:

- — Use of different type form of the letters such as italics.
- — Use of bolder type face for the word or portion of the news item to be emphasised.
- — Underlining the word or sentence.

The portion to be emphasised may be displayed with the wider margin, different colour or a combination of above alternatives.

Desktop Publishing

The Desktop Publishing, the DTP for short, refers to both hardware and software that are involved in preparing high quality prints of pages, once these are composed satisfactorily. The prints are used as artwork, and the actual duplication is done by offset printing, owing to the high costs involved in the DTP operations. The hardware of a DTP includes a large-sized colour monitor of the VDU (Visual Display Unit) and a laser printer apart from the CPU, which is programmed to suit the DTP software. The laser printer involves a high-speed, high-quality printer technology.

The DTP software consist of programmes to compose pages and their layout. These perform the function of the word-processing and automatic margin alignment, providing a variety of type-faces, page-numbering, etc.

Limitations: Although, DTP is considered incomparable when it comes to composing a page according to specifications. It handles the entire process with ease, completing the tasks at a rapid pace. But a few limitations persist in the new DTP packages too, like:

(a) It is not possible to obtain on the VDU an exact copy of the colours, as they would appear in the final print.

(b) The monitor is capable of showing the character in white against a background, whereas the actual product is black and white.

(c) The monitor shows only a restricted areas of each page. Such fragmented views make it difficult for an entire page to be visualised.

(d) A change once made in the typography might not eventually be printed as the package would not be programmed for it.

The appearance of a newspaper contributes to its having greater or lesser readership. There are number of readers who get addicted to their daily papers just because they take a liking to its layout and design. Each publication has a tradition which is flexible enough to accommodate innovative changes in the design layout with the passage of time. However, the readers might welcome such change only to a certain point. Both content and style of presentation matter in attracting readership.

Editing of Electronic Type

Speedy transmission of news is as important as the actual news gathering. It has been made possible by the advanced electronic equipment. News is a perishable commodity. The newspaper staff have to be on their toes to ensure that important news items are processed quickly, to meet the deadlines of publication.

But rapid transmission of news becomes meaningless if information being imparted is inaccurate. In this context, the accuracy of the data and apparently minor details of spellings and language, assume importance. Such correction work is done with the help of the computers and 'fax' machines.

Computers: The computer are an ideal system for storing data in their memory and this data could be retained at a later stage. The computers act as the data banks, and are very useful sources of reference for the newspapers.

A computer is an automatic electronic apparatus for making calculations, besides storing and processing information. For this data along with instructions on how to process the same have to be fed into the computer. That is called the 'input'. The result obtained from the computer after processing of the data is called the 'output'.

The hardware components of the computers refer to all the physical parts, viz. electronic and mechanical parts.

The software components of a computer refer to the set of instructions given to it to perform a specified task. These are fed to the computer in a language understood by it called a 'programme'.

Page Designing: The arrangement of captions, photographs and graphic on a page would have to facilitate easy reading, besides being visually appealing. Certain parameters of format are fixed for any newspaper, such as those of the page size, print area, number of columns, positions of masthead, allotment of articles according to their categories and page titles.

5

Structural Editing of News

In a well-run newspaper the news operation is managed efficiently with few surface signs of tension whether in the reporter's pen, at the sub-editors' desk or the editorial *sanctum sanctorum.*

The bawling editor, the temperamental news editor and the reporter with his feet on the desk are stereotypes found only in American films of the thirties. This is not to say that there are no temperamental news editors or that editors are not to be found who may want to bawl out an erring reporter, but they are rarities. One does not have to yell to haul a reporter over the coals. It can be done with a polite note just as well.

There is no single organisational structure common to all newspapers. Each newspaper has its own structure suited to its needs. On a small district newspaper, the editor oftener than not would be his own news editor and reporter, not to speak of proof-reader.

A newspaper of the size and standing of say, *The Times of India,* which brings out editions from Delhi and Ahmedabad has in addition to an Editor-or Chief Editor-one or two Resident Editors whose task will be to assume complete responsibility over local editions. The Editor lays down general editorial policy which his Resident Editors will scrupulously follow. He is the captain of the team whose wishes are law. It is he who will get editorials written by his junior colleagues-the Assistant Editors-and, in the ultimate analysis, it is he who bears the brunt of public criticism or gathers the laurels.

The Resident Editor handles the issue under his jurisdiction and acts for his Editor though he enjoys a wide range of powers and a considerable amount of autonomy. A newspaper is a live organisation whose functioning cannot be allowed to be stymied by red tape. Editors, in the circumstances, do not, in the normal course, interfere with their Resident Editors unless they have genuine cause to do so.

Process of Editing

What should a sub do when he finds a reporter making value judgements in his copy? Editorialising often crops into copy in the guise of interpretation. Columnists are allowed this privilege since it is an accepted part of columnist's duty to comment on news. But it is no part of a reporter's job to editorialise.

When this becomes absolutely necessary the comments are best kept to a bare minimum. In large newspapers, special correspondents are permitted comment but this should be the exception, not the rule.

It is interesting to note what some of the great journalists of the century have said on this issue. Walter Lippmann, for example, has this to say:

When I first went to work on a newspaper, which was after World War I, the generally accepted theory was that it was the duty of the news columns to report the "facts" uncoloured by "opinions," and it was the privilege of the editorial page to express opinions about what was reported in the news columns.

To this simple rule of the division of labour between reporters and editorial writers we all subscribed... In practice we all, reporters and editorial writers, broke the rule and this led to many disputes, good-natured and some not so good-natured. The news columns would have opinions with which the editorial writers disagreed. The editorial pages could contain statements of fact that the news editor had not certified.

In the course of time most of us have come to see that the old distinction between fact and opinion does not fit into the reality of things the modern world being so very complicated and so hard to understand, it has become necessary not only to report the news but to explain it and interpret it.

In the *Blue Book* of the Associated Press Managing Editors,. 1957, Dr. George Gallup has elaborated on the theme: A strong case can be made for including much more background material, more interpretation of the news. Readers like to be told what is important and what is not important. The I theory that newspaper readers want to make up their own minds, that they want only the bare facts, is refuted by all kinds of evidence. They want help in understanding the news and recognising its importance. They don't want bias. Too many already think newspapers 'slant' the news to suit the editorial view of the paper. But, I insist, interpretation can be free from bias, just as free as the selection of details in the story which purports to be completely free of bias.

Lester Markel, a former Sunday editor of the *New York Times* once discussed this issue at length before the American Press Institute and the International Press Institute-(IPI) of which he was the first president. To the latter group he said:

To report that the Kremlin is launching a peace offensive is news, To "explain why the Kremlin is setting the doves cooing at this time is interpretation. To state that any Kremlin peace offer should be rejected out of hand is opinion. Interpretation is an essential part of the news columns. Opinion should be confined, almost religiously, to the editorial columns. This is a prime point and it cannot have too much emphasis.

The Entirety

On a small newspaper, the editor necessarily is the be-all of the organisation. The larger the paper, the remoter would be the Editor from the general operation of the news set-up, even when he controls its policy and ultimately the contents. Customarily the Editor finds that just running the editorial page is sufficiently taxing a job to wish to interfere with the day-to-day running of the paper. Inevitably he has to delegate responsibilities.

A good editor, of course, would know how to get the best out of his colleagues and put his own stamp on the paper. Necessarily he would stay in touch with all his immediate subordinates, taking an active interest in the presentation not only of views but news as well. In regard to the latter, his chief lieutenant is the News Editor.

A good News-Editor is what makes a great newspaper. It is he who is in overall charge of the actual production of the paper, who will decide what news shall appear where and how, apportion space, assign priorities. It is to him that the Chief Reporter is primarily responsible. The News-Editor will, in consultation with the Chief Reporter, decide what events should be covered and in what-detail and give instructions as to how certain stories should be featured or displayed. He is the chief link between the Editor and the news staff and the sub-editorial staff. As the final authority on the news side, he has power to stop the presses should he consider it necessary to accommodate a fast-breaking news item. For one who is little known beyond the confines of the news room, his powers are impressive.

On a large newspaper, a News-Editor is an institution apart from the Chief Sub-Editor who is the man who actually mans the news desk and distributes "copy" to the subeditors. On smaller papers the News-Editor doubles up as the Chief Sub-Editor. But no matter what role he plays, he is the ultimate arbiter of what goes into a newspaper. He must scan all incoming news, issue directions for appropriate editing and display.of the same and maintain close check on the river of "copy" that comes to his desk. It is he who will, in consultation with the Chief Sub-Editor, prepare the "dummy" of page 1. It is he, again, who commissions photographers or artists, acts as liaison with the Advertisement Department, arranges staff assignment, leave or overtime.

His duties involve administration; he is the father-figure on the news side, a senior journalist guiding other journalists, ready as much to administer a sharp rebuff to an erring junior as to give a shoulder for him to cry on. He would have come to his job after putting several years on the news desk, working on night shifts and experiencing all the joys and heart-breaks of competitive editing. As a News-Editor he is spared night duty, but he is always available, no matter how late the night (or early the morning) to guide and counsel the Chief Sub-Editor whose duty it is to put the paper "to bed."

If the News-Editor is our supremo on the operational side of the news desk, his chief aide-de-camp is the Chief Sub-Editor who is actually in charge of the operations. It is his responsibility to ensure that the flow of copy is smooth, that the sub-editors working with him are engaged, that the headings given are accurate and not libellous, that no important news is skipped or overlooked that the pages are "locked" in time and put to bed at the stipulated hour. He will need a particularly good excuse for going to press late.

Working under the Chief Sub-Editor are the sub-editors-the foot soldiers, so to speak, in the army. No Editor or News-Editor or, for that matter the Chief Sub-Editor can afford to ignore them. In the past they came to the job out of the cold not knowing the difference between Bodoni Bold and Century Italics. They put in a long and difficult apprenticeship before being trusted with copy on their own.

Today, thanks largely to journalism schools, they at least are well-equipped with the rudiments of knowledge and are capable of handling copy without a Chief Sub-Editor looking warily at the final result. We can now go on with the third pillar of the newspaper establishment-the Chief Reporter. He is the one who leads his team of men and women who provide us the core and content of news, day in and day out round the clock. A reporter, like the sun in the skies, is always on duty.

Everything is grist to his particular mill, births, marriages, deaths-what is cynically described as the Hatch, Match and Despatch Department-disaster and tragedy, conflict and confrontation, crime and its concommitant law and order, riots, mutinies and rebellions, wars and pestilence, religion, science, money, mystery and sex, entertainment or just plain weather and food. Nothing human is alien to him.

In a well-ordered newspaper organisation, reporters tend to specialise in their particular fields. The *New York Times* even has a reporter-he is known as Food Editor-to sample and report on restaurants-an especially difficult job for one conscious of his physical well-being. Gastronomy goes frequently with girth.

There is nc substitute for a good reporter. In the final analysis it is he who is the chief contributor to a daily newspaper. A news paper without a reporter is like a well without water. It is immaterial whether the reporter works for a paper or a news agency: what is relevant is that he is the primary source of news, the man who "brings it back alive."

It is the Chief Reporter's job to assign his men to cover events of the day; some assignments are routine in nature. Police courts, docks, the Municipal Corporation (City Hall), the Coroner's Court, the High Court, they have regular reporters to cover them who are aware of the on-going stories and stories likely to break. But news does not come neatly packaged for a reporter to take delivery of a fire breaks in a multistoreyed building, a ship is wrecked, a Cardinal dies in the home of a prostitute (as did happen once in Paris), a celebrity swallows, an overdose of sleeping pills, or a murder is committed. A reporter has to be alert and ready to cover the event at a moment's notice; procrastination is not only the thief of time, it is a sure way to lose a story to a rival. And nothing is more damaging to a reporter's status than the tab that he has missed a story. Missed stories are like missed opportunities, they never recur.

It is part of the Chief Reporter's job-and a very important part at that-to hold an inquest every morning. What stories did the paper miss? What stories were covered adequately? Where did the rival paper score over his? He is accountable to the editor who will question him even more pertinently. Too many stories missed and very soon a paper will get the reputation that it is not *au courant*, in the swim. And that can be the death-knell of a paper.

In the circumstances, a Chief Reporter has to be even more alive to the world around him than any other member of the newspaper fraternity. His *antennae* are out to receive, register and transmute something indefinite and airy into hard news. He must be aware of not only what has happened in the past but what *could* happen in the future. To the extent that he can foresee events and be there-or have his men there-at the right time, he is the right man for his job. To foresee news and to forestall competitors is the hallmark of a truly competent Chief Reporter. He knows-and should know-that editors accept no excuses. Neither do news pages.

Almost alone among his fraternity, the Chief Reporter is the target for pressure groups. Those who want to get into the news will pester him. Those who want favourable news about them and their institutions would want to keep him on their side. Just as importantly, those who want certain items of news kept out would equally want to curry his favour. Among the things he will have to learn is how to say "no," politely and firmly to temptations of all kinds. A Chief Reporter who gives in soon becomes a liability to his newspaper and ultimately to himself. A Chief Reporter who can be bought can have no place on a newspaper. Integrity is all.

He is well advised, in the circumstances, to report to his editor, the names of individuals, societies or governments who come forward with gifts. Information shared is insurance against later charges of malfeasance.

As part of his job the Chief Reporter will look into the copy written by his reporters before it is submitted to the news desk. He will watch out for efforts, conscious or unconscious, on the part of the reporter to "slant" stories and warn him if necessary. It is no part of a reporter's job to fool around with a story. In this case objectivity is all.

Reporters have their own pecking order, though the profession, should admit no caste system within it. Nevertheless one has to face the facts of life and a "liner" cannot possibly be on par with a foreign correspondent. A "liner" is not a full-time reporter. 'More often than not he may be a lawyer or a school teacher living- in a small town who is authorised to send in stories to a newspaper on the understanding that he will be paid by the line. If his story does not appear, neither will his money order. Somewhat better off than him is the "Stringer" who will "string" for a paper and submit news items for publication. Often he would have been retained through payment of a nominal sum to cover expenses. He would not be a full-time employee and would be free to "string" for other papers as well.

By and large he would have been-appointed by virtue of his acknowledged credibility and his status in the society in which he functions. At one level he could be a small town lawyer; at another level he could be a full-time employee of a paper in a metropolitan city. Many Chief Reporters of city newspapers or even assistant editors are known to "string" for foreign newspapers or news agencies. At the lowest level the terms "liner" and "stringer" are used synonymously-especially when the stringer is paid on the basis of the number of lines of a story published.

A metropolitan newspaper may hire full-fledged reporters on a, regular basis at district headquarters though this is still rare. The regulars or "staffers" are those who work at the newspaper's home base. Their salaries and emoluments are fixed and they enjoy' certain rights normally denied to stringers. It is common for the more senior among them to be assigned the more prestigious beats-like the Secretariat or the Legislative Assembly. Usually the crime reporter is the low man on the totem pole, no matter if some crime can be big news.

The aristocrats among reporters are those assigned by news papers to cover the various Ministries of the Government of India.

"Their Lordships" are called Special Correspondents, the only thing special about them being their access to news at the national level. In Delhi they enjoy certain perquisites like accommodation, in government housing. They are "accredited" to different Ministries and are expected to be in close and constant touch with the policy-makers. Generally they are senior men who have made-their mark and have established their credibility as objective reporters. Many of them would have known ministers intimately, having reported on their activities when they were no better than, garden-variety politicians out at the hustings. It is rare for young reporters to be appointed as Special Correspondents though youth is not necessarily a bar to that privileged post.

The *"creme de 10 creme"* of special correspondents are the foreign correspondents accredited to distant capitals like Bonn, Paris, London, Washington or Peking. Some of the major news papers like *The Times of India* run their own news service to supplement the news they get from the regular wire services. *The Times of India* has its own news bureau where news received from state capitals and district headquarters is processed. This processing is done by a team of sub-editors who are really rewrite artists charged with the task of changing dreary prose into lively news items. And that is no mean task. The processed news from the bureau's desk is submitted to the news desk where it will be treated like news from any other source except that as information from the paper's own reporters, it will receive extra consideration.

A typical Reporter's Diary will indicate how news is covered in, the metropolitan area on a daily basis. Take this page from *The Times of India's* Diary, for instance:

March 5, 1979

1. Calls and Coroner's Court-Khalid Mohammad.
2. Esplanade Police Court-Desai.
3. Mantralaya-Raman.
4. Shipping-Dharmarajan.
5. Civic Affairs-Desai and Kamalakar.
6. Legislative Assembly-V.V. Date and Shailendra Ghorpade.
7. Legislative Council-V.R. Padiyar.
8. Morcha to Council Hall by entrepreneurs of cottage industries and small shopkeepers on government land, from Azad Maidan 11 a.m.-Balkrishnan.
9. Yuva Janata procession from Azad Maidan to Council Hall 2.30 p, m.-Balkrishnan.
10. Symposium on Mental Retardation-Balkrishnan.
11. National Society for Equal Opportunities for the Handicapped: lecture by Mr. Henri Viscardi, chairman of US President's Committee on Handicapped, Syndicate Hall, SNDT University 5 p.m.-Carol D'Souza.
12. Maharashtra INTUC Morcha from Azad Maidan to Council Hall 4.30 p.m. -Balkrishnan.
13. Press conference by head of Sarpanchayat of Byendar, Bristol Grill 3.30 p.m.-Anita Katyal.
14. All-India Students' Organisation-chain hunger strike, Hutatma Chowk-Srinivas Laxman.
15. D.N. Kachru, Commissioner of Tourism, Jammu and Kashmir Government to meet the press-Oberoi Sherarton 4 p.m.-Srinivas Laxman.

16. Lions Film Awards Governing Council: press conference to announce results of annual Lions films awards, Radio Club 5.15 p.m.-Balkrishnan.
17. In Office and Afternoon calls-Anita Katyal.
18. Indo-American Society: talk-Behram Contractor.
19. Night calls-weather-Kumar Civic Affairs cover a multitude of events in Bombay such as meetings of the Standing, Education, BEST and Improvements Committees of the Municipal Corporation not to speak of any news-conference that the Municipal Commissioner may want to give. The diary did not put down opening of an art exhibition and a musical concert as these were covered separately by the Art Critic and the Music Critic.

An Assignment: Working an assignment such as a fire or a multiple car accident can be exciting but a reporter can't get much of a job done if he permits himself to get excited. Good reporting under such conditions calls for a calm, reasoned approach.

The first rule in such events is for the reporter to maintain his cool like a surgeon at the operating table. The reporter observes, but never intrudes, studies without being fussy, is detached. Objectivity is all. In reporting public speeches by politicians the reporter must always be fair no matter what his own personal feelings are. The technique of *suppressio veri suggestio falsi* can have the place in honest reporting.

While estimating numbers at a public meeting it makes no sense "to indulge in wild guesses. "An audience variously estimated at five to ten lakhs" makes no sense either. The reader would like to have a fair approximation of how many came to listen to the speaker. There are experts usually available who can give a pretty good estimate.

In covering major conference the reporter has to remember that space allotted to his assignment is limited. He must first check with the News Editor as to the amount of column space-or word age-that is expected of him to fill. He can then streamline his efforts to suit his papers needs. What 'angle' is he expected to take? News agencies, because they have to meet the needs of news papers of all shades of opinion provide what is known as "straight' copy" which tells the full story as it is with no pretence at taking sides.

In fact, taking sides is frowned upon. An agency reporter who indulges in such practices may find himself put on the mat in no time. But that does not hold true for reporters working for newspapers of a particular persuasion. Mr. Ashok Mitra, West Bengal Finance Minister in 1979 used to complain that he was routinely misquoted by a Calcutta paper; if true, that cannot be-described as good journalism but journalism as is, regrettable but an example of what editors expect of their reporters.

Access to News: Does a newspaper or radio reporter have any legal right to get the news? Does he have the right to attend and, report any kind of meeting? If the meeting is a public one, the.answer is yes. If it is a private meeting, the answer obviously is no. How does one tell the difference? A public meeting is any meeting open to the general public. A private meeting is one open only to members of the organisation or a club. Its proceedings are not open to the press.

By agreement among members of the organisation's executive the press, of course, may be briefed by a responsible member of the executive. But a press reporter cannot claim the right to attend a private meeting, as he can to attend and report the meeting of the municipal council, the legislative assembly or Parliament or the Courts.

In the case of the latter, on the judgement of the presiding officer, certain proceedings may be declared as closed, in which case reporting them may make the reporter liable to contempt of court proceedings. But these situations come under the chapter on the press and the law.

There are times when police officials ask that the identity of an arrested person be not divulged in order to rope in all the criminals. In such instances-as indeed on all occasions when a reporter has been requested by parties to withhold information-it is not his, but his superior's judgement that is final. The reporter should keep his Chief Reporter or News Editor or Editor informed of all such requests.

Rewritten Story

How often have we not heard a petulant reporter tell his colleague that a particular story written by him had been "botched" or "butchered" by a sub-editor? The charge of "butchering" by a sub-editor-the autocrat of the blue pencil-is a common complaint among reporters. A poor sub-editor may be guilty of such a charge but a good sub-editor is a reporter's best friend.

The fact of the matter is that all stories destined to appear in a daily newspaper, whether written by staff reporters or coming from the wire services go through the hands of sub-editors (also known as copyreaders) who are the anonymous and frequently unappreciated collaborators of the writer. Reporters may squirm at the free use of the sub-editor's blue pencil but many have remained grateful to the subs for making their copy sing. The subbing desk is headed by the Chief Sub-Editor.

Sub editors, like children, are neither seen nor heard; they are read by an unsuspecting public which oftener than not is ignorant of their very existence. In essence, a sub-edit or's job is to "prepare" or "sub" copy to make it suitable for publication. In that sense he is a creative artist. It was Northcliffe who said "Reporters write the paper; sub-editors make it." How true.

"Subbing" requires a special kind of talent. It involves knowledge at various levels. A reporter may be-and often is-a specialist. But the man at the desk needs to be a rgeneralist. He handles all kinds of copy. A reporter may b excused for making a mistake. A sub-editor who fails to correct it does not deserve to be one. For his, by definition, is the critical eye. He is the first to read copy submitted to him, to check on facts, style, grammar, accuracy. Necessarily, he has to be as well if not better informed than a reporter on a wide range of subjects. In that sense, his reponsibility is greater than that of a reporter.

What are the qualifications of a good sub-editor? Here are a few:

He should be well-read.

He should have a sound current-affairs background.

He must be able to follow mass interests and have a nodding acquaintance with sectional ones as well.

He must have an analytical mind.

He must be able to visualise not only how a story maybe developed but its impact on the readership.

He should have a good knowledge of the mechanical processes of newspaper production.

He must know how to summarise and boil down a long and tedious report.

He must have an eye for accuracy.

He must be a "team-man" and not a loner.

He must be physically fit to survive long working hours, especially at night when physical tiredness can easily make him journalistically "accident-prone."

He must have the power of quick and accurate work, the ability to make swift decisions and the gift of concentration.

He should be able to rewrite bad copy and make it readable.

He should have a good grasp of law-especially laws pertaining to libel.

In other words he should have all the qualifications sought in a reporter-plus some more.

When he picks up copy passed on to him by the chief sub, his first task is to check whether it is accurate, fair, complete, clear and has news value. If the copy has no news value, it is not worth printing, no matter how accurate it is and how well-written. This is where sub-editorial discretion comes into instant action. But he does not have all day to make his assessment. If the copy is not news worthy, it is "spiked."

If it is newsy the sub moves on to make other value judgements. If the copy is too long and involved, the next step is to condense it. Condensation applies not to ideas but words. The fat is trimmed but not the meat. A good sub must know the difference between the two. To start with he must approach all copy with a critical eye and mind. No copy is sacrosanct; and the sub should allow himself to be brow beaten into submission to any authority except the chief sub. He should put himself in the position of the reader and ask himself whether the copy makes sense. If it doesn't make sense to him, how can it be expected to make sense to anyone else?

So the sub must read the copy carefully and thoroughly; he must give it the once-over. He must, as the saying goes, get "on top" of it and have control and mastery of what has been written. That done, the rest is almost routine: double checking for facts, correction of spelling, grammar and syntax, condensation when and if necessary and dotting the i's and crossing the t's.

In the end it should be seen that only a "dean" copy is sent down to the printer. This implies that whatever corrections are made are done legibly, paragraphs are marked and all pages properly numbered.

A good sub is a sworn enemy of cliches. These should be excised with no mercy Shown. Escapes may be "narrow" but they are seldom "miraculous." A "shark-infested" sea is best drained quickly, and a "nation-wide hunt" is worth calling off in the interest of effective subbing.

Similarly, a sub will watch out for words that are frequently over-worked like "drama," "disaster," "horror" and "crisis." Used carelessly a sub will not only devalue them but in time will destory the credibility of his paper. Crises are more often in an over-taxed mind than in a given situation, And tragedy "strikes" only when a sub is struck for word. Words, indeed, must be used carefully and with full understanding of what is sought to be conveyed.

All Customs offences do not necessarily constitute smuggling. A person is only bankrupt when there has been an adjudication order. Every prisoner is not a convict. Condensation is an art and is its own reward. How does one condense? Here's some well regarded advice:

Cut out all the extra trimmings

Boil it down

Skim it well, then skim the skimmings Boil it down

When you're sure 'would be a sin to Cut another sentence into

Send it down and we'll begin to

Boil it down.

"In the near future" can easily make way for "soon." "The prisoners made good their escape" can be shortened to "The prisoners escaped" and nobody would be in any doubt about what the prisoners did. As to "because of the fact that..." won't "since" do just as well?

A sub should never presume that the reader knows the full background to a story. He must work on the basis that the reader comes fresh to it. Repetition is tedious, but backgrounding completes a story. Long-forgotten or half-remembered happenings can be brought to life for the reader by an alert sub.

When reports of Jayaprakash Narayan's "demise" turned out to be false and premature, a good sub would have inserted into a reporter's copy instances of a similar nature. This would flesh out the story and make it stand above other reports of the same blunder. That is where good reading and memory come in handy. In the first place a sub must work on the premise that the average reader has no memory. This has to be supplied to him.

Books for Reference

A good sub will also remember that his memory too might be faulty. In the event he is wise to consult the necessary reference book which should always be available close at hand.

Among these books can be mentioned:

An English Dictionary.

A Dictionary of Quotations.

Modern English Usage.

A Thesaurus of English Words and Phrases.

An Encyclopaedia.

A Dictionary of Biographies.

Contemporary Archives.

A Year Book.

Encyclopaedias are costly and are regularly updated. *The Dictionary of National Biography* goes into several volumes and supplements and there are Indian variations of the same like *The Statesman's Who's Who.*

There are several things that a sub must watch out for in his effort to cleanse copy. One is bias. Let him, for instance, beware of the reporter who sometimes consciously and just as likely unconsciously, introduces bias against a person, institution, ideology or political party in his copy. In the interests of good journalism this should be neatly incised.

It is not part of a reporter's job-unless he has been specifically instructed to the contrary, in which case it is a different story-to sit on judgement on the events he has been sent to cover. Should a reporter forget this, it is the duty of the sub to keep him on the straight and narrow path.

A sub will do well not to be over-enthusiastic and try to be ahead of the news when matters are in a fluid srate. The *Chicago Tribune* came out with an extra on election night, 1948, that proclaimed Thomas E. Dewey President of the United States when it was Harry Truman who won. *The Chicago Tribune* had to eat crow the next day and that is not an edifying exercise.

The New York Times, another great paper, published an early edition report on election night, 1954 that Averell Harriman had: been elected Governor of New York by an over-whelming plurality when it later developed that his winning margin was only 11,000 votes. Harriman, of course, did win but the early edition report did not exactly redound to the credit of the *New York Time.* All India Radio came out with a report that Jayaprakash Narayan was dead in March 1979, when he was still very much alive and undergoing dialysis. Similar instances could be multiplied and in all such events a wise sub will use his caution before, he launches on enlivening his copy of the front page.

Unintentional Remarks

Inadvertent comment takes different forms. M.V. Kamath cites the instance when he was summoned by his editor S. Natarajan to explain what he meant by describing a man as "elderly."

"Young man, how old is elderly?"

"Sir, the man in the story is forty-two."

"Well, I am forty-two and I do not consider that I am elderly at all. I suggest you stick to giving the man's age and leave it at that. Let's have no more editorialising in copy."

Unclearness

Reporters are frequently guilty of vagueness because they have had no time to enquire, and get at facts. Where does vagueness creep in? It does so in statements such as these:

"Morarji Desai today addressed a massive audience in front of the Red Fort."

"The weather was surprisingly warm for this time of the year."

"An important meeting was scheduled today by All-India Students Federation."

Consider this list:

Designation	*Miles per hour*
Calm	Less than 1
Light air	1-3
Light breeze	4-7
Gentle breeze	8-12
Moderate breeze	13-18
Fresh breeze	19-24
Strong breeze	25-31
Moderate gale	32-38
Fresh gale	39-46
Strong gale	47-54
Whole gale	55-63
Storm	64-72
Hurricane	Above 72

What exactly is a "massive" audience? How many were present at the meeting? Ten thousand? A hundred thousand? Two million? What is a stardard-size audience that would normally come to hear Morarji Desai when he delivers an address from the ramparts of the Red Fort?

Why would the weather at that time of the year be considered "surprisingly warm?" When would it be considered just plain warm and what should the temperature be to be described as "surprisingly warm"?

In what way can the All India Students Federation meeting be said to be "important"? Wouldn't it be more to the point to simply say that the All-India Students Federation was meeting to discusss the course of action to be taken following a steep rise in college fees announced by the university and leave the reader to decide whether it was important or not.

One of the most common error reporters make is in announcing weather. A newspaper must be precise in using terms such as storm or a tornado.

According to Beaufort's Scale, devised by Sir Francis Beaufort R.N. in 1805, a hurricane is a wind of more than 70 miles an hour velocity. Actually, hurricanes, tornadoes, cyclones and typhoons are all members of the cyclonic family. A cyclone is a system of winds that may be several hundred miles wide and circulate about a centre of low barometric pressure. It travels 20 miles an hour or more. A tornado is it small but violent cyclone-a rotary storm of small diameter that devastates a path only a few hundred yards wide-and 10 to 40 miles long. It is accompanied by a funnel-shaped cloud within which the winds may reach estimated speeds of 500 miles an hour. A hurricane is a tropical cyclone, accompanied by rain.

Short Forms

When are abbreviations permissible and when are they not? A lot depends on a particular paper's style book but, here is a short guide:

(1) Names of states in the United States immediately following geographical terms such as cities, towns, air bases, etc. Thus, Seattle, Wash, or Randolph Air Force Base, Tex., are correct. But if used by itself, spell out the name of the state in frill, such as Washington or Texas.

In India states are not abbreviated in the US style; thus, Allahabad; Vt. Pra., makes no sense while Allahabad, UP does.

(2) Abbreviations are used for government agencies after they are first spelled out, with the abbreviation in bracket, so that the reader knows what the copy refers to. Thus, the first mention would be European Economic Community (EEC) thereafter just EEC.

(3) Agencies, groups, military or civil organisations have their abbreviations used without periods. Thus, AP, UPI, PTI, YMCA, YWCA, AFL-CIO, AFP, DPA. But Reuters has never been abbreviated.

(4) Permitted in business copy are abbreviations such as Corp. Co., Inc., Ltd., Assn.

(5) It is correct to use St., for Street, Ave., for Avenue, Blvd., for Boulevard and Pl., for place when giving addresses as in 54 Tilak St., or 48 Raj Blvd. But when used by themselves in copy street names are writen out: Hornby Road is closed for traffic.

(6) Figures are written differently for addresses and dates. Thus, 12th Road, but July 12.

(7) Abbreviations are used for titles before names, such as Mr., Dr., the Rev., Gen. The title Mr. must never be used with the full name, except on a society page-and we don't have that in India. Mr. is customarily used with the last name only. Thus, Morarji Desai said today but if the Prime Minister is referred to.again, it is as Mr. Desai; not as just Desai.

(8) Write abbreviations with periods in such lower case designations as a.m., p.m., c.o.d., *f.o.b.,* m.p.h., etc.

(9) Use B.A. for Bachelor of Arts, Ph. D., for Doctor of Philosophy.

(10) Spell out names of foreign countries. United States, United Nations and United Kingdom are spelled out when used as nouns, but may be abbreviated when used as UN Security Council or US Mission to the UN or the UK Delegation.

(11) Religious titles:

Protestant: the Rev. Dr. John David Sutherland or the Rev. Samuel A. French. If the names are repeated say Dr. Sutherland or Mr. French, but never the Rev. Sutherland or the Rev. French,

Roman Catholic: the Rev. Francis Xavier or Father D'Souza (but never Mr. for Catholic priest). The Rt. Rev. Armando Menezes or Msgr Menezes; the Most Rev. Mario Miranda, bishop of the diocese or Bishop Miranda; Francis Cardinal Spellman, Archbishop of the New York archdiocese; Cardinal Spellman. Nuns may be addressed as Sister Mary but not as Sister D'Souza.

Jewish: Rabbi and Cantor are never abbreviated. The title Dr. may be used singly, where it applies. Thus, Rabbi Abba Hillel Silver, Rabbi Silver or Dr. Silver.

(12) Units of measure, preceded by numerals: loft. 3 in.

(13) Some abbreviations differ from the names of organisations and should be used as designated.

United Nations Children's Fund-UNICEF Pan American-Grave Airways-Panagra.

(14) WAC is the abbreviation for Women's Army Corps, but a Wac is a member of the corps. The same is true of WAVE and Wave.

(15) Most military titles are abbreviated (Gen., Lt. Col., Maj., Capt., etc.) except when they are not commonly known or under stood.

The following should not be abbreviated:

(1) Days of the week. It shall always be Monday, Tuesday, Wednesday, etc. and never Mon., Tues., or Wed.

(2) Given names. You do not write Wm. for William or Robt, for Robert but Venkat for Venkataraghavan and Tiru for Tim. malai are permissible, provided the person is known by these.

(3) Names of centuries (tenth, fifteenth, twenty-first, not 10th, 15th, 21 st) and cities.

(4) Points of the compass, except with appropriate figures (north east winds, southwest monsoon, not NE winds and SW monsoon).

(5) Per cent, except when used in tabulations.

(6) Such words as detective, commandant, commodore, field' marshal, general manager, postmaster general, vice president, mathematics, building and chaplain, though there is an increasing tendency to use maths for mathematics.

(7) Numerals, never begin a sentence with an arabic or Roman numeral. Spell these out. Twelve persons were killed in an accident today and not 12 persons were killed in an accident today.

(8) Spell out numbers through ten inclusive, but use numerals thereafter.

Capitalising Letters

The following should be capitalised:

(1) All proper nouns.

(2) Street designations, when preceded by name.

Hornby Road

Marine Drive.

Netaji Boulevard.

King George Avenue.

(3) Titles preceding (or part of) names.

Rao Saheb Patwardhan.

Sir Jamesetji Jeejeebhoy.

Padma Shri K.K. Hebbar.

(4) Cabinet, Supreme Court or specific court titles, of specific legislative bodies such as Municipal Council, Maharashtra Legislative Assembly, Parliament, official names of government departments. (Ministry of External Affairs, etc.).

(5) Regional, local or geographic descriptive terms (such as North Korea, West Germany, Middle East, Orient, Promised Land).

(6) Days and months (Monday, Tuesday, September, December, etc.) but not seasons except in a poetic sense ("When Winter comes, can Spring be far behind"?).

(7) Sun, moon and earth, but only when used with other astronomical bodies like Mars, Jupiter and Saturn, but otherwise in the lower case.

The earth is round Among the planets are Jupiter, Mars, Earth, Moon, Venus.

(8) All sacred writings (The Gita, the Holy Bible, the Koran) 'and faiths, Islam, Hinduism, Christianity.

(9) Proper names of animals (Cocker Spaniel; French Poodle).

(10) Official residences (the Kremlin, the Vatican, the White House).

(11) Sports events such as the Irish Sweepstakes, the Kentucky Derby.

(12) Specialised groups of military men (Swiss Guards, Marines, Bengal Lancers).

(13) All military decorations (Victoria Cross, Param Vir Chakra).

What not to Capitalise?

(1) Common nouns that originally were proper nouns: India rubber, plaster of paris.

Indefinite use of college, high school, etc.

He attended high school for three years.

He attended Barda High School.

(2) Scientific names of plants, birds and animals.

Punctuation Corrections

If you are writing in Devnagari, you do not use punctuation marks the way you would if you are writing in English. These marks are not used haphazardly but with specific intent.

Proper sentence construction requires that you use these marks with discrimination and care. What are they?

Full stop (.) Comma (,) Semicolon (;) Colon (:) Question mark (?) Exclamation point (!) Hyphen (-) Apostrophe (') Quotation marks (" ").

The Full Stop: Use a full stop at the end of a sentence that tells something or just makes a statement. Such a sentence is called a declarative sentence because it *declares* a fact.

I am going to work.

I do not enjoy over-eating.

Use a full stop after a sentence that expresses a command or a request.

Please pass the salt.

Do your sums.

Use a full stop to show that words have been abbreviated; as in: Days of the week: Tues. (Tuesday), Wed. (Wednesday).

Names of Months: Jan. (January), Nov. (November).

Titles used with proper names: Mr. (Mister), Dr. (Doctor), Sen. (Senator).

Names of Things: Ave. (Avenue), St. (Street).

Use a full stop when writing initials as part of a name:

C.K. Narayanaswami

Gopal S. Pohekar

Use a full stop as a decimal point:

Rs. 267.75

78.5 kilometres.

Use a full stop to show time:

2.30 p.m.

7.25 a.m.

Warning: Use a full stop after Mr. and Mrs. but never after Miss except at the end of a sentence.

Sharada is married but Laxmi is still a Miss.

The Comma: There is more confusion in the use of the comma than in anything else. A comma is used to clarify meaning by separating words and figures when necessary. A comma is used in writing dates, to separate the month from the year.

On August 15, 1947, India became free.

The month and the day form a single part. The comma is placed only after the day. Since the year is not the last word in the sentence, a comma is placed after it to separate it from the rest of the-sentence.

A comma is used to separate the different parts of an address.

She came here from Bonn, West Germany.

The comma separates the city and state.

His address is 40 Diamond Court, Nepean Sea Road, Bombay 6.

A comma is used to separate two nouns that mean the same thing or person.

The bridge was declared open by the Home Minister, Mr. Charan Singh.

The Home Minister, Mr. Charan Singh, declared the bridge open.

The Semicolon: The semicolon may often be replaced by a comma but is used chiefly to separate phrases containing comma to avoid confusion.

On the international scene, rights and duties apply only to the states, and they result from contracts, not from superior rule; there are vast gaps and ambiguities in the regulations, the authority of the world judge is limited, and enforcement is a polite word for self-help.

Commas follow the words yes, no, well, and oh, when they are used at the beginning of a sentence.

Yes, I am hungry.

Oh, I didn't know about it

Web, what do you know?

Commas are used to separate the exact words a person has said from the rest of the sentence.

Shenoy said, "I am leaving my job soon."

"Shucks," said Narayan, "let him go!"

"That's what I told him," said Costa.

Commas are used in several parts of an informal or personal letter.

Dear Ramesh,

Very truly yours,

Yours sincerely,

A comma is used to separate the two parts of long compound sentences before conjunctions, such as and, but, or, nor, and for.

I would like to go, but your company is pleasant.

The men played badminton, but the women rested.

The Semicolon: A semicolon is used in compound sentences if the conjunction is omitted.

Madhav used one exit and Usha used the other.

Madhav used one exit; Usha used the other.

A semicolon is used in a series of names and addresses:

Ram Nayak, Calcutta; C.S. Rajan, Madras; P.K. Bannerjee,

Dhanbad; Vallabbdas Gopaldas, Ahmedabad.

The Colon: The colon's principal use is to introduce listings, or io introduce statements.

Send me one each of the following books: *David Copperfield* by Charles Dickens; *India and British English* by Nihalani; *The News Machine* by Thompson.

It is used in writing time.

He ran the mile in 3:59.

It is used in introducing a resolution.

Resolved:

It separates chapter and verse in scriptural references.

Quotation Marks: Quotation marks, it is needless to say, are used in pairs. If such marks are used, it is assumed that the words they enclose were actually said. When in doubt, do not use the marks. You may be doing an injustice to the person you are allegedly quoting.

Quotation marks are used before and after the actual words a person has said:

Jayaprakash said, "It is sad, very sad!"

"Have you called for a taxi?" the General Manager enquired.

When the persons name is used in the middle of the words he speaks, the quotation marks are placed around each set of words the person has said.

"I am sorry," said the Editor, "but the article cannot be used."

In breaking up what should go into quotation marks, see that the break makes sense.

"I am sorry but," said the Editor, "that article cannot be used" does not make sense.

Use a new paragraph when the conversation of several people is reported.

"How many of you went to see the play?" asked Mr. Desai. "I did," said Mrs. Desai, "and I liked it!"

"I did too," added their eldest son, Ramesh, "but I didn't!"

When there are several paragraphs of continuous quotations, each paragraph should be started with a quotation mark, but it should be omitted from the end of all paragraphs except the final one: If there are quotes within quotes, the interior quotes take single quotation marks (' ').

Title of books, plays, movies, operas, statuary, paintings, etc., all take quotation marks.

The Apostrophe: An apostrophe (') is used to show that some thing belongs to one or more persons. It is used to show ownership, possession.

This is Laxman's cartoon.

Here are two adults' books.

An apostrophe is used in writing the plurals of numbers and letters.

There are four 7's in the license number.

There are three d's in the word added.

An apostrophe is used to write a shortened form of two words as one word.

I have heard it said...

I've heard it said...

Other examples:

We've

You've

Let's (Let us)

Isn't (is not)

But beware of the word 'It's. This is not to be confused with the word 'its'.

It's not clear what its meaning is.

Hyphen: A hyphen (-) is used to divide words at the end of a line:

Most experts don't mind talking to a layman, so long as
he understands what has been said.

In breaking up the word, however, see that it makes sense.

Thus:

Under

stands

makes sense, but not

understands

A hyphen is used to separate two or more words when they are used to mean one thing in describing a noun.

He is a well-educated peasant.

It was a three-week holiday.

We have up-to-date machinery in our plant.

The hyphen is used in writing compound numbers.

Twenty-one

ninety-nine.

The Dash: The dash marks an abrupt change of thought.

Most experts don't mind talking to a layman-so long as he's intelligent.

Punctuation is important. The following statements show how punctuation can completely change the meaning of a sentence:

1. *(a)* He ate a half-fried chicken.

   (b) He ate half a fried chicken.

2. *(a)* Don't break your crackers or roll in your soup.

   (b) Don't break your crackers, or roll in your soup.

3. *(a)* We'd like you to see our students work.

   (b) We'd like you to see our students' work.

4. *(a)* Mr. Desai, the Prime Minister, is two hours late.

   (b) Mr. Desai, the Prime Minister is two hours late.

5. *(a)* When the critics say that we object.

   (b) When the critics say that, we object.

Punctuation should be effective, but it should be sparingly used.

This is what the Associated Press Style Book has to say:

Punctuation is the visual inflection. The marks should clarify meaning and, like shouting, should be employed sparingly. Skillful phrasing avoids ambiguity, insures correct interpretation and lessens need for punctuation. When punctuation is used, it should be employed-solely to bring out what is intended. If punctuation does not clarify, it should be omitted.

Every sub at some time or the other comes across a situation where he has to ask himself whether words are used to convey what is meant to be conveyed, whether, in fact, the words used are right for the occasion. Good usage or correct usage is the selection of words that best describe what is intended to be said in conversation or writing.

Let us start with some common errors one is prone to make in regard to the use of:

Can, may.

Affect, effect.

Accept, except.

Loan, lend.

Principal, principle.

Leave, let.

Fewer, less.

Healthy, healthful.

Teach, learn.

Their, there.

Can indicates ability or willingness to do something. *May* indicates that a person is requesting permission.

Can he do the job?

May I bring chocolates for the children?

Affect means to influence or change something. *Effect* is the *result* of a change.

How has he been *affected* by the change of weather?

The effect is all for the good.

Accept means to receive or acknowledge. *Except* means to exclude or leave out.

I intend to *accept* your invitation.

All of us are going to Simla *except* mother.

The word *lend* is a verb. It means to allow the use of or to give out. The word *loan* is a noun. A person may seek a *loan* from a bank; the bank *lends him* the money.

When the word principal is used as a *noun,* it means the chief person or bead. When it is used as an adjective it means main, chief, leading or most important.

Mr. Sunderam is the *principal* of S.T.E.S. High School.

Sickness was the *principal* cause of heavy absenteeism.

Principle is a noun meaning a basic fact, a theory, or rule of law or of conduct.

We must study the *principles* of grammar in order to write well.

He never gives alms to beggars as a matter of *principle.*

Leave means to move away from. *Let* means to allow or permit.

May I *leave* you for a moment?

Don't *let* him get away with it.

Fewer is used with the plural forms of words. *Less* is used with singular words. A person has *fewer* possessions than another, but you have *less* money than someone else. *Fewer* modifies *possessions,* which is plural. *Less* modifies *money* which is singular.

Healthy is an adjective used to describe the state of being of people and animals; healthful is also an adjective but suggests the producing or bringing about of health.

He is a very *healthy* specimen.

Amul milk powder is supposed to be a very *healthful* food.

You *teach someone,* but you *learn something.* You teach a man, a dog or a child; but you learn science or music or astrology.

There is an adverb.

The chair should be placed *there.*

Their is a possessive pronoun.

Their children are very happy.

Consider some other puzzlers like

Sit-set.

Lie-lay.

Real-very.

Rise-raise.

Good-well.

Adapt-adopt.

Between-among.

Should-would.

Loose-lose.

very-too.

You *sit* at a table. You *set* a table (keep the china and cutlery).

The sun *sets.*

What *lies* ahead of you? *Lie* down. The hen *lays* eggs.

Real attests to the truth. *Very* signifies quality.

What is *real* and what is unreal?

This is *very* sweet.

The sun *rises.* You get a *raise* in your salary.

Good refers to quality, a state of being.

He is *good* to his servants.

Be *good.*

Well pertains to health or improvement.

He is *well. Well* done.

A man *adapts* to a situation; but he *adopts* a child.

The difference here is between a transitive and intransitive verb. *Between* is used to signify two people or things; *among,* more than two.

Between you and me, nothing should stand.

You are *among* friends.

Should and *Would.* In the case of the former there is the element of command.

He *should* be sent to prison.

In the case of the latter, it is an expression of willingness.

He *would* be happy to leave.

If you have plenty of coins you have *loose* change; if someone steals the change, you *lose* your money.

Very and *too.* He is *very* good (This is a compliment), He is *too,* good (this is not).

Articles: There is a notion among some newspapermen that they can dispense with articles as there is among some criminals that they-can get away with murder. Both notions are erroneous and can lead to trouble for their adherants.

The wise course is for a proper respect for "the" "a" and "an" and for their judicial use wherever that is called for. Except in headlines where omission of.articles is excusable, elsewhere a good sub will restore them to their proper place.

False Attraction: There is frequently a tendency among writers- when plural nouns come between a singular subject and the verb, 10 make the verb plural instead of singular, a tendency which grammarians call "false attraction."

A whole series of shocks, each lasting for several seconds, *were* recorded. The subject here is *series* and the verb to be used is *was* and not *were*. Usually, of course, a multiple subject requires a plural verb, as in.

He and I *are* friends but when the separate words of a multiple subject, taken together,-express a single idea, or (when they require Singular verb, the verb is often singular. Examples:

Thine *is* the kingdom, the power and the glory.

And now *abideth* faith, hope, charity, these three.

The tumult and the shouting *dies*.

Hostility and civil tumult *reigns*.

Collective nouns (flock, fleet, team, crowd, Cabinet) maybe, treated as either singular or plural, according to the meaning to be communicated and here American and British usage differs, the latter more often than not opting for the plural. The important thing is to stick to anyone usage throughout a paragraph. It is obviously wrong to say:

The team *was* well chosen but *they* could not score.

When two singular nouns are joined by *and*, they form a plural subject requiring plural verb; but if joined by any other word, the first noun is usually the subject and the verb must be singular.

The King and Queen *were* present.

The King, with the Queen, *was* present.

In the matter of *either* or *neither nor*, where one of the alternative terms is used with two subjects in a sentence the verb agrees with the nearer word.

Either she or her sister *is* coming.

Neither she nor her sisters *are* coming.

Neither her sisters nor she *is* coming.

The Use of Pronouns: *I, he, she, we* and *they* are nominative; the corresponding accusative forms are *me, him, her, us* and *them.* Transitive verbs and also prepositions have to be followed by the accusative case (*me* and not I). In the following pairs of examples, the wrong version is given first, followed by the right version:

He invited my wife and *I* to dinner. He invited my wife and *me* to dinner.

Between you and *I,* he is wrong. Between you and *me,* he is wrong.

Who did you tell about it? *Whom* did you tell about it?

He is the man *whom* the police think can help them. He is the man *who* the police think can help them.

Remember *who* you are talking to. Remember *whom* you are talking to.

Distributive adjectives or distributive nouns like *anybody, everybody, nobody, either, neither, each, every, none-are* singular.

Anybody who needs food *is* welcome

But beware of the word *none.* Sometimes it is more natural to use the word as plural. Thus:

None of the men *were* hurt.

It must be stated, however, that this common colloquial usage is frowned upon by staid grammarians.

Split Infinitive: Infinitives are best not split, but to be a superpurist in such matters is to invite ridicule. Winston Churchill's rage when some purist tried to improve his language is easily understood when he said that the alleged improvement was some thing "up with which he will not put." Yet, take this sentence:

Air Force scientists at Cape Kennedy said they intended to use the installation to better develop intercontinental ballistie missiles.

As will be immediately noticed, the foul deed has been done. The infinitive has been split. But how awful would it sound to say "'better to develop"! That is being needlessly to be guilty of strained effort.

Usage: Some words and expressions are frequently misused by writers and a good sub will keep a sharp look-out for them. Below are some that have achieved notoriety:

All-India: Gavaskar is playing for an All-India Eleven; *not* All Indian.

All Right: Often incorrectly spelled *alright.* The expression is two words, like *under way* and *per cent.*

Allude: Should never be confused with *refer.*

Anyone: It is one word, like *everybody, nobody.*

Banquet: Usually a dinner in grand style. "There has not been a dinner in Bombay worth calling a banquet in years."

Bride: A woman about to be married, as well as a newly-married woman. Her husband is *not* a groom but a bridegroom.

Broadcast: Present and past tense of the verbs are identical.

Broadcasted is wrong.

Burglar: There must be breaking and entering before a larceny can be called a burglary. The act of stealing is a theft or robbery.

Capital: Washington D.C., is America's capital. The building is called capitol.

Citizen: A man may be a citizen of India, but not a citizen of Britain. He will be a British subject.

Collision: Avoid saying two cars were in collision. It is better to write that they collided.

Comprise: Do not confuse with compose. Comprise means to include.

Critical: A person may be in a critical condition but this does not necessarily mean that he is dying.

Data: This is plural but the singular, *datum,* is seldom used.

Etc.: It means "and other things" and should not be used in connection with human beings.

Finalise: This is plain, bad English. Do not use.

Forecast: Like broadcast, present and past tense of the verbs are identical.

From: A man does not die from heart failure. He dies of heart disease.

Hanged: A man is hanged. A picture is hung.

Pass Away: A man no doubt will pass away, but it is better to say that he will die.

St: James's: India has a High Commission at the Court of St. James's not St. James.

Scot: The people of Scotland are Scots. They drink Scotch and soda sometimes.

Sustain: Injuries are received or suffered; not sustained.

Towards: The final "s" is dropped on towards, afterwards; forward.

Try: This is a verb, not a noun and to say "that's a good try" may be sound effort but is bad grammar.

Widow: A man who dies is survived by his wife, not his widow.

The Repetition

Beware of words that are redundant, as for example in:

At the Present Time: The time is now, or at present. Biography of his life: Well, that is what a biography is. Combined together: You put things together or combine them.

Consensus of Opinion: A consensus means opinion.

Early Pioneer: How late is pioneer?

Knots per Hour: Knots measure speed per hour.

Present Incumbent: drop the 'present'. The incumbent is right there.

Repeat Again: That is what repeating is-again.

True Facts: When are facts false?

Two Alternatives: An alternative refers to a choice between two things.

Well-known: If a man is, well-known, he would feel insulted to be so described.

Sierra Nevada Mountains: Sierra means mountains.

Cross-checking the Copy

A common error committed by subs is in-the matter of names. To this day many American papers spell the word "Gandhi'" wrongly. Whenever a difficult name like Dag Hammarskjold or AU Sastroamidjojo crops in it is common precaution to have the spelling checked for accuracy. The name Jayaprakash Narayan is spelled in at least six different ways. The important thing is to know how the leader himself wishes his name to be spelled and to accept that as the last word. Many newspapers have their own style book which lays down set rules of punctuation and spelling of proper names and even such mundane things as how to use S or Z in words like "realise"-all this in the interest of consistency.

Another error is in regard to figures. A *Times of India* reporter writing about an educational institution in south India in March 1979 said that eighty lakhs of rupees had been spent in celebrating the birthday of the institution's founder. Apart from the fact that this was inconceivable, the reporter bloated gaffe further by suggesting that the sum was drawn from institutional funds. In this instance the sub double-faulted not only in not checking on accuracy but also in the matter of personal bias.

6

Presentation of News

A news is a report of a recent or current event or an information published in a newspaper or other periodicals. In its final analysis, news may be defined as any accurate fact or idea that will interest a large number of readers; and of two stories the accurate one that interests the greater number of people is a better news. In a news strangeness, abnormality, unexpectedness and nearness of an event, all add to the interest in the story but none of these is absolutely essential.

Similarly, freshness, enormity, and departure from the normal also add greatly to the value of a news, but even these are not absolutely essential. The only requirements are that the story should be accurate and contain facts or ideas interesting to a considerable number of readers. Thus, the news is an information about an event, some development plans, movement of important persons, announcement of Government policies, etc. The news, of course, should be meaningful and have some importance for its readers. But a news should be an information that is both important and meaningful for the people. There is no doubt that an information may have importance for some people while it may have no significance for others. In fact, to become a good news, an information should have importance for a considerable number of readers.

Although, the factor of timeliness may not be absolutely essential, yet it does matter. A hot burning news is more eagerly awaited than a stale and old news. Immediacy of the news arouses the interest of the readers. Nevertheless, it does not mean that the past events can never become a good news. For example, if a new light is thrown on past happenings, even this may become a news. The quality of a news is in reality determined by many factors. Sometimes, proximity of an event may increase its importance for the readers. Similarly, stories of human interest and local problems may make a very good news.

Sometimes, the novelty or unique picture of an event may add to the importance of a news. Unusual events always make good news. The information factor in a news is also very important. Whatever adds to our knowledge about which we had no prior information makes a good news. The stories with human element are gaining much importance now-a-days due to their news value. These stories with human element arouse the emotions and sentiments of the readers and create an interest and sympathy in them for the human beings involved in these stories.

Relevant Characteristics

A guide to advanced techniques in journalism prepared by the Editorial Study Centre of the Thomson Foundation lists 20 categories of what makes news.

Let us examine them:

Novelty: Man bites dog. Wife beats husband. Cripple scores goal. Something that could happen but had never happened before. Mini-skirts were news when they became a vogue; so did flared trousers. And in an earlier era bikinis were hot news indeed.

Personal Impact: What interests the average reader in his daily life. Bombay Dyeing paying a bonus. Raj Kapoor's son getting married. Stories about people like himself (or herself) which gives the reader a chance to identify with them.

Local Interest: A local bus crash with three dead can be more interesting than 60 dead in a plane crash on the others side of the world.

Money: The budget (national, state, municipal) is news; so are taxes, fall in commodities prices, salary increments and economic crises.

Crime: Especially murder which has a morbid appeal. The Abhyankar murders, the Billa-Ranga kidnapping case are of steady interest, even to those who profess that they don't read crime stories. More often than not, they do.

Sex: This is of perennial interest as can be gauged by the number of even the most respectable magazines that cater to this aspect of life. Also, the more sordid the sex, the greater the curiosity about it.

Conflict: Conflict between man and wife resulting in divorce cases, between nations resulting in war, between man and nature resulting in the failure of one or the conquest of the other brings out reader interest. Thousands climbed Mount Everest with Tensing and Hillary.

Religion: Even an agnostic is interested in the election of a Pope; a Cardinal found dead in a Paris prostitute's apartment made news in a big way. Maharshi Mahesh Yogi, Rajneesh they all make news because they appeal to our emotions.

Disaster and Tragedy: The *Titanic* sinks with all aboard. French expedition to *Annapurna* fails. Lal Bahadur Shastri dies on the morrow of a successful peace treaty. A volcano erupts bringing in its wake death and destruction. "It could have happened to me" feels the reader.

Humour: H.V. Kamath is inform in Parliament making light hearted comments on his colleagues or even against himself. Raj Narain does some monkeying to catch attention. R.K. Laxman,draws a cartoon that daily draws a chuckle.

Human Interest: Ordeals suffered, happiness experienced, love's labour lost, stolen money recovered. A Prime Minister's daughter is arrested for drunkenness. A wolf boy is found in the jungles of Uttar Pradesh.

The Underdog: Charlie Chaplin's tramp in all variations in real life. The peasant who wins a case against a rapacious money lender. Stories illustrating *satyameva jayate.*

An example of a human interest story:

New Delhi, March 19 (PTI): A man in Pune went to buy meat worth Rs. 2. The butcher asked him if he had a bus ticket. The puzzled man asked why?

The butcher said the prices had gone up so high that he could wrap up meat worth Rs. 2 in a bus ticket.

The man produced the bus ticket and the meat was wrapped in it. By the time the man reached home, the meat had fallen through the punch hole the conductor had made in the ticket.

The Rajya Sabha heard this story from Congress-I member Vithal Gadgil, who narrated it during the discussion on the general budget in support of his contention that prices had shot up.

Or take this story:

Teheran, March 18 (Reuter): A woman received 100 lashes and a man 25 after being caught committing adultery in the Caspian Sea town of Amlash, newspapers reported today.

The woman fainted as the sentence was being carried out yesterday, the papers said, similar sentences have been ordered by Islamic tribunals in several towns since last month's revolution which toppled the Shah. Both the items were carried as box items in *The Hindustan Times.*

The second item carried the headline: Woman gets 100 lashes, man 25. And that, of course, was the reason why the news got a box.

Mystery: How did it happen? Where was the body? Who discovered it? Under what circumstances? Suspense can keep a story running for days. Remember the Billa-Ranga Murder Case. Or the Nagarwala story.

Health: Miracle drug, medical advice columns are always popular items. Any time there is a story of a cancer cure, it invariably finds place in the news columns. So do stories of *hatha yogis.*

Science: Space flights have triggered the most sluggish imaginations into demanding more information. John Glenn, Yuri Gagarin made the headlines. Winners of state prizes for scientific discoveries make stories. Nobel Prize winners, of course, are always good for top billing.

Entertainment: Show business makes news. Who is making what film? Why was a certain play banned? What is Amitabh

Bachchan's newest role? What is Satyajit Ray currently busy with?" 'The world of entertainment always holds a fascination that is perennial as the stars and the heavens above.

Famous People: People, especially famous people, make news. Whether they are film stars, sports heroes, musical prodigies or men in high office, their doings never fail to catch the attention of the reader. Famous people are especially newsworthy if they fall from power, fall from grace or fall into evil times. Jackie Kennedy Onassis continues to draw attention, so do the Shah of Iran or Mrs. Indira Gandhi, Ravi Shankar, Sunil Gavaskar and Vinoba Bhave.

Weather: They say that in Britain, the weather is an almost neurotic interest. In India there is a sense of impending doom if the monsoon is delayed or fails.

Food: Next to weather, food and drink is of abiding interest. Shortage of food is news, so is a glut. Have the prices fallen? Are they going up? What about hoarding and black marketing?

Minorities: In every country there is invariably a minority community and their treatment or problems are of especial interest. Blacks in the United States, Harijans in India or Christians in Orissa-as minorities and groups, they are in the news most of the time.

News Items of Interest

Newspapers now-a-days are also giving a lot of news in which their readers are particularly interested. Some newspapers even hold opinion polls to know in what columns their readers are more interested. The readers are also interested to read news about the day to day common problems which concern most of them.

Because of this, a lot of news about water shortages, electricity breakdowns, inadequacy of transport, scarcity of essential commodities, rising prices, etc. appear in the, newspapers quite often. The letters to the editor column is also a very good indicator and mirror of the problems and the interests of the readers.

The Needs

There are four requisites of a successful news story. These are the power to estimate news value, the stories to write, the ability to work rapidly and the power to represent facts accurately and interestingly. Of course, recognition of these news values implies the need for a "news nose".

Without it a reporter may not be able to achieve much success in his career. There are numerous examples of reporters who could not achieve success in their career because they lacked the quality to recognise news.

While writing a news, the reporter should remember the following points:

(i) The first essential of news writing is its accuracy.

(ii) Every reporter should remember that a newspaper's reputation for fairness and reliability rests upon an accurate presentation of the facts.

(iii) You should also keep in your mind, while writing about the facts, the number and class of people who would be interested in them as well as the need for printing them while they still have news value.

(iv) The geographical nearness of an event does add to its interest.

(v) The readers have a lot of interest in all sorts of contests.

(vi) News stories regarding the miseries of the people, helplessness of old people, children and animals also never fail to have an emotional appeal.

(vii) News concerning the well known local, national or international personalities is also welcomed by the people.

(viii) Even the stories that touch upon the domestic problems faced by the people, business interests of the people and industrial unrest, also command the attention of the public.

There is no doubt that all the features mentioned above are quite important and any of them will contribute greatly to make a story news-worthy. But you should always remember that none of these is absolutely essential. The main essential pre-requisite is that the news should be based upon facts and it should present a new situation or problem or even a new face of an old situation or problem.

Tiniest Peace of News

A professor of journalism was telling his students that "news" had to have a mix of religion, royalty, sex and mystery. He then asked them to write a news report. One answer went thus: "My God!" said the Duchess, "I'm pregnant! whodunit?"

Ask any ten newspapermen what they understand by news and you are likely to get ten different answers. Everyone has heard of the familiar cliche: "When dog bites man, it's no news; when man 'bites dog it's news."

Think of other definitions. "North, East, West, South, what comes fram there makes news."

"News is something revealed."

"News is something which somebody wants suppressed." "News is anything you didn't know yesterday."

"News is any event, idea or opinion that is timely, that interests or affects a large number of people in a community and that is capable of being understand by them."

"News is what the newspaper prints and radio broadcasts." "News is a compilation of facts and events of current interest or importance to the readers of the newspaper printing it."

"Sex, money, crime-that is news."

"News is anything and everything interesting about life and materials in all their manifestation."

"What is new in news."

These are definitions actually provided by distinguished news papermen. They are not necessarily contradictory. News has no "geographic boundaries. News is always revealing. News is what interests popple. News is news.

No news interests all people. Without consciously realising it, mast people read only part of the paper they buy. In others words their reading is highly selective. They read what *they* consider is news. This need not tally with the news editor's own understanding of what makes the front page. Too often the average reader's interest does not go beyond scandal, murder, crime of all sorts, and sex. Also the unusual (man bites dog), the incongruous and the unexpended (the cow jumps over the moon).

Foreseeable News Items

Some news is predictable. Some can be anticipated. But all too often news is unpredictable. What is predictable should be marked in advance by the Chief Reporter for adequate coverage. Failure to do so is inexcusable. Parliamentary or legislative sessions, enquiries by various committees, trials, international conferences.

I all these would have been announced in advance. So would news conferences, fashion and trade exhibitions and the like. Everyone knows when Diwali comes around and a pre-Diwali story literally writes itself.

Dates of strikes are often made known days or weeks ahead. What is involved in the strike? How many workers will be out of work? What is the strike's likely duration? A strike is a rich news vein to exploit for the competent reporter.

Some news can be anticipated, such as the completion of a waterworks, the extension of a roadway, the appointment of a cabinet minister, even the coming of the monsoon. Some of this involves intelligent guesswork based on knowledge of people and personalities, prior promises and research in the newspaper morgue.

News of Unpredictable Type

The unpredictable news is what stumps most reporters, and it is in their ingenuity in handling such news lies their real talent. The murder of a politician or a president, the collapse of a building, the eruption of a long dead volcano, a truant hurricane that leaves a trail of destruction in its wake, the sinking of a ship in mid-Pacific, the theft of a priceless painting from a famous museum, these are situations that are unpredictable and tax the strategies of the reporter's desk.

For everyone of these unpredictable events there is a sequential chain of enquiries to be made that a competent reporter knows how to handle. Information sources are easy to identify: official, such as the District Collector, the District Superintendent of Police and their respective offices, the local Janata (or Congress or Communist or any parallel) party office, the offices of relief organisations (Servants of India Society, Ramakrishna Mission, Church missions), the mamlatdar or petty revenue officials, the postmaster, the headmaster of the local school, the local lawyer.

In big cities there is a wider range of information sources available, both official and non-official. It is knowing how to collect the information, have it double checked for accuracy and writing it that distinguishes the competent from the incompetent, the smart from the dullard.

The Follow-up: News is not merely the reporting of one day's events. If that were so, there would be no need for a newspaper. Gossip could suffice. After all, if a plane crashes off Bombay's seas, the news gets known in no time, a daily or no daily. What is important for the reader is not merely the reporting of an event, but its follow-up.

On 9 August 1942, the All-India Congress Committee meeting at Gowalia Tank, Bombay, passed its famous Quit India resolution. It was the biggest event of the month, if not the year. But what followed was even more sensational. The Congress leaders had hardly gone to bed that night when they were picked up, one by one, by the police, herded into cars, driven to a train that was being kept ready for their arrival and taken to Poona. As much as the passing of the Quit India resolution was the report of the arrest of the leaders and their subsequent incarceration important.

There is therefore much truth in the comment that the follow-up is not only an essential part of an active newspaper's function but it often leads up to a more important story than the original. In fact, in this instant, the follow-up story never ceased to interest the reader until the country became free.

Follow-up implies continuity. This is not difficult in the case of major stories such as a Cabinet shake-up, an aircrash or a shipwreck. In the case of the latter two, it can never always be easy to get the full story at first shot. Lists of passengers are usually incomplete and in order to keep faith with the readers it will be necessary to balance out what was, very likely, an incomplete story that first broke out. Readers would be interested to know who the survivors were, what happened to them and whether they have been adequately taken care of. There will also be interest in why the accident occurred and what is likely to be done to see that there will not be a repetition of it in the future. In fact a newspaper which follows up and positively investigates what had happened takes its rightful place in the community.

News of Big Type

What is Big News? Here are a few examples: The re-induction of Charan Singh in the Desai Cabinet. The *faux pas* committed by the Prime Minister in prematurely announcing the "death" of Mr. Jayaprakash Narayan. Test cricket. The visit of Prince Charles to India, or of President Carter. The "blackout" in Calcutta. The toppling of the Karpoori Thakur Ministry in Bihar. The revolution in Iran. The defeat of Idi Amin. But what have they in common? Competition, conflict, confrontation. These invariably make Big News.

Spot News: Spot news is what it says: news gathered on the spot, live, recent, immediate and fresh with the reporter being able to say: "I was right there!" Spot news is not something that was expected or scheduled. It has an element of the exciting and the new.

News Story: Take any news story that appears in a newspaper. It will be noticed that it consists on a superficial look of three parts: the headline, the first paragraph usually set in bold and the remainder of the story.

The headline is the first to attract the reader. Giving an appropriate headline is an art in itself. Choosing the length and size of the headline is to make the first choice as to its importance and relevance. The headline's message is terse, abrupt and often startling. The whole idea is to makee the reader stop and look. The headline seeks to hold attention and compel the reader to read the story.

But an effective headline is not sufficient unto itself. A great deal depends on the first paragraph. It is called lead because it leads the rest of the story. It is also called the intro because it introduces the rest to the reader. If the lead or intro is not sufficiently arresting, interest will lag and the reader's eye may wander-on to another headline and another story. Hence, the importance of writing the catchy first paragraph.

Convention requires that in the lead the reporter must answer "the five W's: Who, What, When, Where, Why and the one H—How? But that was in the old days.

These days it is a convention honoured more in the breach than the observance. In fact a religious observance of the convention would make a lead paragraph unwieldy and heavy. The practice nowadays is to write a lead of not more than 30 words. The former International News Service's style book instructed its staff to write the lead in three lines or less. Any good reporter can tell you that the news can be told effectively within these set limits.

But what exactly is expected of a good lead or intra? The follow*ing* general points are almost universal:

1. The intro should be appropriate for the story.
2. The intra should make the reader want to read the rest of the story.
3. The intra should be kept short whenever possible.
4. The intra should normally be based on the key point of the story. One news editor summed it all up tersely in eighteen words. "Spill the whole story in the first paragraph and maintain the interest for the rest of the copy." It is a sound advice.

To begin with the first rule, appropriateness. Obviously a serious news story calls for a serious intra and a flippant story a flippant intra, unless of course a writer desires to treat a serious story in a light-hearted manner. One does not write about the death of a politician or any citizen in words such as: "Shri Blank blank kicked the bucket early this morning," however much he was held in contempt by the reporter or the public. The best intros are those which make a reader want to read the rest of the story. It is common knowledge among reporters that few readers go beyond the sixth paragraph in any news story but a poorly written intro may inhibit the reader from reading even paragraph two.

The short intra is easier to read and by its very nature may goad the reader to read on. But it is the fourth rule that about sums up the ideal intra, namely, its insistence on telling what the central or "key" point of the story is all about, in the very first lines. This is harder to observe than one thinks. In the first place there may be more than one "key" point to a story. Should the story, then, be broken up into separate stories? Given the constraints of time and column space, how should the rule be observed?

In the second place this does not take into account the need for a "delayed intro" which a writer may want to use to "get the stage" for the key item to be presented later on in the story.

The "delayed intro" does not mention the key point but only gives a bare hint of what is to come and is in the nature of a "teaser" or a "come-on." Such an intra is not commonly in use in Indian papers which have no column space for the elaboration of a story and the use of gimmickry. Take this intro, for example. Bombay, June 4: Nineteen year old Shriman Narayan climbed out of his bed about 6.00 a.m. picked a gun that he had hid under his pillow all night, walked over to his parents' bedroom and opened the door.

Well, what was he up to? Was he about to kill his parents? Was he merely playing a practical joke by wielding a gun? Was he about to commit suicide but only anxious to take one last look at his dad and mum? The delayed intro does not tell us, but the reader's curiosity is firmly aroused. This, needless to say, is the opposite of what is known as the "inverted pyramid" style of news story writing where the key point is quickly noted in the very first paragraph, as below:

Bombay, June 4: A 19-year old student today shot his aged parents in the early hours of the morning.

Or

Bombay, June 4: Shriman Narayan, 19, a student of Blank High School today shot himself to death in the early hours of the morning.

A story with multiple 'key points' can either be broken up in parts or told chronologically with the headlines telling the facts.

Take this story about a meeting of the AICC (I) held in New Delhi on 21 April. Here ate its main ingredients:

The meeting was the first it held since the Congress split in 1978. The meeting saw a clash between Indira Gandhi and Devraj Urs. The meeting also saw a clash between Mrs. Gandhi and Tarakeshwari Sinha who walked out of the meeting in a huff.

The meeting issued a strong indictment of Janata rule in a resolution passed unanimously.

This is how *The Times of India, The Free Press Journal, The Press Trust of India* and *United News of India* wrote the story:

The Times of India

New Delhi: April 21. A threat' by the Karnataka Chief Minister Mr. Devraj Urs, to expose those partymen who surreptitiously went to Mr. Sanjay Gandhi to get things done by his mother and a clash between Mrs. Tarakeshwari Sinha and Mrs. Indira Gandhi, the Congress (I) president, marked the first day's nine-hour long session of the A.T.C.C. (I) here today.

The *Times* report then went on to detail the proceedings in chronolological order but nowhere did it give in its l8-paragraph copy what exactly was the nature of the clash between Mrs. Gandhi and Mrs. Sinha.

The Free Press Journal of 22 April led off with its own correspondent's report of the AICC (I) proceedings, but gave two separate reports from the PTI, one concerning Mrs. Gandhi's clash with Urs and another with her clash with Mrs. Sinha in the inside pages:

FPI Correspondent

New Delhi, April 21: Differences on the role of Mr. Sanjay Gandhi leading to an open clash between Mrs. Indira Gandhi and Mr. Devraj Urs, Karnataka Chief Minister, as also between Mrs. Gandhi and Mrs. Tarakeshwari Sinha, marked the proceedings of the AICC(I) which began its two-day session here today.

This was the first AICC(I) meeting since the Congress split in 1978. Mr. Urs who moved the main resolution on the political situation, at the end of his one-hour speech referred to the talks of emergence of Mr. Sanjay Gandhi into politics and said these were mere gossip. He had earlier paid tributes to the leadership of Mrs. Gandhi.

Seen visibly annoyed at the reference to Sanjay, Mrs. Gandhi indicated that Mr. Urs should conclude his speech. He did, but soon after Mr. Urs and Mrs. Gandhi were engaged in a heated discussion as observed from their gestures (nothing of their talks was heard) from the Press Gallery. Soon after, Mr. Urs left the talks. He, however, returned late in the afternoon to wind up the debate. Both inside the AICC(I) pandal and outside, groups of people were engaged in sharply criticising Mr. V rs and demanding his expulsion from the party.

Mr. Urs had threatened to 'expose' all those who went to Mr. Sanjay Gandhi for various work.

Mrs. Sinha also got up and said that the Congress (I) should beware of such persons who went to Mr. Gandhi and such people should be removed from the party. She also said that Mrs. Gandhi was surrounded by an evil circle (Shani chakra).

Mrs. Gandhi who was presiding, pointedly told Mrs. Sinha that the session was caned to discuss policies and programmes and not personalities. She denied Mrs. Sinha's charge but the latter persisted and said that shops were being run in the name of either Mrs. Gandhi or Mr. Sanjay Gandhi.

This led to the clash and Mrs. Sinha left the session in a huff.

The Press Trust of India treated the story of the AICC(I) session in two parts (as published in *the Free Press Journal).*

In pursuance of its policy to give a "straight" report of the events, the PTI was careful not to seem to be editorialising. The Gandhi Sinha tiff was reported thus:

New Delhi, April 21 (PTI): Mrs. Tarakeshwari Sinha threw her papers on the dais today and walked out of the AICC(I) meeting after heated exchanges with Mrs. Indira Gandhi.

Exchanges took place after Mrs. Sinha said, "People have formed a Saturn's ring round you" and "some people are trading on your name and on the name of your son."

Mrs. Gandhi snapped at her: "This session has been convened to discuss issues and not personalities. I will not allow anybody to discuss personalities. This happened also in the morning and I am not going to allow it." (She was obviously referring to Mr. Devraj Urs' remarks about Mr. Sanjay Gandhi).

Mrs. Sinha retorted that she was not mentioning personalities but only raising relevant issues.

At this stage, Mrs. Sinha was heckled by a section of the participants.

"Do I have no right to speak?" she asked. When heckling 'continued, Mrs. Sinha walked out in protest saying she was not being allowed to have her word.

Mrs. Gandhi remarked, "I am sorry Mrs. Sinha walked out in a huff. I did not stop her from speaking."

The UNI report was bland and chronological to the point of being unreadable. As published in *The Economie Times,* it went 'thus New Delhi, April 21 (UNI): Congress (1) president Indira Gandhi slid here today that an air of "uncertainty and instability" pervaded the country which virtually threatened its unity and integrity. In her opening remarks at the two-day session at the All India Congress Committee (I) she said poverty and backwardness could not be fought unless the country's security and unity were ensured.

The UNI report went on for 19 more paragraphs before the Gandhi-Urs and Gandhi-Sinha clashes were presented, as from the PTI. The PTI report, incidentally quoted the actual words used by Mrs. Sinha in Hindi which annoyed Mrs. Gandhi to impart a flavour to the clash.

The story of the meeting of the AICC(I) lends itself to illustrate several possible intros.

Summary Intro: New Delhi, April 21: Differences on the role of Mr. Sanjay Gandhi led to an open clash between Mrs. Indira Gandhi, Congress (I) president and two of her supporters Mr. Devraj Urs and Mrs. Tarakeshwari Sinha today.

This lead summarises a key point or points. It does not "spill the whole story" but imparts a sense of what was the central issue at the AICC(I) meeting, which was the undercurrent of unease among many delegates over the role that Sanjay Gandhi had in the past played and was likely to play in the future. To attempt to write a more comprehensive paragraph would only lead to lengthening it without necessarily making it more readable.

Figurative or Colour Intro: A second possible intro for this story is the figurative or colour intro:

New Delhi, April 21: Mrs. Indira Gandhi quickly doused an anti-Sanjay Gandhi fire which threatened to break out at the first meeting of the AICC(I) today by refusing to let two of her supporters strike the match.

The figurative intro makes use of figures of speech-in this instance, setting a fire and quickly dousing it-that is, common uses of words in the figurative rather than the literal sense, which is rather eye-catching though somewhat irreverent.

Oddity Intro: A third though somewhat odd intro makes an effort to draw attention to the story by an unusual approach:

New Delhi, April 21: Wanted: Supporters to Mrs. Indira Gandhi, president of the AICC(I) who will unquestioningly accept her leadership and will not challenge her son Sanjay Gandhi's pretensions at being her heir-apparent.

Quotation Intro: New Delhi: April 21: "Mrs. Indira Gandhi, is our unquestioned' leader" Mr. Devraj Urs, Chief Minister of Karnataka told a meeting of the AICC(I) today.

In the light of reports that Urs has been openly meeting Janata Party president Chandrasekhar and the implications sought to be drawn that this could lead to the former defection from the AICC (I) camp, this short intro makes the firm point that the Karnataka Chief Minister is still devoted to Mrs. Gandhi

A general rule in using quotation intros is to use them sparingly, since they are too easy to write and can become "an easy way out." A quotation intro that is more brusque can run as follows:

New Delhi, April 21: "She is my unquestioned leader."

But this must be immediately followed by a para which identifies the persons involved, in this case Mrs. Gandhi and Urs and the context in which the comment is made.

Question Intro: The question intro is more apt for a background feature to the news story. But consider this intro appropos the AICC(I) story:

New Delhi, April 21: Who would have thought that the hegemany of Mrs. Indira Gandhi, president of the AICC(I) would ever he challenged by two of her most vocal supporters of the past, Mr. Devraj Drs and Mrs. Tarakeshwari Sinha?

Here the reporter has sought to involve the reader in what he believes is the key issue at stake. The question intro has its uses, but like the quotation intro it is best used sparingly, and only when the question asked really illuminates the story. In this example, the second paragraph would have to explain the intro some what like this:

This is the question in many minds today as first the Karnataka Chief Minister and then Mrs. Sinha clashed with Mrs. Gandhi and the leader walked out of the session in a huff.

Dialogue Intro: New Delhi. April 21: "People have formed al Saturn's ring round you and some people are trading on your name and on the name of your son." Mrs. Tarakeshwari Sinha told the president of AICC(I) Mrs. Indira Gandhi today.

"This session has been convened to discuss issues and not personalities. I will not allow anybody to discuse personalities." Mrs. Gandhi replied from the chair.

A dialogue is always eye-catching and direct quotes are more attractive than an indirect statement. But the trouble with a dialogue intro is that the story has to be needlessly lengthened in order to explain the situation to a reader.

Descriptive Intro: New Delhi, April 21: Hundreds of citizens milled around the AICC(I) pandal here today as delegates to the session inside fought bitterly over whether Mr. Sanjay Gandhi's intrusion in to Congress politics was to be welcomed or not.

The idea behind the descriptive intro is to take the reader on to the scene and provide him with a feel of the place, with people milling around, words and biows flung at each other, chappals flying and the conference site in disorder. The descriptive intro is best used when the story lends itself especially to description and where the description adds a great deal to the mood and content of the story.

Bullet Intro: New Delhi. April 21: The battle over Sanjay Gandhi was over.

The bullet intro is a very short sentence-usually a flash message which carries impact. It comes in most handy when an event of earth-shaking importance takes place as when Mahatama Gandhi was assassinated or President Kennedy was killed. In the case of the latter the bullet intro could be:

Dallas, Texas: The President is dead.

It tells the story simply, with no pretensions at embellishment because no embellishment is necessary. When Prime Minister Nehru died, the pews was conveyed to Parliament by C. Subramaniam in the words, "The Light is gone." It was the phrase used by Nehru himself to describe the passing away of Mahatma Gandhi. In a cricket story, one can imagine a bullet intro such as:

London, July 6: The Aussies regained the Ashes.

Staccato Intro: New Delhi, April 21: Angry words. A call to order. More recriminations. Heckling. And then a walk-out.

This is an example of a staccato intro, with words being used like bullets from a machine gun whose noise is invoked in the phrase. Ideally the staccato intro should be constructed as to give a certain rhythm to the whole paragraph so that a certain mood is established, of dissidence, noise, disruption, anger. Incidentally this can also be a descriptive intro which only goes to show that two or more types of intros could be combined effectively by the trained reporter.

Writing an intro is an art by itself. In some offices the intro is written not by the reporter himself but by a senior who has gone through the mill. But no 'matter who writes it, presents a difficult task to the writer. It is his big moment. He is making a grand entrance into the main current of the story. On the intro depends the "life" of the copy and in the circumstances he cannot dither with it. There is about it a feeling of "now or never."

A reporter frequently finds that if he gets the intro right, the story comes right too. There is considerable truth in the saying that the best of the story, if told in the intro, makes the story glow. A beginner must learn to write intros to as many stories as possible until he writes the intro that fits the story.

Some reporters hurry back to their offices ready to start writing. Some others prefer to take a break and spend some time doing something else in order to let the story sink in their minds. Each reporter has his own way of approaching that magic moment when he has to submit his copy and start writing. There is no precise way to write an intro though the choice should usually be clear-cut to a trained reporter. But some approaches are manifestly wrong and should be avoided.

The negative approach:

New Delhi, April 21: Sources close to Mrs. Indira Gandhi would neither confirm nor deny that there has been a major rift between her and Mr. Devraj Urs. *(wrong)*

Better say:

New Delhi, April 21: A rift between Mrs. Indira Gandhi and Karnataka Chief Minister Mr. Devraj Urs was clearly noticeable to many delegates as the first day of the two-day session of the AICC (I) ended here today.

The inverted sentence:

New Delhi, April 21: As she walked to the dais dressed in a blue-bordered sari and a rudrakshimala hanging round her neck, Mrs. Indira Gandhi was loudly and vociferouly cheered by a section of the delegates. *(wrong)*

Better say:

New Delhi, April 21: Mrs. Indira Gandhi received a rousing cheer as she entered the-venue of the AICC (I) session today.

The cluttered sentence:

New Delhi, April 21: Mrs. Indira Gandhi, Mr. Devraj Urs and Mrs. Tarakeshwari Sinha were involved in battle of words at the 2-day session of the AICC (I) held here

> today that resulted in a behind-the-scene tussel between Mrs. Gandhi and Mr. Urs and an angry walk-out by Mrs. Sinha.

Here there are too many names and too many situations all strung together in one paragraph. Better say:

> New Delhi, April 21: Mrs. Tarakeshwari Sinha walked out of a meeting of the AICC (I) today after a tiff with Mrs. Indira Gandhi.

All intros, of course, must reflect the content of the story. If a bank raid is foiled, then HOW is probably worth the intro. If it was pulled off, then WHERE and HOW MUCH would be more in order. Always to be avoided is over-dramatisation and the use of words' such as "exciting," "nerve-tingling" and "sensational." Let the story itself provide the excitement and the sensation.

Part Played by Newspapers

A newspaper's role is to reveal the why and wherefores (background) and not merely the whos and whens and whats. This implies that it keeps up with a story until everything falls in its place and for all practical purposes its significance has been understood and appreciated. A newspaper that fails to follow up a story merely prints a series of unrelated events, never projects life as a pattern. A newspaper's approach must be holistic, not frog monetary.

In a good newspaper office the News Editor or the Chief Reporter or the Editor himself (depending on how large the staff is) will carefully go through every item in his own or a rival newspaper looking for possible follow-ups. One will invariably find them. It is better to have those items clipped and pasted on to a sheet on which instructions could then be written. It is important that the sheets are "marked," which means putting down the name of the paper, the date on which it was published and the page number for future identification. It is usual to mark the clipping in red ink.

Those clippings that may not be of immediate use, but could provide information for a likely story in the weeks ahead should be put into a folder for future reference. In all large newspaper offices there is usually a clipping service that provides ready reference. Smaller offices that cannot afford such a service must maintain their own, no matter on how small a scale.

The Curtain-raiser: A curtain-raiser is a story on what is likely to happen and not a report on what has happened. It raises the curtain to show what is on the stage and how the drama will unfold itself. It is to a news event what an appetiser is to a meal it whets one's appetite to know what is going to come. A curtain raiser is based on past events and the reporter's understanding of what is likely to come on the strength of his information on what had happened in the past. Take this example:

Patna, April 21. A split in the Bihar Janata Party seems imminent judging by the letter die outgoing Chief Minister, Mr. Karpoori Thakur, is believed to have sent to the acting governor, Mr. K.B.N. Singh.

The letter says that Mr. Thakur and his 104 associates will not support the government headed by Mr. Ram Sunder Das if anyone having links with RSS is sworn in as a minister in his Cabinet.

A sealed cover containing the letter was delivered to the acting governor a few hours before the swearing-in of the two member Cabinet headed by Mr. Das.

Mr. Thakur's letter to the governor at this stage has far-reaching implications. Mr. Thakur specifically states that until the RSS is cleared of the charge of its involvement in the Jamshedpur riots by a three-man panel suggested by him, no persons having links with the RSS should be included in the Cabinet.

The letter was drafted in consultation with Mr. Raj Narain and Mr. S.N. Mishra who have been camping here for the past three days. According to knowledgeable circles in Mr. Thakur's camp, a split in the Janata Party is a foregone conclusion.

The group has decided to show its strength on the floor of the house at the June session of the Assembly if the party does not formally split before that.

This was the lead story in *The Times of India* (22 April 1979) by its Special Correspondent. It is evident that the correspondent had close links with the Janata Party and especially the Chief Minister Mr. Thakur. The first paragraph or "intro" suggeste that the Bihar Janata Party may split and that the split is imminent. It bases the prediction on what the correspondent knows-in this case a letter sent by the outgoing Chief Minister to the Acting Governor of Bihar. The correspondent then moves on to dissect the likely results if the threat implied in the outgoing Chief Minister's letter is met. The only "hard" news in this story is the fact that Mr. Thakur has sent a letter to the Acting Governor. The correspondent had obviously been told about its contents. His "curtain-raiser" is thus based on what is known to move on to what is likely to happen.

A curtain-raiser is generally careful not to be too specific. It is couched in such terms as "The likelihood of " "Possibilities were raised" "it seems obvious that" "the question is expected to be raised" all of which suggesting the reporter's grasp of how a given situation may develop.

Sometimes the reporter would have been briefed by an official source on what is yet to come. Take this example from *The Economic Times:*

New Delhi, April 21: The Union Government proposes to undertake legislations to provide safety for workers in building and construction industry and to regulate the conditions of work of inter-state migrant workers to prevent their exploitation by contractors, according to the annual report of the Ministry of Labour for the year 1978-79.

The Ministry is planning amendments to the Mines Act, the Plantation Labour Act and the Employees Provident Funds and Miscellaneous Provisions Act.

In this instance, the Ministry of Labour's report would havebeen made available to all reporters who would have been briefed on what the Ministry proposes to do in the future.

A curtain-raiser, to be sure, is scheduled on the day a meeting is to take place so that it has an aura of freshness. When the curtain is raised, there must be someone on the stage for action to begin. *The Economic Times* story comes under the category or Predictive Coverage, *The Advance Story.*

The Local Follow-up: It is important for a reporter to read overseas journals and magazines to keep tag of events that would necessitate local follow-ups. Thus, when it became known that several hundred women in Europe had given birth to malformed children es a result of taking thalidomide during their stage or pregnancy, it is the reporter's task to find out whether authorities in India have been apprised of the birth of malformed children in any significant numbers, whether thalidomide or any other drug of a similar chemical composition is available in the market and who is doing the marketing. A report in *The Times of India* that suggested that severe illnesses had been encountered in Japan as a result of taking enterovioform resulted in enquiries made of doctors in India as to whether similar illnesses had been observed among their patients. The enquiry showed that Indians, for some reason, seemed better conditioned than the Japanese.

The Hidden Story: Reporters have often to plough through long and laborious speeches and reports that taxes their patience. But ploughing through them with care and thoroughness can be very rewarding. In the mid-1950s, Secretary of State John Foster Dulles made a lengthy speech to the UN General Assembly dealing with great issues of State, but tucked in somewhere half-way was the barest of hints that Goa was part of Portugal.

Unless a reporter went through the entire speech which was several thousand word long it was likely that this reference to Goa would be missed and it was probably the intention of the US Administration that the reference-and its significance-would be missed by reporters but not by Lisbon for whom it was evidently meant. All western news agencies which covered Mr. Dulles' speech missed this point, either unknowingly or intentionally but the Press Trust of India's correspondent in the United Nations got on to it and made it his lead.

Understandably it was the lead story in all Indian newspapers since India was concerned about American support to Portugal on the Goa issue.

Jawaharlal Nehru once addressed an AICC session and covered a lot of ground in a lengthy speech. He wanted, however, that one policy statement should be highlighted in the press. He therefore asked the senior PTI correspondent covering the AICC session to come and see him. Nehru then,handed him a slip of paper on which he had written down the policy statement with the suggestion that the PTI lead with it. The next day, according to Mr. T.V. Parasuram, the correspondent in question, several delegates asked him whether Mr. Nehru had indeed said the things the PTI had attributed to him. Nehru, needless to say, had carefully wrapped up his controversial policy statement in a lot of rhetoric in much the same manner as Mr. Dulles had covered his policy, statement on Goa.

Almost any report, if carefully persued, can give excellent leads for stories. It is the reporter's duty to go through reports page by page and line by line. *The Times of India's* Washington correspondent, going through the *Congressional Record,* soon after the Bangladesh war was over, learnt that the Pakistani submarine *Ghazi* with ten torpedo tubes which had been sunk by Indian-action off Visakhapatnam had been an American submarine on Joan which had been in Pakistan's possession illegally, the loan period having been exceeded by 18 months. His story made the front page lead on 27 December 1971. Reading the voluminous *Record* systematically paid off.

The Other Side: Politicians are apt to give only their version of, an event which is only to be expected. Rival politicians inevitably will have *their* version of the story to give which provides the reporter with fresh copy to file. On occasions, the other side may provide even newsier information which the first side had wanted to suppress or otherwise keep out of the press. The other side is the simplest form of follow-up. A reporter is advised never to take the word of a politician, no matter how highly placed, as final. There is always another side to a story and not infrequently it could be the more exciting one.

Enlargements: More efforts are spent in hiding the truth while, giving answers to written questions in Parliament than most readers are aware of Reporters should read the written answers and the supplementaries-very carefully for possible leads. Some of the replies could conceal a good news story if developed. What is being sought to be concealed? And for what reason? Who are the people who could provide the necessary background for an investigative report? The first thing for a reporter to do is to contact the Member of Parliament who had submitted the question and to see who his contacts are:

Elements Deciding Value of News: Four main factors determine the value of news: Timeliness, proximity, size and importance.

Timeliness: The reader wants his news to be new. That is why he buys his paper or listens to the broadcast. A newspaper that publishes stale news soon ceases to have any meaningful circulation. News coming out of the press must be really hot, in the sense of being not only exciting but new not till then known. The saying "stale as yesterday's news" is its own comment.

Proximity: The reader finds more interest in a minor event close at hand than in a more important event miles away-James Gordon Bennett Jr., when he first published his Paris edition of *The Herald'* gave his reporters this principle in the epigram. "A dead dog in the Rue de Louvre (the paper's address) is of more interest than a flood in China." This may be exaggerating a bit, but it makes the point nicely. But proximity is both geographical as well as emotional. The murder of an Indian diamond merchant in New York is news in Bombay, not only because the merchant happens to be an Indian but because he may be having friends in Bombay. The murder of the wife of an Indian official in the World Bank in a Washington suburb similarly made the headlines in Bombay papers, especially because the murderer happened to be the official's Indian domestic servant.

Size: The very small and the very large draw attention. If Mrs. Indira Gandhi addressed ten people at a wayside village it is unlikely to make news but if she called on Capt. M.M. Chopra and his wife following the murder of their two children Geeta and Sanjay, it is news. If Morarji Desai failed to get a sizeable audience at Ram Lila grounds it becomes news even as it becomes news if Mrs. Gandhi attracted large crowds when she was taken in procession through the streets of Old Delhi in 1979.

Similarly, if a Tiger Moth crashes while a cadet is under training, the accident may be dismissed in a brief paragraph while the crash of a Boeing 747 carrying 400 passengers would make the headlines.

Importance: In the final analysis the question that a News Editor will ask is whether what has been submitted to him is really important. While this is subjective, it has direct bearing on the kind of audience that the newspaper has in mind. What sounds important to *Blitz* may not be important to *The Statesman,* and *vice versa.*

In the context of the political situation prevailing in April 1979, a dinner meeting between Karnatak Chief Minister Devraj Urs, then a prominent Congress (I) leader and supporter of Mrs. Indira Gandhi with Chandrasekhar, president of the Janata Party assumes special meaning and significance and makes news. For that matter Mrs. Gandhi's call on Charan Singh when the latter was out of office following his dismissal from the Morarji Desai Cabinet made news because of what it could mean in terms of a approchement between Mrs. Gandhi and Charan Singh.

7

News Communication

Communication Tools

The following are the important telecommunication tools:

Telegram: A written message supplied to the department of telecommunication which in turn sends the message by telegram.

Telegraph: A system of sending message by telegraph using either wires and electricity or radio.

Telegraphist: Also called Telegrapher. He is a person who operates a telegraph and acts as intermediary between communicator and recipient.

Telegraphy: With reference to telecommunication telegraphy is the process of sending a message by telegraph. Telegraph wire by which telegraph messages are sent.

Telepathy: A quite different style of communication of ideas and thoughts directly from one person's mind without the use of audio or visual help. Telepathist is a person who studies or practises telepathy.

Telephone Booth: Other names used are telephone box, call box. It is a small room or compartment established at a prominent public place containing a telephone for public use.

Telephone Directory: The directory is a specially prepared type of volume containing names and addresses of a particular group. The telephone directory is a special book containing a list of names, addresses and telephone numbers of a group of all the people in a particular area who have telephones. The list is arranged in alphabetical order.

Telephone Exchange: A centrally controlled system through which telephone calls are directed. The telephonist in a telephone exchange on being given a number connects. The use of the telephone exchange is necessary in case of non-STD and in the absence of direct dialling operations.

Teleprinter: A machine in a communication system. Teleprinter is a machine, a specialised type of type-writer. A telegraphic system or instrument by which messages are sent out at one place and received at another place in a printed form. The typing is connected to a telephone line and the message typed at one place transmits electrical signal over wire and the same message is simultaneously reproduced, printed at a distant place by the machine. It is used as a private circuit or through the post office telex service system. The post offices give teleprinters on rent to form a part of private telecommunication.

Tele type: An electronic system of transmitting information in typewritten form. Used in operation of the various public relations, newswires, as well as by the Associated Press and United Press International.

Telex: Sending messages by teleprinters. Detailed discussion is given under the teleprinter paragraph.

The most popularly used speedy forms of external communication and mechanical devices are telegrams, cablegrams and telex messages. It is pertinent to remember that these tools are commonly and widely practised techniques of communication in every organisation irrespective of the form and nature of the business organisation. These communication instruments are used when the message must reach the receiver on the subject matter which is more important and urgent. Indeed it is to be noted that with the increase in the area of operation and the urgency of the matters on which decisions have to be taken telegrams, cablegrams and telex techniques are widely practised. The advantages of these techniques are that they help to get rid of the problem of distance, save time and the receiver draws immediate attention to the central theme of the matter. But while using these techniques care should be taken to frame the message correctly.

The essentials of a good telegram, cablegram and telex are that they should be concise, clear, simple and selective with appropriate words conveying the correct theme of the matter to avoid ambiguity. The words are selected in such a way so as to economise the cost of sending messages. Undoubtedly, therefore, the transmitter of the message is to be well versed in precise writing, to follow certain principles to make the communication really effective. The message to be effective, the central idea should be identified, sentences should be short and economically worded.

Communication of News

Written documents containing messages or subject matters are to be transmitted. The question often arises how to transmit written messages. In use there are two methods of transmitting messages.

By Messengers: This is a manual method of transmitting written message by the communicator to the receiver. A messenger is an employee meant for delivery of a message from one person to another person or from one department to another. The communicators call the messengers by using signals or a buzzer and instruct them to deliver the message to the directed person or department. Though, a primitive method of communication it is still being used in all organisations.

Every organisation has an internal mail service under which a messenger or messengers are required to meet regularly at a particular place like a department or desk or both, to deliver written communications brought from other departments or desks, and to take the message relating to other departments or desks.

The Advantages

1. The time of the executive is saved.
2. Executives are assisted by messengers who bring messages from other desks or departments.
3. Under this system timely decision is possible.

4. There will be many messenger services of not less than 4 to 5 deliveries in an hour.

5. Messengers service method can be used for many purposes. For instance, messenger services from executives to individual subordinate. Similarly messenger services from one department to another.

Mechanical devices are also introduced for transmission of written messages. Mechanical instruments carry messages from one place to another. Therefore, mechanical devices are broadly categorised into four types for transmission of written communication within the office. They are:

A conveyor is a mechanical device that conveys communication. A moving conveyor with moving belt of rubber, metal used for carrying papers and documents from one place to another. The messages are put on the conveyor which travels on fixed routes where papers and documents are picked. Conveyors are most useful when forwarding a large volume of papers and documents. They operate by a motor driven belt under them, moves along its routes and stops at fixed stations. Overhead write conveyors, horizontal conveyors, roller conveyors and vertical conveyors are the various types of conveyors in use in offices.

A chute is a sloping channel for sending objects. A structure of wide diameter pipes or channels running downward from top to bottom or from upper level to lower level. A chute is made of metal or wood. This device can also be used for transmission of papers and documents in larger quantities from one place located at an upper level to another place at a lower level.

Devices operated electrically or hydraulically used to raise or bring messages. A small enclosed platform that moves up and down, as operated, carrying articles. The written papers or documents or files can be transmitted between floors continuously. Lifts for transmission of messages are most useful in case of an organisation located in a multi-storied building.

When pneumatic devices are desired to be installed, a cylindrical pipe is connected to various offices. The cylinders containing papers and documents are transmitted by suction from one department to another within the office. Plastic conveyors are also now in popular use. Pneumatic tubes may be of a radial type, or of a continuous loop type.

Others: (a) teleprinter, (b) Telewriter, (c) Telefax, (d) Television.

General Methods

External communication is a part of the communication network of the organisation. Most external correspondence is through written communication. It is by post. The postal department is the important department of the Government of India which has established a wide network of communication services throughout the country.

The communication services provided by the postal department is of immense value not only to the business community but also all sections of society. External communication is between the organisation and outsiders. In this mail service the department is very essential for smooth functioning and work. If the mail is delayed the office work is also delayed. If communication services are inadequate it leads not only to late delivery of correspondence but also disrupts office work.

Mail service keeps work effective and workers with work. Therefore, it can be said that efficient communication sciences must be provided by the postal department. A business house may receive several letters and may correspond with them. The object of the mail service is to carry written communication. The message so transmitted should be interpreted and the decision is taken to act on that. In order to meet the needs of different businesses the postal department has been rendering different types of communication services. These services are most useful, particularly for external written communication. The important communication services are listed as under:

Prepaid Postage: Prepaid means payment in advance to the postal department. It avoids the work of affixing stamps on each letter. It is an arrangement with the post office department to facilitate this work. Under this scheme the person or the institution availing this facility has to pay postage in cash. In case there are a large number of standard letters to be despatched the postal department provides this facility.

Value Payable Post (V.P.P.): The post office value payable postal service is more useful particularly to mail order business houses or book publishers and sellers. In this service the post office acts as an agent in collecting money or value from the customers. For instance, a book publisher may despatch a book under V.P.P. service. This means the price of the book is collected by the post office for and on behalf of the publisher or seller.

Certificate of Posting: This is a mail service, under which the post office gives a certificate of posting. This certificate is evidence that a particular letter has been actually posted. For this service the post office collects a requisite fee. In all ordinary mail posted no certificate is issued. It is an additional service of giving a certificate which serves as proof in case of dispute regarding communication. Company meeting notices, interview cards, etc., are generally posted under certificate of posting.

Post Box Number: The postal department gives a separate post box number. It is also known as post box, letter box or mail box. This service helps to take delivery of the post direct from the post office from the post box without waiting for the postman. A business organisation, institution or individual with an arrangement with the post office gets the number allotted. Their mail is directly put into the box provided the post box number is written in the address.

Business Reply Cards: Business houses engaged in the mail order business usually use business reply cards. The reply cards help the receiver place the orders in accordance with the requirements of the business. With arrangement with the post office under licence, this facility can be availed of. But a certain sum of money as fee is payable for this service. The postal department may prescribe certain standards and business reply cards or envelopes should conform to the standards.

Concessional Postage: Concessional rates of postage are another important mail service rendered by the postal department. A company engaged in a large number of letters, bulky, more weight and printed matters can avail of the facility of concessional rates of postage. The department extends concessional rates of postage in respect of books, samples, patterns, printed magazines and journals, registered newspapers, etc. Thus, concessional rate is very helpful to certain business houses.

Registered Post: This service helps provide security for delivering communication provided the correct address is given. Remitting money by money-orders, remittance through bank-drafts, cheques, etc., can be despatched either through registered or insured letters.

Acknowledgement Receipts: When a particular letter is sent by registered post, with acknowledgement due, the post office gives the acknowledgement receipt of the addressee. This serves as evidence in case of dispute of communication.

Telegraphic Address: An abbreviated telegraphic address can be used in transmitting a message by the communicator to the receiver. The telegraphic address is to be registered with the post office. A word containing 10 letters or less is to be registered; it serves as a telegraphic address. In cases where a telegraphic address is used, the full address is not required to be written on the telegrams. This facility saves a lot of time and cost.

Cipher Telegrams: This is a fast communication service through telegrams. This message is transmitted in code language and the recipient has necessarily to decode the message. The receiver finds it difficult to decode the message, for which he should be acquainted with the code language.

Phonogram: A phonogram is used for sending and receiving the message through a telegram. The subject matter of the message is dictated over the telephone at either side. The cost of the phonogram will be included in the routine telephone bill.

Recording Process

One of the important merits of written communication is that written message can he preserved as records and reference source. It has the capacity of being stored as a record. At times the records can be used as evidence. Reports, circulars, notices, manuals, memos and other printed written or typed documents can be filed and preserved for future reference and can be produced as legal evidence.

So filing of written communication is obviously important because there is a very large number of papers and other media of written communications which have to be handled and preserved. Generally, however, serious attention is not given to filing of messages because some people think that it is not a useful activity, but this is not a correct understanding of the importance of filing written messages. There are a number of advantages which a business house can derive from a proper system of filing.

Filing is a process of collection of papers of particular subject. Filing with reference to written communication is the systematic arrangement of keeping every business correspondence and records so that these may be found and delivered quickly when needed for reference in future. Thus, filing written messages performs a library function and information service. Filing includes classification of messages, preservation of letters, circulars, forms, memos, records and other documents.

Filing also performs an administrative function by maintaining, supplying and protecting records, forms, circulars and other documents necessary for formulating broad business policies and objectives and preserving them for future reference and use. The efficiency of office administration depends upon the efficient and scientific way of preserving messages and quickly making them available when required. Messages of any media must not only be maintained systematically but also preserved with great care so as to prevent them from damage, loss, theft, or mutilation. Human memory is poor and limited. Sometimes one should not rely on one's memory for past messages which have no official support or which cannot be legal evidence in case of a dispute of a particular message. The important functions of filing messages are to:

(1) preserve messages,

(2) perform library and information functions,

(3) know precedences,

(4) help in framing business policies, etc.

There are various methods in use which can be used for filing written messages effected by any media of written communication.

All filing methods may not be useful to all organisations. Some methods may have only limited utility and some are only useful for small organisations. Some methods of filing communication are useful only for large concerns where the volume of written communication is comparatively large. So a method can be used in some concerns most efficiently in comparison with others. Old methods of filing may be replaced by modern methods. Filing methods can broadly be classified in two categories, namely, old methods of filing and modern methods of filing.

Old methods of filing in practice are more popular and are still used in small offices where the volume of communication is comparatively small.

The following are the old methods of filing:

Metal folders and guard book are used as a method of filing. Under this method papers, letters, documents, circulars, memos, instructions, etc., are held together by metal folders or are pasted in bound books in chronological order. They serve no special function and the work of filing is inconvenient and difficult. The same function is served by a letter register. So these filing methods of messages have been discarded by most of the big concerns.

Under this method packets are used to file messages. Expanding alphabetical cases are numbered packets in which written documents like letters and other media can be placed alphabetically. The alphabetical cases or packets can be used for sorting out correspondence or keeping documents collectively only for a temporary period. However, this is a good method but not suitable for large volume of papers as it does not serve as a permanent record. Before despatch documents can be kept in these cases or packets for the time being.

Also called a wire file or pillar and post file. Under this method a spike or wire is fixed to a wooden stand or a wall. They may be placed on the table or hung on the wall near the table. The documents are punched and fixed into a metal spike. Another method of this type is each paper is punched with two holes to fit on the spikes and clamped down in its appropriate file. The file opens like a book and can be opened when necessary.

Boxes are used for filing documents. Cardboard boxes about three to four inches deep are used for filing papers. A box file is used but only for a temporary purpose. The boxes are fitted with spring clips to hold the papers down and the papers are placed under the clip. Sometimes papers may be placed in manila folders which may be kept in a box file. Though, under this system documents remain fully secured, box files are not suitable for permanent storage of papers.

***Pigeon Holding*:** Also called docketing. It operates with the help of a cupboard. Under this system a cabinet containing some compartments is required. It resembles pigeon holes so it is named as a pigeon holder. Each compartment is allotted a letter of the alphabet. All papers before placing into holes are sorted, folded and tied into bundles easily identifiable. A brief description of the folder is written on the outer top. The writing of particulars on the outer top is called docketing. Docketing means writing on the outer top the subject of correspondence, residence, date and name of the correspondence. Though, the system is popular, particularly in small organisations it is unsuitable for modern offices. Hence, many companies have discarded this method. The Post office even today uses this method for sorting letters.

All communications which are transmitted out are copied in a book marked for this purpose. A press copy book may be divided either on an alphabetical or on a geographical basis. Since particulars are entered in a book the press copy book serves as good evidence in case of dispute of communication. However, this is a very old method and is not in popular use in modern organisations. Old methods of filing were popularly used where the volume of communication was comparatively small.

The importance of these methods of filing has declined by the passing of time. Some of the methods have been fast replaced by modern methods. Modern methods are found suitable and perform more efficiently in comparison with old methods. With a view to meeting the requirements of large organisations, new and improved methods of filing have been devised and introduced. Consequently, old methods of filing became outdated. All large sized business organisations have now come to use modern filing methods.

Modern methods of filing can broadly be classified into two broad categories. They are flat or horizontal filing and, secondly, vertical filing.

Horizontal Filing: It is called horizontal filing because the documents are kept in a horizontal position or in a flat position. It means one on top of the other. First papers are inserted in files or folders and these folders or files are kept in a horizontal position in drawers or shelves. The horizontal method of filing takes the following two forms:

> Under the flat file method the papers are kept in a flat position under a file liver. The files are made of cardboard or thick paper. Each cover is allotted to each customer or allotted to a particular subject. All papers relating to a particular customer or relating to a particular subject are put in the cover in the order in which they are received. In cases where a particular message relates to more than one file, more copies of the messages are made out so that each file may have a copy. A punching machine is used to punch the papers to be filed. The files are placed in the cupboards or drawers one on top of the other. Easy location of files is possible by preparing an index. Thus, under the flat file method papers are arranged horizontally and in chronological order. But proper numbering of files and indexing is necessary.

Also called the pilot or liver arch files. These files are either made of very thick cardboard or have filing cabinets. It is called a liver file because it is operated by a liver. It opens and closes when the liver is operated. Cardboard files are opened by a liver. "Era" file and "shannon" file are examples of this type. When a letter is to be filed the liver is moved upwards and after inserting the paper the liver is pressed down. The special feature of liver file is that a paper can be inserted at any place between two earlier papers without disturbing the order of other papers.

The Merits: The following are the merits of horizontal filing method:

1. Filing of messages is simple.
2. There is easy access to the document.

3. There is no risk of losing the documents filed.
4. Misplacement problem does not arise once the paper is inserted in the file.
5. Quick and easy reference is possible without disturbing the order and without removing from the file.
6. The operation of the arch helps to avoid mixing of papers.
7. Papers are fixed on the arch and there is no chance of changing the order.
8. Files are kept in chronological order so it is easy to find out a particular letter with the help of the index, or if the date is known.

The Demerits

1. There is no scope for expansion.
2. It is not possible to trace a filed paper at short notice because of its horizontal nature.
3. Flat files involve trouble removing the papers on the top in order to take out a particular paper.
4. Keeping a complete drawer or tray for each classification causes difficulty.
5. It takes more space compared with the vertical system.
6. The system is not very efficient for a larger business concern.
7. It is difficult to maintain data for each letter or paper to trace a particular paper.

Vertical Filing: Also called the upright system of filing. Vertical filing is the most modern system of filing. As such it removes the drawbacks associated with the horizontal filing system. It has gained importance essentially out of the limitations and defects of the horizontal method because under the horizontal method papers are arranged in such a way that it is very cumbersome to refer to them at short notice. Owing to its defects vertical filing has come to be adopted by most modern organisations. It ensures efficiency in record keeping. The papers and the files cont ıining them are placed vertically in position or in a standing upright position hence the name vertical file.

There are two parts in vertical filing. The equipment needs two parts. They are:

Folders: The basis for vertical filing is a folder. A folder is a folded sheet of manila or some other strong but flexible substance. The back of a folder or a tab attached to it is slightly higher than the front sheet. The extended edge of the back sheet is used for writing the description of the contents kept in the file. The description takes the form of the name of the subject, number, etc. A separate folder may be kept for each subject.

All the papers relating to a particular subject or correspondence are kept standing in chronological or other suitable order in the folder. Any particular paper can be removed or inserted without disturbing other papers. Usually clips or folders are used to keep the papers fast and together.

A wooden or steel cabinet is the second important part required for vertical filing. Folders are kept in the wooden or steel cabinet with a suitable number of drawers depending upon the volume of papers to be preserved. Hence, the folders are to be placed in a standing upright position. The drawers must be deep enough to accommodate the folders. The folders are placed vertically on their left hand edge one on top of the other. It has a mechanism called expander which slides backwards or forwards and holds up the folders. A memorandum card is put in the place of a particular folder which is removed from a drawer for any reference purpose.

The Merits: The following are the advantages of vertical filing:

1. Messages filed in a vertical system have the merit of quick reference.

   The facility of ready reference is not possible in horizontal filling.

2. Any particular document can be removed easily as compared to a horizontal filing system.

3. Easy to find the records, contents of each folder are visible from the extended edge of the back sheet.

4. It accommodates handling of large volume of correspondence more conveniently and easily than the flat filing system.
5. Vertical filing system has the advantage of saving time because there is no need to punch the papers.
6. The advantage of cost saving or economy cannot be overlooked. A large number of papers can be arranged in drawers meant for the purpose. When files are arranged vertically they accommodate more papers. Thus, it ensures economy of space and expense.
7. The system has inherent merit which offers scope for expansion. There is a provision for expansion in the drawers. It has a mechanism of expander which facilitates accommodating increase in correspondence.
8. Vertical filing system has the advantage that there is no fear of mixing up correspondence of one person with that of the other. Because they are kept separately for each individual.
9. The vertical filing system is more adaptable to any variety of classifications. The folders can be arranged subject-wise, area-wise, alphabetically or in any other suitable basis.
10. Safety of papers can be achieved under this system. Papers are kept safe from dust and insects in the manila folders and steel or wooden drawers.
11. It has the merit of side applicability. Vertical filing systems can be used for preservation of all media of written communication such as letters, folders, orders, memos, and other documents.

One-shelf Filing: To find a paper in a cabinet, one has to lean over in a cabinet to open it. It also takes more floor space. In view of these difficulties, there is a recent trend towards open shelf filing. It is in popular use in the USA. This is particularly so where materials have been accumulated in packets or large envelopes. The drawbacks of folder and cabinet method can be solved by making the shelves nine to ten feet high and providing ladders to the operator.

The Essentials: A good filing system is one that facilitates easy reference, preservation and maintenance. The following are the essentials of a good filing system:

Simplicity: The purpose of the filing should be clear and simple. It must be simple to understand, so that all clerical workers may operate it without any difficulty. The system must ensure quick reference, without any training and knowledge of filing.

Suitability: A particular type of filing should be followed which will meet the requirements of the organisation and which is in conformity with the nature and objectives of the organisation. No particular type is suitable for all types of organisations and as such, it is the problem of the management to devise a suitable system according to the needs of the business.

Accessibility: The written messages so filed should facilitate ready accessibility to documents, so that the communication required may be available quickly as and when required. The messages may be picked up without loss of time.

Economy: Budgeting of filing of communications is the important factor in selecting a particular filing system. The cost of labour, equipment, and overheads should be reasonable. As such filing should be economical. The cost should not be more than the benefits derived from it. Space is a problem; the filing system should not take too much. Economising space, and preserving documents but not beyond their proper life are the two important principles.

Compactness: A good system must ensure that the area must be compact so that only the required space is occupied. In big cities the cost of office space is very high.

Flexibility: The system of filing should consider future requirements. So it should be capable of expansion to accommodate the expanding needs. When the activities of the concern expand, an inflexible system is useless. The system must be suitable even after a certain limit is crossed, and adaptable to meet changing circumstances.

Identification: The system should be in a position to permit ready and quick location and identification of messages otherwise the system is not only a waste but also costly.

Cross Reference: Cross reference of filing is yet another essential of a good filing system. Sometimes communications may be filed under two different heads. The messages should be classified under various headings with cross references. The cross reference helps the clerks to find out the message in another file where it is kept.

Classification: A communication filing system should follow a suitable classification. There are many methods of classification of messages such as alphabetical, numerical, geographical, subject-wise, alphabetical, numerical and chronological. A proper and suitable classification should be adopted.

Safety: One of the merits of written communication is preservation of messages, which serve as future reference and evidence. *So* a good filing system is one which must try to achieve this objective. The system must provide safety to documents and prevent unauthorised persons from tampering with them. It should protect them from the dangers of insects, rain, rats, and white ants.

Indexing: A ready guide to locate a particular file is necessary. A good filing system should facilitate introduction of a good index system. The system of classification of files and the type of filing method adapted will decide the method of indexing to be followed.

Movement: Communication movement from one place to another is a common feature in the organisation. An indicator or guide is to be used when a particular message is removed from a file. The indicator should be inserted in its place with particulars of the part of the message removed, date, to which section it is sent, etc.

Serviceability: It is obviously important that a good filing system should be capable of filing papers speedily and traced speedily. This is what is known as convenience of filing or serviceability of filing.

Up to Date: The messages should also be filed to date. This is possible to achieve with an efficient office forms control.

Mechanical Ways

Modern mechanical equipment and machines play an important role in efficient and speedy communication. Mechanisation of communication work is fast taking place. Messages are required to be transmitted to the inside tall network and flat network as well as to outsiders. It is no exaggeration that there are rapid changes in communication management because of growing scientific and technological innovations. The age of communication has brought about many changes in different fields, to keep pace with mass communication. Also to transmit messages to distant places with considerable speed, accuracy and quantity of messages to enable quick and correct decision making.

All this has necessitated the installation of a number of time and labour saving electrical and electronic mechanical devices in written communication. These machines right from the typewriter to the sophisticated computers and teleprinters are required for transmitting information.

Network for Communication: Mechanisation of the communication network is for the accurate and speedy communication of messages. Even office work inside the organisation is mostly indoor desk and manual work. The process of communication is routine, continuous and monotonous in nature. The routine manual work may adversely affect efficient performance.

This also necessitates the adoption of certain equipment and machines suitable for efficient written communication. Therefore, the most appropriate communication work can be done with machines at a comparatively minimum cost. More accuracy and speed not only improve general efficiency, but also increase the goodwill of the organisation among its visitors and other outsiders.

Today a wide variety of writing and communicating machines are available in the market. A management has to procure and install suitable machinery depending upon organisational requirements and working staff. There are a number of advantages associated in mechanisation of communication, like saving in cost ensures accuracy and speed in transmission. This reduces monotony, achieves uniformity, better appearance and easy record and reference. The various types of machines which are available for the purpose of written communication are listed below along with a brief description.

Type-writer: The type-writer is a machine with keys for printing letters on a piece of paper. The type-writer is the most popular and commonly used machine in all types of communication work. Type-writers are now available not only in English but also in regional languages. In every organisation the type-writer is seen as a basic requirement now a days. The typed copy is the writing produced by the type-writer. It is called a typescript. Different companies make type-writers with different type faces. Type faces are a set of letters for printing, cut in a particular style. A typist is a person whose job is to type. Type-writing, *i.e.,* writing produced by a type-writer is a form of written communication.

There are various types of type-writers which are used in type-writing.

Standard Type-writer: It is the most commonly used type-writer in all organisations. It is most suitable for routine business correspondence and general typing work. Typing work can be done with considerable speed. It is more compact and more matter can be typed on a page comparing other types. The typescript is easier to read, clear and, if necessary, a clear carbon copy can be produced.

Portable Type-writer: A machine of comparatively small size, a portable typewriter can be carried or moved easily from place to place. A handy, lightweight machine. It can be used mostly for personal work of limited quantity. It contains all fundamental elements of the standard typewriter. Economically also it is cheaper.

Noiseless Type-writer: This typewriter produces no noise or less noise compared to the standard typewriter. Type faces are pressed rather than stamping and produces less noise. So it is called a noiseless typewriter. Generally used in meeting rooms or executive chambers where there is always some disturbance with telephone calls. A greater number of carbon copies cannot be produced.

Electric Type-writer: This typewriter is operated electrically by the typist. This kind of typewriter is basically in the structure of the standard type-writer but connected with electricity, fitted with an electric motor. It saves the energy of the typist and reduces monotony. The semi-electric machine is another variant form.

There are different types of type faces with various sizes, shapes and styles. Now a days a machine has been developed by which typing of letters with types of various sizes, shapes and styles is possible. The name itself indicates that it performs variable functions. The machine has differential space justification.

Automatic Type-writer: This type of typewriter functions with the help of punched paper type or paper roles or cards known as master cards. An automatic type-writer types individually typed matter from a punched tape or paper tape or roles as the case may be. The tape or roles are placed on the machine and the matter punched on the tape is automatically typed on the paper.

Type-writer with Other Devices: The machine facilitates continuous typing of standard and routine work. It is a common standard type-writer with a special fitted device. Continuous stationery can also be typed provided such stationery is inserted in the machine.

Teleprinter: Yet another type of typewriter is the teleprinter. The teleprinter not only types but transmits electrical signals over wires. At receiving point at the same time a machine prints the matter. It is used for transmitting messages to distant places. A machine in a communication system. A teleprinter is a machine, a specialised type of typewriter. A telegraphic system or instrument by which messages are sent out at one place and received at another place in a printed form. The typing is connected to a telephone line, and the message typed at one place transmits electrical signals over a wire and the same message is simultaneously reproduced and printed at a distant place by the machine. It is used as a private circuit or through the post office telex service system. The post office gives teleprinters on rent to form a part of private telecommunication.

Stenographic Type-writer: This is not in a strict sense a standard typewriter. Though, is appears to be like a typewriter, not only is it portable but also makes less noise. It is used by a stenographer to take down short-hand dictation. It reduces monotony and work can be done at a considerable speed.

Continuous Stationery: This is stationery of long run routine forms, a long strip of paper folded in a zig-zag manner. A separate part called an attachment is fitted to the typewriter carriage. When there is a large quantity of work, continuous stationery is used to cope up with the volume of work. It ensures speedy typing and the greatest cleanliness.

Duplicating machines are used in offices and facilitate reproduction of a number of copies of letters, reports, circulars, memos, notices, etc., for circulation. Duplicating machines ensure reproduction promptly and efficiently with secrecy.

They are a substitute for printing. Usually these machines are used to produce more copies which an ordinary standard typewriter cannot produce. With the help of a master impression, a number of copies can be obtained. There are various types of duplicating machines. The important duplicating processor and machines used in offices are us under:

Hectograph

(a) Flat Bed Type

(b) Rotary Type

(c) Mimeograph

(d) Multigraph (Photographic Film. Electronic Stencil)

(e) Offset-Litho Duplication

(f) Copying (Photostatic Process. Diazo microfilming)

Imprinting Machines: Imprinting machines and their process contribute an addition to the existing copy. The difference between imprinting process and duplicating process is that the duplicating process merely reproduces a number of facsimile copies. They include:

Impression Stamps: Rubber stamps. For instance, stamp bearing impression as "paid", "date", "numbering", etc.

Addressing machines are useful when a number of letters are to be posted. When hundreds of bills, circulars, notices or wrappers are to be addressed, addressing machines are used.

Addressograph machines are used for the respective printing of the same address. They are of two types:

(i) Fibre stencils and

(ii) plates.

Metal plates are prepared on special embossing machines called graphotype. These plates when prepared can be preserved for future use and repeatedly used.

Signature Machines: These machines can be used for imprinting signatures on cheques, circulars or notices.

In order to affix stamps over covers or letters franking machines are used. The machines are used for imprinting postage marks in large numbers. The posts and telegraph department supplies these machines on hire for use in business premises. A cover is inserted in the machine and with the help of a handle it is possible to mark the letter with the required denomination of the postage. It saves time handling large quantities of stamps. There is no scope of risk of theft and mutilation in stamping.

The date and time recorder is used so that all incoming mail is stamped with the date and time of its arrival in the office. The mail is inserted in the recorder which automatically prints the time and date. It is used both for incoming and outgoing mail.

These include computing, accounting, tabulating machines, mailing scale, folding machine, inserting machines, sorting devices, adding and listing machines, billing machines, book keeping machines, punch-card machines, and other statistical or tabulating machines.

Telefax: This machine is used for transmitting sketches or drawings. The chart or diagram is originally drawn on a paper. The paper is wrapped round a cylinder in the machine. The machine upon switching on transmits the facsimile to the machine at the other end where it is reproduced simultaneously.

Telewriter: Also called a Telautograph or Tele-autorgraph. It also operates on the principle of a teleprinter. A message is written on a metal plate attached to a machine which is reproduced electrically on the machine at the other end.

Indexing: Communication is a continuous process involving the original message, followed by clarifications, explanations, corrected messages, etc. We have presented a detailed picture of methods of filing communication, classification of documents and the essentials of a good filing system. Unless a particular filing system itself has an index, every filing system must be supplemented by a well designed index plan. The method of index to be adopted will depend upon the nature of organisation, media of communication in use and system of classification of files. So indexing is the most important and one of the essentials of a good filing system.

Indexing with reference to communication files refers to something which indicates or points to a particular piece of fact, figure, idea, opinion, etc. In other words, it shows the indices. It is an alphabetical list of correspondence at the end of the file or beginning or on separate cards.

The index is a guide which helps to locate the required file or records. In a business concern with the help of the index it is possible to ascertain names, subject and other particulars under which documents are to be filed. The index helps to find out documents easily and without delay.

It indicates as to where communication in detail will be available. So from the above discussion on classification, it is clear that indexing and classification are different. Indexing indicates and points out the location. But classification is only a method of filing. For instance, when files are arranged alphabetically that itself serves as an index. In all cases where files have self-indexing there is no need to have separate index. But still it is good to have a good indexing system even if the files are arranged on a self-indexing system. The only purpose of an index is to facilitate the location of the papers. A condensed record of the customers, credit rating, etc. Indexes are used with ledgers and accounts. It is common to have indexes in libraries, banks, insurance companies, etc.

Types of Index: Different types of indexing are in use. The following are the various kinds of index systems in use.

This is also called an ordinary page index or bound book index. As the name indicates it is in the nature of a bound book or register. The book is divided into alphabetical divisions in which names of customers or correspondents are entered into. Each page or more pages is/are allotted to one letter or more letters of the alphabet. Each page or section has pages cut away at the right hand side, so that letters are visible at a glance. All entries relating to a particular letter will be arranged on the same page maintained for it. The arrangement is in the strict alphabetical order. The index may be maintained by different methods such as:

(a) an index in the front of the book,

(b) an index at the back of a book,

(c) an index in a separate book or

(d) a series of loose sheets inserted in front of each section of a file.

Advantages

(i) Under this system of indexing it is very easy and simple to operate.

(ii) It is not an expensive system.

(iii) It is possible to maintain the records for a long period.

(iv) A bound index is not generally misplaced.

(v) No scope for torn pages, lost or disarranged.

Disadvantages

(i) The system is not flexible or elastic and cannot meet the changes and expansion. Increase in correspondence cannot be accommodated in this system. More entries cannot be entered.

(ii) There is no scope for any other information to be inserted in bound book index.

(iii) Deletion of ceased and outdated entries of certain correspondence makes the system ineffective.

(iv) It also needs some knowledge to operate.

(v) Under utilisation of book is a serious problem in many cases.

This is an improved method of the bound book index method. Each page indexed for a particular letter is divided into six sub-divisions and each sub-division is earmarked for a vowel captioned A, E, I, O, U and Y.

Each sub-section has a separate page of letter 'A' and then a separate part of the page is allotted. The name of each correspondent is entered on one page reserved for its initial letters. The sub-division is meant for the first vowel in the name after the first letter. For example, the name Ranjit will be recorded in the section reserved for 'R' and in the vowel of section 'A'. Though, the method theoretically appears good it suffers from certain drawbacks. For instance, entering of names on each page must be in sequence in which they have first occurred. Similarly the system is not flexible and elastic and does not permit addition of new entries. This is similar to loose leaf ledger. It is a variant form of a book index. Under this system individual sheets can be inserted into metal, hinges, or scrows. It permits the pages to be taken out or to insert additional pages. The book index may simply be unscrewed and anew leaf can be inserted. A loose leaf book index has certain advantages such as:

1. The system is elastic and flexible, meets changing needs.
2. It is easily adaptable to meet different circumstances.
3. The system operates with locking so that no leaves are taken out without proper authority.
4. The loose index sheets may be inserted at the beginning of each alphabetical section of a book.

The card index system was invented by A. J. Rozier. The book index and vowel index have certain difficulties it their operation. In order to overcome the limitations the loose card index system has been introduced. Under this system a separate card is allotted to each *message. Here a card index is an index in which each item occupies a separate card.* All cards are in uniform size. The cards are arranged in some classification like alphabetical, numerical or geographical. The card index method is followed in libraries, banks, etc. The cards so prepared are put in steel or wooden drawers. Generally a rod is put through them to hold the cards in their places. Forms can be put either in a vertical or horizontal position. On each card is written the name, address, number and other particulars.

The cards are arranged in such a way that the top portion of all cards bearing the main subject heading will be visible simultaneously. The cards are generally of uniform size, say post-card size or four inches into two and half inches. A card index is used particularly for the following purposes:

1. The addresses of the customers are maintained.
2. Index cards of books according to title or according to the name of the author in libraries.
3. Banks maintain a card index to keep specimen signatures of customers.
4. Index to the ledgers in which accounts of various customers are maintained.
5. Index is used to record employees particulars.
6. To record financial position.
7. Card index of store items.
8. To maintain particulars of title deeds, contracts and other documents.
9. Indexing of price list, catalogues.
10. To keep the accounts of stores items.
11. To maintain record of investment particulars.
12. For maintaining the record of transactions relating to hire purchase and instalment sales.
13. To maintain a record of the period of credit to be granted.

Advantages

1. New cards can be inserted easily and quickly.
2. The system is more flexible and elastic, so accommodates increasing work.
3. Adding and insertion do not disturb the order.

4. Old cards or cards of ceased customers can be removed from the drawers.
5. The system is easy and simple to operate and understand.
6. Any card can be taken out for reference. It is also helpful to find out a particular card. The sub division under the vowel index further facilitates reference.
7. As the cards are arranged in alphabetical order it saves time to locate any name or subject.
8. Card indexing is cheaper compared to the bound index method which takes more renewal cost.
9. Cards can be grouped and regrouped in any manner and in any order.
10. Cards can be ruled according to convenience or to the particulars desired to be recorded.
11. Different coloured cards can be used to classify various purposes.
12. It is possible to maintain the system neat and tidy.
13. Indicators or guide cards may be used to group cards to draw attention.
14. Blank pages will appear in case of a bound index. There is no need to insert blank cards in the cabinets.
15. A number of persons can use the index simultaneously.

Disadvantages

1. A serious draw back of the system is when cards are lost, misplaced, etc. It is very difficult to find them.
2. The system is also known for delay as many cards have to be seen before the desired card can be traced.
3. It cannot be afforded by small concerns since the installation cost is very high.
4. When cards are kept for keeping the ledger there is a danger of fraudulent substitution, concealment, etc.
5. At a time only one card can be seen, as all the cards cannot be seen at a glance.

6. When cards are freely taken out, checking is very difficult
7. The facility given by guide cards and dictionary arrangement is thus reduced

Visible Card Index: To overcome the difficulties of the card index method, the visible card index system has been introduced. If the visible card index method is adopted, the operational difficulties associated with the card index can be removed.

Under it a large number of cards cannot be seen at a glance, as pointed out earlier. Under this method, the cards are laid flat in a shallow or in metal trays. In other words, cards are put in transparent covers and then arranged in trays. Each card is arranged in such a way and fitted into a metal hinge so that it overlaps the one before it.

Overlaps its neighbour in such a way that a narrow strip at the bottom containing the name or title remains visible. The trays may be fitted horizontally or attached vertically to metal stands. The cards can be classified either by usual systems like alphabetical, numerical or a combination of them. There are two variant forms of visible card indexing such as "card wheel" and "Strip index".

Advantages

1. This system saves considerable time.
2. A large number of cards can be kept at a time.
3. It permits speedy reference of cards, because the names or subjects are visible.
4. Easy location and speedy posting in cards is possible.
5. The system operates in a very compact way and occupies less space.
6. It is possible to write on each card either in front or on the reverse without removing the card from its place.
7. Speedy and ready reference and information enables the management to control effectively the sales, purchases, credit, etc.
8. Listing of correspondents or subjects can be done smoothly.

The Categorisation

There are different forms of classification of papers or other written messages. In order to make communication messages available promptly, it is indispensable that pieces of communication messages be properly classified or divided and grouped according to some prescribed basis and by giving proper titles. The purpose of written communication can be achieved only when the documents are properly classified. On the other hand, the success or failure of a filing system largely depends upon the selection of the most suitable method of classification of documents. The following are the main methods of classification of papers and documents placed in files.

Various Manners

Alphabetical classification of files is popular, and the method is most widely used in every organisation. With this method, each file containing papers bears the name of the correspondent. The arrangement is in strict alphabetical order of the surname. It starts with the first letter with which the surname of the correspondent begins. Each file bears a letter like A or B or C, etc. All the letters of customers whose surname begins with 'a' Are put in the file bearing letter A. And all those beginning with letter 'b' are placed in the B file. This method is very easy for the clerks to operate.

Advantages

1. Alphabetical method is simple and easy to understand.
2. There is no need to have separate indexing. The system itself is the index.
3. The system is flexible and more elastic. It accommodates changes and expansion.
4. It can easily be operated.
5. Any method of filing like vertical or horizontal can be adopted.

Disadvantages

1. The system takes a longer time for filing.
2. It may not be suitable to a larger organisation.

3. Confusion arises when spellings are not correctly given.
4. Congestion under common names is a serious problem.
5. Wrong filing of documents is possible under different headings.
6. Forecasting of documents under each letter is not possible.
7. If there are a large number of names of a particular letter more files are to be kept.

Numerical: As the name indicates this classification facilitates operation with numbers. Under this method each customer or correspondent is allotted a number. In other words, a number is allotted to such a file. All documents relating to a particular customer or subject are put in one separate file which has a distinct number. For instance, 'A' is allotted number 25. All papers connected with him are placed in the number 25.

The files are then placed in cupboards according to their serial numbers. But this system calls for comprehensive indexing. Index cards are maintained, which are also arranged in alphabetical order. A variant form of this system is that the filing cabinet is arranged in pigeon holes according to the alphabetical order.

Advantages

1. This is the simplest method to operate and understand.
2. There is greater accuracy in filing.
3. It facilitates and accommodates all kinds of communication media.
4. Under this system, it is possible to know the total number of customers or correspondents.
5. It is sufficiently adaptable to meet changing circumstances. It is more elastic and flexible.
6. Files can be arranged in an orderly way and can be easily located.
7. Any paper of a particular customer can be traced easily without disturbing the sequence.
8. The index is a full list and can be used for as an index address.

9. This system helps to expand or increase the number of files with the increase in the number of customers.
10. The files of ceased, old and irrelevant customers without any dealings can be removed

Disadvantages

1. It takes more time of find out when a particular number is given to a particular customer.
2. A separate index has to be prepared.
3. Documents of a miscellaneous nature, or residual category are difficult to arrange.
4. It takes more space.
5. Errors occur in filing in cases of transposition of figures.

Classification of messages under this method is a combination of the alphabetical and numerical method as discussed above. While filing, documents are classified in alphabetical divisions and numbers are then allotted to different classified documents. Giving numbers to alphabetical classification serves the purpose of their sub- classification. This combined system can be used suitably because it has many advantages.

Guide cards or index cards can also be used to subdivide the holders into divisions or groups which help their speedy location. For instance Z_1 may refer to Mr. Kulkarni, Z_2 may refer to Mr. Saxena. This method is more popular and is commonly used in libraries for classification of books, and in banks for filing specimen signatures of the customers. This method combines all the advantages of the alphabetical and numerical systems of classification. This classification avoids serious problems of similar names arising in the case of the alphabetical system.

Under this classification documents are filed according to their geographical area or location. This classification is adopted when an organisation wants to keep the records according to the area. So this system facilitates that correspondence relating to a particular territory which is collected or pooled together and then classified according to alphabetical or numerical order.

The documents are classified according to villages, towns, cities, states, countries, etc. Under this system correspondence is maintained according to customers, records of the various areas and filing correspondence according to a geographical area. The sales department of an organisation can suitably classify sales particulars according to areas.

This is the suitable method for all organisations which extend their area of operation to a wider area. Transport companies, export houses, mail order business houses, banks, insurance companies, etc., can adopt geographical classification of documents properly. A company which has its business all over the world may classify documents according to the area or country. In home trade files can be classified and arranged according to state, district or taluk. These can again be classified and arranged in alphabetical order.

Advantages: The advantages of this method are:

1. The sales of each area can be known for planning.
2. Under this method documents can be easily located.
3. This method is very simple and easy to understand and operate.
4. It can be applied to all types of documents where area classification is necessary.

Disadvantages: The disadvantages of this method are:

1. It is very difficult to know all the addresses. Unless one knows the addresses it is not possible to locate the file.
2. It requires a thorough knowledge of geography.
3. Geographical locations are very difficult to know.
4. Sometimes a separate alphabetical index may be needed.
5. It is costly as clerks have to be trained to understand geography.

The subject matter of a message is important in the classification of documents. This method is adopted where the subject matter of the correspondence is important. The names of the correspondence and geographical area are of secondary importance. Under this method documents are classified and arranged in accordance with the subject matter like sales, purchases, royalty, taxes, commission, rent, etc. Therefore, all correspondence relating to a particular subject may be collected together and put in one file. Similarly, documents of contracts, legal proceedings, income-tax, etc.

Advantages

1. This method is most useful to lawyers, architects, educational institutions, etc.
2. It automatically reveals useful information about the subject.
3. This is the simplest method and can be easily understood by all.
4. Ease of reference and location.
5. It can be adapted to changes. This system is more elastic and flexible.

Disadvantages

1 Difficulties may arise if the subjects are not fully known.
2. Under this method it is not possible to arrange miscellaneous papers
3. When a particular subject is allotted to a classification has to be found out, some time has to be spent.
4. A separate index is required to be prepared.
5. Sometimes cross reference may be needed.

This method operates with dates. Under this method documents are collected together and put into a container according to the date. Papers are kept in files date-wise. Date-wise classification takes place in case of newspapers, magazines, shipping lists, share price, market report invoices, and this method may also be used in filing vouchers. So chronological classification is useful for files of letters which have answers outstanding. The system is useful if dates are known.

Goals and Aims

The systematic filing of written communication is one of the important aspects of communication work. Filing along with indexing is necessary because of the limitation of the human mind and memory. The object of preserving written messages is to provide necessary information readily and without any delay and when needed. However, the following are the main objectives of keeping messages:

Future Reference: The limitation of the human mind and poor memory cannot be overlooked. Changes of seats on account of transfer of employees also causes problems. Written messages can be preserved as records and reference source. Various media of communication can be filed for future reference. Thus, keeping records is essential for continuous operation of the business.

Record of Evidence: Word of mouth is not believable and in a number of cases oral messages have no legal sanction. Written messages have the capacity of being stored as records. At times the records can be used as evidence. Papers can be produced as proof in case of dispute of communication.

Measurement of Progress: Properly filed messages are useful to know the progress of the concern. The records provide relevant and basic information; from this it is possible to know the progress of the organisation. It also facilitates comparison with previous years and also comparison with other firms. In other words, filing messages serves as a barometer of progress which supplies information for the purpose of preparation of annual reports and other periodical reviews.

Precedents: Maintenance of communication provides necessary information on earlier activities and decisions. Past messages are helpful for future decision making. They may act as a guide or rule in the future. In making decisions the decision maker has to follow a precedent set in the organisation earlier.

Avoiding Mistakes: In transmitting messages earlier records help in reducing mistakes and errors. So there is no need for correction, issue of amended messages, instructions, clarifications and explanations. Effective internal control is possible. So keeping and maintaining written messages minimises the chances for errors and prevents the occurrence of fraud.

Effective Decision Making: Old documents help effective decision making in a great way. The decision making process becomes easier if old records are available. Because the messages provide necessary information for the decision making purpose. Decisions may go wrong if the old communications are not followed. Past records may serve as a guide in the decision making process.

Organisational Efficiency: Organisational efficiency cannot be achieved with confusions and lack of guidance. Those records are most useful which guide the employees to take decisions to motivate effective internal control. Preparing classification of messages and suitable filing and indexing in this respect would be helpful in maintaining organisational efficiency.

Legal Requirements: There are certain documents which are required to be preserved compulsorily under the provisions of different legislations. To meet legal requirements the documents should be preserved and maintained. For instance, the maintenance of certain records and books is compulsory under the Indian Companies Act, 1956 and the Banking Regulation Act, 1949, etc.

Relevant Elements

Lajuana Williams Lee, Sallye Starks Benoit, William Colins and Celests Standfield Power, predict the importance of written communication in the future in the following way:

(1) The direct approach will be used more and more to save time and energy for the busy executive.

(2) The use of visual aids will increase and the text decrease in written reports and oral presentations.

(3) Research will be faster and more economical through technology's expanding data-based systems.

(4) Use of office memorandums for dissemination of information will increase.

(5) Increased data provided by advanced technology will demand skill and competence in handling and storage on microforms will eliminate heavy file cabinets.

(6) Information will be disseminated through computers Equipment will display information on screens, which will enable persons to correct errors before messages are sent. Teletypewriters transmitting electric impulses over telephone systems will reproduce written messages simultaneously on machines in neighbouring or distant offices.

(7) Computers will maintain the majority of business records. Primary storage will be in computers and in microfilm equipment.

(8) Business will begin to move closer to a paperless society. There will be electronic delivery rather than postal service deliver. Business letters and reports will be read from machines, not just paper.

Black and white is the most important vehicle used in communication in all organisations. Information through paper can be transmitted in a written form. Written communication as a means of gathering and disseminating information is generally used more extensively particularly in formal communication. A considerable part of the executive's time is saved. Thus, written communication enjoys certain advantages over verbal communication; some of the useful merits of written communication may be outlined below:

There is no scope in written communication to be influenced by self-interest and attitude. The employees have to care only for their work. The subordinates have to pay great attention to the written matter and the messages are formal or official, directly relating to their work.

Written communication is more reliable, and one can trust it. It has official recognition. Oral communication is not believable but written information is correct and reliable. This principle is equally important otherwise at times it tends to reduce the effectiveness of the message; Thus, reliability of the communication in the mind of the receiver is a factor of great significance. The dangers of oral communication are that they may lead to distorted information without any official sanction.

Written communication does not suffer from the dangers of being distorted. In every tall network there is organisational distance, written communication is the best media. But in the same structure oral communication may lead to possibility of distortion which goes up with every increase in the organisation structure.

Written communication is a formal method of transmitting messages and they are best suited for long distance communication. This is the only way out if both the communicator and recipient are located geographically in far off places beyond oral communication media, or even beyond mechanical oral device range.

Written messages can be preserved as records and reference source. They have the capacity of being stored as records. At times the records can be used as evidence. Reports, circulars, manuals and other printed, written or typed documents can be filed for future reference and can be produced as legal evidence.

A bulky message cannot be transmitted fully and clearly by oral media. But a lengthy message can be effectively circulated in black and white. The problems of missing points, forgetfulness, lack of memory and use of improper words in speaking are the problems which can be avoided in written communication.

A number of business transactions takes place through writing, where oral communication has no place and is not believed. Written communication covers all kinds of subject matter like notices, deeds, minutes, resolutions, contracts, complaints, financial statements, legal documents, proposals, pleadings, charts, communication intelligence, memoranda and articles of association, and many other transactions concerned only with paper work.

Written communication usually carries no rumours and inaccurate and partial information. It has official sanction and may not even turn into gossip and rumour. It is routine, formal and will continue to exist for all time to come.

The written media are also useful for dissemination of certain information which cannot be transmitted through oral channel. There is every possibility that word of mouth is heard by others. Secrecy can be maintained in written communication.

As pointed out earlier, in real world situations oral communication does not always save time. Written media not only save time but also cost. The cost is greater in case of conferences, and meetings. In oral media the time of many people is wasted in conversation, but in written communication copies of written messages can be placed on the desk of the employees.

It has permanent value. It promotes upward communication for clarification, correction of error and other amendments. It is more orderly and binding on subordinates and superiors.

The Demerits: The purpose of communication is to understand the message. Written communication may sometimes lead to confusion and misunderstanding. The chances of communication being misunderstood are more. Everyone may not have the same understanding capacity. Written communication is comparatively less effective because there is no instinct of personal contact. Everything is in black and white and better and immediate impressions cannot be created. It takes more time to see clarifications and explanations. There is no scope for exchange of feelings freely, and reactions cannot be understood immediately.

One-way communication implies giving information flowing from top to middle, and from middle to operating level. Most written communications are orders and instructions issued by superiors, imposed and enforced. The communication to be effective must be a two-way channel. One way directs in a definite manner the employees to understand what the management intends them to do. So it is rigid and lacks the quality of flexibility.

The importance of informal communication cannot be overlooked. Written communication is purely formal and generally expressed in writing in manuals, orders, reports, etc. There are many messages which in the general interest of the organisation cannot be put in black and white. In such cases informal oral media are more useful. The executives should make effective use of the grapevine for the purpose.

Written communication moves 'comparatively' with little speed and often not faster than oral communication. Messages get disseminated improperly and impersonally. The element of personal touch is absent. It does not offer the executive insight into what the subordinates think and feel about the message. The absence of personal interaction makes it difficult to get clues of the reactions of the receiver of message. The written communication represents no natural desire of people in the organisation to interact and communicate with each other. It does not grow up spontaneously and lacks flexibility.

Feedback is one of the important essentials of good communication. In written communication in respect of many matters, like objectives and policy matters, there is no scope for feedback. Feedback in the process of communication calls for making it a two-way process. Feedback is an inherent quality in oral communication. The communicator cannot ascertain whether the receiver accepted or rejected the message. The reaction of the receiver of the message can be assessed effectively in oral communication rather than through written communication. Getting feedback information is easier in verbal communication.

Written communication does not give subordinates a feeling of belonging and a sense of a personal importance. So it does not help in morale building and motivation. In times of insecurity and uncertainty there is not an outlet in written communication freely to express their fears, attitudes and thoughts.

The characteristic of bureaucratic administration is another drawback of written communication. It leads to delays and redtapism. Executives act in a bureaucratic way and do things officially, strictly according to the letter rather than the spirit.

Incompleteness of the message leads to a chain of clarifications. This delays action and the decision-making process. Organisational efficiency is dependent not only on effective writing but on clear interpretation by the receiver. Owing to the problem of the language, the receiver of the message does not interpret it in the same manner as the communicator. Differences in status, in formal education, vocabulary and the cosmopolitan nature of the organisation, etc., make the written communication ineffective.

Verbal Expression

Among various forms of communication, oral communication is considered to be the earliest and common medium of communication. In oral communication, speech is a widely adopted tool of communication. The ender, the medium, the receiver and the message are the four basic factors associated with communication.

Socrates and Demosthenes were great and renowned in giving speeches. The world is busy with speeches. Everyday, in educational institutions the students and the taught come into conversation. In offices the superiors talk to the subordinates, the subordinates to superiors, superiors among themselves. In productive and service organisations the customers come into conversation with the suppliers, lawyers, doctors, auditors, consultants, etc., with their clients and so on and so forth.

Majestic Ways

Either in business communication or otherwise the oral communication should be clear and effective to achieve the objects of communication. Speech is an art for which there are no fixed rules which can be uniformly followed always and in all circumstances. There are a number of factors which influence effective oral communication. Factors like the conversation style of the speaker, language, medium, the temperaments of the receiver and speaker, size of audience, importance of message, fear of superiors, etc. are important. For instance, an important person appearing on TV or Radio or at a public meeting chooses his words selectively because if words are wrongly selected and used they may damage his image.

Human relations is the fundamental element of public relations. It is with speech to get along well with the public both internal to the organisation and external to the organisation. The public stands divided into three categories of people:

(a) There are those who know you and like you.

(b) There are those who know you and do not like you.

(c) There are those who neither know you nor care for you.

The technique involved in the process of communication is through speech to do business with all types of people. The essential basis of all cross sections is the communication process. It is the transfer of information from one to another. The message is transmitted by spoken or written words or by image or a combination of these or other media such as music, colour, mimicry, design, odour, and sense of touch.

In a competitive and dynamic market economy there are information gaps which cannot be filled up by the interaction of supply and demand through prices and costs. This is where Communication activity steps in.

Fundamental Problems

The capacity to communicate effectively and clearly is an important skill. The speakers have to make the message clear and easily understandable both in work and outside. In any profession it is not possible to get through without communication. Communication is a valuable asset for most people in the modern-day busy world such as for lawyers, teachers, auditors, consultants, administrators, politicians, business executives, parents and children, etc. Thus, speech or talking is basic and indispensable in any group activities and civilized society. Speech is for others to understand. The confusion and misunderstanding in conversation are due to ineffective and bad speech.

There are no standard rules to be followed in oral communication once and for all time to come. However, effective oral communication calls for certain principles to be followed. Whatever the circumstances, however, the following are essential ingredients of good oral communication.

The essential of good oral communication is clarity. Clarity of message is of the first and foremost importance among principles. The three most important qualities of oral communication style are: first clarity, then clarity and then clarity. Before you start talking think and rethink ideas till they are clear to the speaker. Then put ideas in conversation in a clear-cut order. Clarity can be achieved with simple words, short sentences and common words. Daniel Defoe, the author of Robinson Crusoe, said that clarity is a matter of style in which a man speaking to five hundred people of all common and various capacities, idiots and lunatics excepted, should be understood by them all.

A message must be brief. Lengthy sentences confuse and may lead to misunderstanding. It should be a short one. One can achieve brevity by taking pains and framing sentences to serve people rather than indulging in lengthy and complex ones. We do come across people who give speech short in a sentence.

Conversation in short sentences gives the listener time and opportunity to follow what the speaker endeavours to pur across. Using precise words, simple and familiar words and avoiding superfluous words are important factors in effective communication.

Precision is the most important principle in effective communication. Using precise words mean speaking in exact detail. Using right words at the right place in the context will alone convey the meaning intended by the speaker. In oral communication the precise words which are often the concrete words express the real and correct meaning.

As far as possible using vague words should be avoided. But in practice it is difficult to replace one word for another. No two words give exactly the same meaning without changing or diluting the meaning. People may substitute a simple word for a difficult one. It is better to have full knowledge of synonyms and antonyms of words.

Cliche means a phrase which is used too often, and has some meaning. The cliches are now stale in oral communication. An effective good communicator avoids cliches. A speaker may use them unconsciously when he is involved in a serious mood of conversation. Examples of cliches are 'I mean', 'oh really', 'ok', 'quite fine', 'yes', etc.

Presentation of matter in a logical sequence is yet another important principle of effective communication. The speaker does not jump points or change the sequence. Consistency, continuity and logical development of the subject matter should be there. The manner in which a speaker said something is more important than the matter itself in communication.

In our conversation we must be conscious to avoid jargon. Jargon is a field applicable or relating to a particular section of a profession. It means language or terminology relating to law, commerce, sports, defence, etc. It may be called legal jargon, military jargon, commercial jargon, etc. Only people who are versed in a particular subject can understand. But in public and general conversation the words used must be clear to other people as well.

To convey meaning is more important than using superfluous words. Verbosity in oral communication is a great danger in conveying a message. Using more words does not assure greater clarity. Using more words will take more time and the time of an audience is wasted. The listener may tire and may misunderstand the meaning.

Seven C's of Communication: Francis J. Bergin advocates that there are seven C's to remember in spoken communication. They are:

1. Candid,
2. Clear,
3. Complete,
4. Concise,
5. Concrete,
6. Correct,
7. Courteous.

Use of unnecessary prepositions should be avoided. For instance, all employees must follow the safety regulation in regard to work. Here the word " about" can be used in place of " in regard to". Some other examples are: in connection with, with reference to, in relation to, with regard to.

Adjectives and adverbs should be used where necessary. They emphasis the meaning with the degree of importance. For instance, the problem is under *active* consideration; a *positive* decision will be taken; *definite* results; *comparatively* the results are poor.

Varied Means

Certain techniques should be followed to be a successful communicator. He must build into his speech an element of goodwill to which the listener will react favourably. A speech creates goodwill provided a message produces a favourable reaction from the listeners. A positive favourable reaction from the listeners can be achieved by promoting a friendly, kind attitude, cheerful consent towards listeners. Listeners are many and human, of all common and various capacities, idiots, lunatics. They should be treated as such, and the message capable of being understood by them all. A favourable effect of a message is important. One principle is being courteous, which is fundamental in all oral communication and good relations.

> "Courtesy consists of putting yourself in the other person's place and showing every consideration, as well as showing good common sense in getting along with other people. It is an attitude of mind based on kindness, respect and understanding. It comes naturally to people who are considerate of another person's feelings, needs, and reactions, and impresses the other person favourably."

However, the following are the important techniques in oral communication to be successful:

Friendly Atmosphere: It is the responsibility of the speaker to create a friendly or kindly attitude, benevolent atmosphere at the place. A sincere speech should be in a conversational manner. The message should be capable of being put into writing. Cheerful consent, feeling of warmth of the listener are necessary.

The speaker must use a personal greeting while starting a speech, the salutation in oral communication to the listener.

It is always desirable to call the person by name say "Dear Mr. Saxena" but not "Dear Sir". Use the person's name once or twice during oral conversation.

Showing appreciation towards listeners is a technique for building goodwill. It involves being grateful to the audience. The speaker must wish to show his personal appreciation for what they have listened. It means giving thanks to an appreciative audience. Every listener likes to be appreciated. The success of speech depends entirely on the speaker's satisfaction with his listeners. The listener likes to be treated as an individual and to feel recognised as a person.

Showing awareness and interest in listeners as individuals is the desirable quality of successful communication. He can say: It gives me great pleasure to inform you. I am happy to learn that you are joining the organisation. He must make honest efforts to make the other person feel better or more important.

The communicator has to open his speech with a smile. It involves showing pleasure. It is an act of a smiling speech or the resulting facial expression. It gives clues to feelings and meanings. In the process a happy frame of mind when speaking means that pleasantness and friendliness will pass through what is spoken. This is particularly necessary when taking favourable action. It demands a happy attitude to be apparent from the very beginning.

Another technique for building goodwill among the audience is to make the listeners feel important. Due importance should be given to the listeners. The purpose of speech is to make them understand the message. This can be achieved by showing appreciation for listeners and by taking a personal interest in listening to them and clarifying their doubts. It is an art and tact of the speaker to make them feel important. Speaking from their point of view and mentioning various practical instances also makes them feel important.

Goodwill is a friendly and kindly attitude. A listener's goodwill is a major object of oral communication. Indicating acceptance of suggestions by the listeners will go a long way towards achieving a successful speech. Indicating attention and acknowledgement of what is being suggested will produce positive and favourable reactions from listeners. It will create a friendly confident feeling towards the communicator. Creating impression is a very difficult task. It is reciprocal and can be applied in all speeches. A speech can be given, but one must remember the listener's goodwill.

Empathy is important in a speech to a group or audience. Empathy means ability to understand and share the feelings, experiences, opinions, etc., of listeners. A certain empathy must exist between the speaker and the listener. It is necessary to show every consideration for the listener that will create interest and persuade the listener. To show empathy with listeners is the projection of one's personality into the listeners in order to understand the listeners better.

Language is very essential in good communication. A person can adapt his own language but should speak at the listener's level. This will make message pleasing and interesting. An individual listener is interested in listening to anything which satisfies his purpose and desire. A pleasing message not only puts the speaker at ease but also relaxes his listeners.

Honesty: If the speaker is genuinely interested in the listeners' viewpoint, then the speaker should be honest in his response. Honesty in speech promotes confidence among the listeners.

The style in which a speaker dresses communicates something to listeners. Communicating with acceptable and gentle dress is one of the most direct and silent ways of communication.

John Molloy believes that the way a person dresses communicates something to others. He is a dress consultant with major corporations. In his interview with a series of questions of more than hundred top company executives revealed many interesting features on communicating with good personal appearance. Some of his findings in his book *Dress for Success* are as follows:

(1) "He showed executives five pictures of men each wearing expensive, tailored, but high-fashion clothing. He asked the executives if this was proper dress for a junior business executive. Ninety-two said no, eight said yes.

(2) He showed them five additional pictures of the same people neatly dressed in conservative clothing and asked if they were dressed properly for a young executive. All said yes.

(3) He showed them five additional pictures of the same people obviously dressed in lower-middle class attire and asked if these people were dressed properly for a young executive. Forty-six said yes, fifty-four said no.

(4) He then asked the executives if they thought that the people dressed in the middle-class suit would succeed better in corporate life than those dressed in the lower middle-class suit. Eighty-eight said yes, twelve said no."

How physical movements or keeping still stand in relation to the audience one is communicating with has a real impact on communication. A message or idea is often communicated through action. A person's gesture also communicates meaning. The movements give us clues to a person's self-confidence or interest in the topic. If a person is not interested in a subject he may more likely lean on chair.

The technique of being amusing is a very important characteristic that most good communicators possess. The ability to amuse people when speaking means that pleasantness and friendliness will permeate what is spoken. Especially, when taking any decision, or action, let a speaker's humorous attitude be apparent from the very beginning, opening with a smile. It is the most desirable feature of oral communication. Being amusing, conversation and speech naturally not only puts the speaker at ease, but also relaxes his listeners. Understanding the right situation and using the technique of humour whenever an opportunity arises will increase the speaker's speaking ability.

Making a speech humorous or witty is a technique to build goodwill, provided the wit is relevant to the context and effective. Jokes or anecdotes are recommended when used carefully otherwise the image of the speaker goes down. Corwin's Law: "Never make people laugh. If you could succeed in life you must be solemn, solemu as an ass. All the great monuments arc built over solemn asses." "Never try to make people laugh at the wrong time or just for the sake of being entertaining make joke teach a point." Markel says "Humour is okay, wit can be dangerous, wisecracking is disastrous."

Sometimes, it may be necessary to use visual or audio-visual aids in support of speech. Their use is recommended for effective presentation of matter. It is practically possible to use electrical or electronic tools. The speech is nearly always combined with media like charts, graphs, tables, TV, visual projections from equipment, etc. The speaker must see where they can be used rightly, and use only those aids which will carry the message. Prepare a brief note of the subject matter of the speech and distribute it to the audience. Handouts serve the audience and act as permanent reminders of the speaker's message. Whatever is heard in the meeting may be forgotten soon after the speech is over.

Accent is another important factor to be achieved in good speech. It is a thing which may prevent meaning from being clear. If a person is speaking in an accent which is not familiar to the hearers, they may be worrying about the meaning of a word which he has used while he is saying the next phrase, and so they do not even listen to the second phrase. The word accent covers two separate meanings. It is used in some contexts to mean extra breath-force on a word or syllable (stress): it is also used to indicate the differences of pronunciations heard in different parts of our own country.

Now we all hear our own voice and speech from inside ourselves while other people hear us only from the outside, so it is difficult to know, without a mechanical aid, how we actually do sound to others. Now that so many people own tape-recorders, it is a good idea to listen to ourselves through one of these useful instruments. Listening to a record does not, in itself, make speech better; it only makes us aware of good and bad points in our own voice and speech and in our use of speech, as mumbling, hesitation, dullness and repetition are noticeable on a record especially in an unprepared conversation. When we have become aware of our faults, hard and concentrated work is usually required in order to alter our habits.

A point about speech which is beyond the very practical points raised above, is the actual quality of the voice itself. Some people are more sensitive to this than others, or perhaps it would be truer to say that they are more consciously so. A beautiful voice in itself is interesting and pleasant to listen to, but here again another warning must be given: the owner of a lovely voice often takes great pleasure in listening to himself and anyone who does this is apt to go off the track. Another point is that he may be talking of something ugly or unpleasant, and then the unsuitability of a lovely tone makes him sound insincere.

In fact suitability of voice and speech to the subject is even more important than the acoustics of the room. In addition, the style should be suited to the audience and to the situation: a good speaker uses different styles when he is speaking, for instance, to small children, to adult students interested in his subject or to the guests at a wedding reception.

Dressing by people differ from place to place and from country to country like the dress of army men, naval personnel, airport personnel; dressing by religious heads, political leaders, lawyers, doctors, sports people, etc. Likewise thoughts are so dressed by speakers as to gain the attention and interest of the audience. This is a fundamental principle of motivating the audience. Swami Vivekananda began his address at the Parliament of Religions in Chicago as "brothers and sisters"—Not "distinguished ladies and gentlemen", as others did before Swamiji's turn had come. Similarly it is more appropriate to quote the speech of the great Congress leader Chittaranjan Das to a vast audience, "I feel the weight of iron chains over my body, the handcuffs in my wrist; it is the agony of bondage; the whole of India is a vast prison...."

Guiding Principles

Audience: The communicator should know his audience and accordingly put ideas across. If the audience or listeners are not able to understand, it is an ineffective communication.

Ideas: The transmitter should have clear information to be communicated. One must be clear about the ideas, opinions, facts to be communicated, otherwise one cannot make these clear.

Ambiguity: Using words in current use is important and to avoid words which convey vague meaning. A vague communication gives confusion in communication.

Conditions: Necessary physical conditions, facilities and environment are to be provided to both the speaker and listeners.

Not to Talk and Talk: Speak only that much sufficient to convey the central idea of the subject matter. A verbal communication should be short, clear and simple to pass message.

Gestures and Tone: The style in which the message is conveyed is as important as what is being said. There must be an integration between facial expression, voice, gestures and mood to the action of what is said.

Not to Talk to Impress: The purpose of communication is not to impress but to express, to inspire confidence and to make people understand. Expressing and conveying a better message makes an impression. It is not a good communication if the speaker tries to conceal, confess, intimidate and to impress.

Feedback: Feedback is probably the most important method of improving communication. Two-way process ensures feedback. The communicator has to obtain feedback from the receiver.

Emphasis on Purpose: The subject matter and its theme should be greatly emphasised to draw the attention of the listener.

Avoid Extremes: Some subject matters are too good or too bad. It is desirable to avoid extremes in speaking.

Cultivate Listening: Listening is different from hearing. Listening and understanding require a lot of reasoning and attitude. The reasons of non-listening are boredom, bias, fear, interruption, etc.

Clarify Ideas: The communicator has first to clarify his ideas himself before: think on the message clearly and clarify ideas to ensure effective communication.

Purpose: The purpose of communication is to make others understand the subject matter. The communication is ineffective if the purpose is not achieved.

Physical and Human Setting: An atmosphere of confidence, mutual trust is to be created in the process of communication. It is mainly the responsibility of the superiors. The informal relations is the best weapon to promote physical and human setting in the organisation.

The Basis

In oral communication, the important question arises is as to what are the different forms of tools of oral communication. Media of oral communication means tools or vehicles of communication. The instrument or instruments used or applied in conversation, speech, talk to convey a message is/are termed as medium/media of communication. The problem of misunderstanding in group activities or improper implementation of business objectives or broad policies laid down by the top management arises from poor communication. The aims of an organisation can be achieved with effective communication. Transfer of message by any medium available is essential in any organisation like, private, public, productive, service, educational institutions, Government departments, undertaking, assembly, etc.

However, it needs to be emphasised at this point to account for the important and popular media of oral communication.

To make communication effective, appropriate medium or media may be selected to meet a particular situation which the speaker endeavours to put across. All media may not be useful in all circumstances. A particular medium or instrument may be more useful as a conveyor belt carrying a message to a particular group. Any medium may be considered good only when the listener receives, understands and responds to that or acts accordingly. Diverse educational background, mental aptitude, position occupied, responsibilities, importance of the message, urgency, etc., call for different media of oral communication. As such a particular medium of communication cannot be applied to all cases.

The chief executive's medium of communication is different to a medium applied by a foreman. Similarly, the medium of communication would certainly vary when the politician wants to convey his ideas. Similarly, the medium of communication would also vary when the Government wants the public to be informed about the welfare and development programmes and achievements during a particular period. Again, the medium of communication would definitely vary when a teacher wants to convey a message or to educate about a subject.

In this connection it is, therefore, very necessary to choose an appropriate medium, because the success of communication depends upon the selection of an appropriate instrument or instruments to make effective communication. Oral communication has mostly and primarily been adopted as a media for many purposes. The forms of oral communication are many and varied which may be briefly discussed below.

The Debate

Face to face conversation is the most effective type of communication. It has certain advantages. Certain things can be done orally more effectively than written communication. Though, modern scientific machines like telephones are used as a device for verbal communication it is not a face to face communication. There are many media in oral communication in which there is no personal contact. It is only in face to face communication that information can be satisfactorily conveyed. Explanations, notes, etc., as used to written communication need not necessarily be used in this method because necessary clarifications, explanations and doubts can be exchanged orally without loss of time. A face to face communication gives an opportunity of observing facial expressions, reactions and gives effective feedback on the matter. When the communicator and the recipient are talking together sitting face to face there is a definite understanding. Opinions can be expressed freely, opposed, offers and counter offers and clarifications take place then and there only which are most essential for effective decision making. The verbal words are more direct and personal. Word of mouth exposes feelings and actions. The acceptance or rejection can be better understood and necessary clarifications can be given. But the communicator must choose words so that the receiver will be sure to understand them correctly. The following are some of the important principles of effective face to face communication:

1. To avoid waste of time and thought of both.
2. The message must reveal the necessary facts.
3. The vocabulary level of the receiver must be considered.
4. To convey the message in the way we feel towards the receiver.
5. The manner and style and temperaments are equally important.
6. Appropriate fitting words to be chosen to convey the central message.
7. Short sentences, clear words, currently in use should be used.

Benjamin Balinsky put it: "If there is any short-cut to executive effectiveness, it is the mastery of the art of face-to-face communication."

Telephonic Conversation

A telecommunication device. A communication device for speaking directly to someone at a distant place. The instrument may use either an electric current or radiowave.

The telephone is an instrument for speaking to someone from a distance. The message is transmitted using either an electric current which passes along a wire or radio waves. One speaks to another by means of a telephone. A telephonist is a person who operates a telephone switchboard at a telephone exchange. Telephone exchange is a central control through which telephone calls are directed. Under the direct dial system one can speak to someone from a distance directly without the assistance of the telephone exchange. Telephonic communication is very essential to create a good impression. It has a good potential for providing two-way interaction between the speaker and listener.

This medium is particularly useful when people are scattered over a vast area in an organisation or otherwise. Telephone has thus in recent years come to be used for direct contact. Under this one can hear a natural voice and is more clear in telephonic communication. It is recognised that the telephone is one of the oral communication devices to save time and get things done quickly. But in telephonic communication one should be precise, clear in presenting the message. Similarly it is not desirable to allow the telephone to ring for long because it leads to annoyance. In recent years in many organisations the intercom system has been introduced. Intercom is a system of communication within an organisation usually by means of microphones and loud speakers. The telephone directory is a book containing the list of names, addresses and telephone numbers of all the people in a particular area who have telephone facilities. It provides quick reference of a particular number required. The directory may be compiled covering a limited local area, a taluk, district, state and may also be a national telephone directory.

The Gatherings

Another medium of oral communication is a conference. A conference means a meeting for discussion. A conference is the pooling of thoughts of two or more individuals to assist in solving problems. The conference of political leaders, conference of chief executives, conference of press reporters, conference of scientists, etc., is convened to discuss and find a solution to the problems of their interest. In a conference mutual problems constitute the subject of discussion. Eminent and expert participants contribute their thoughts and experience in solving a problem. It is a joint effort of the people gathered. They interact, exchange with others, teach each other and learn together.

Thus, a conference is an assembly of a group of persons gathered to exchange information for some particular purpose. The words conference and meeting are generally used interchangeably. The group may be small or large. Similarly there is no difference between speaking in a conference and a meeting. A conference is also called a convention when it is attended by a large number of people. In a conference the speaker speaks his own ideas and opinions on the subject on which the conference is conducted. All the speakers present their own solutions or opinions and the leader of the conference summarises the proceedings. In this type of oral communication the success is based on the thought process and how well the members are stimulated.

Press Meet

It is a gathering of journalists and press reporters. In a press conference journalists and reporters from various news agencies are invited to participate and to listen and cover in the press. A press conference may be with politicians, Government, corporate executives, local bodies, educational institutions, voluntary agencies, etc. The purpose of a press conference is to appraise a situation, problems, achievements, progress, public matters, etc. Press reporters are supplied with pamphlets covering information and statistical data so as to enable them to cover in the press. The conference enables the press to carry messages to the public. The press is entitled to raise questions and solicit replies or explanations. In a democratic set-up the press conference is the powerful media of mass communication.

Functional Deeds

Action and message is a communication medium called a demonstration. This media is mostly adopted by corporate marketing strategy. Demonstration is also used to educate the voter as to how to exercise his franchise. The demonstration is the part of the sales presentation where a salesman proves that his company's product will do all. The purpose of the demonstration is to maintain the interest that was aroused on previous occasions and to build desire in the mind of the prospect.

The salesman shows and states the benefits that the prospect will receive, supported by facts. He places the product in the hands of the prospect for his examination. The demonstration gives the prospect the opportunity to experience for himself the benefits to be obtained from using a particular product. Everyone would rather enjoy a pleasant experience than just be told about it by another person.

Radio's Importance

The radio is a vehicle of a mass medium. It is a type of communication technology. Radio is extensively used for broadcasting many programmes mainly because of its wide accessibility and relatively low cost. It is a one way communication system. But some institutions in the advanced countries like New Zealand and Australia have evolved radio tutorials and radio conferences. It is the only audio medium. Nassif suggested that the audio-visual electronic programme used must be complementary to other media. The effective use of radio for correspondence courses began in Japan in 1976.

Recording is a process which involves recording a programme at a particular place. The process of making a record of something like a message, talk, interview especially on a record or on a tape. A record player is an electrical instrument which reproduces the sounds recorded on records. The information or statements recorded are intended to be repeated or made public. It is written down or recorded for future reference. Recordings make it possible to capture a speech or radio programme and replay it by radio before an audience or over a public address system anywhere. Some recordings are made on the spot at special occasions or events. In other cases special programmes are deliberately produced at a recording studio.

In-oral communication a mechanical dictating machine is called a dictaphone. It dictates correspondence read for another to write down through the dictating machine. Dictating machines by a combination of electronics and mechanical means record the voice. The transcriber reproduces the voice. The machines are most popular and used for dictation of correspondence, recording of proceedings, conferences, recording of interviews and are used for market research. The advantages of using dictating machnines are:

(1) They save time.

(2) Reduce the cost involved in corresponding work.

(3) The mistakes in hearing by typists are avoided.

(4) Speed and accuracy can be achieved.

(5) Personal presence of the typist or stenographer is avoided.

(6) Because of inter-room connections dictation is possible without the presence of a steno.

(7) The advantage of centralisation can be achieved.

Thus, there are many types and models of dictaphones. The main function is to record the dictation and transcribing to play back and transcribe the dictation by switching on the machine which is recorded on a magnetic tape or plastic disc. Making use of the dictaphone to be effective in communication demands and calls for following certain norms. They are:

(1) Clear pronunciation,

(2) clarity,

(3) simplicity.

(4) short sentences,

(5) stop when interruption takes place.

(6) avoid pipe, gum, cigar in mouth while dictating, and

(7) dictation should be read back.

In a real world situation meeting are yet another media of oral communication. In a democratic set-up meetings are a common method. In a restless age of communication meetings are business. A message can easily and understandably be communicated through the media of meetings. Message is carried in family meetings, street gatherings, samiti meetings, panchayat meetings, parishad meetings, municipal meetings, municipal corporation meetings and political meetings. Assembly and Parliamentary meetings.

Meetings may be convened regularly and in extraordinary circumstances. In corporate management we frequently come across company meetings. A company may conduct several types of meetings to convey the ideas of the company for the purpose of taking decisions. The usual company meetings are statutory meetings, annual general meetings, extraordinary general meetings, Board of Directors meetings, shareholders meetings, debenture holders meetings, creditors meetings, etc.

Meetings are gatherings of groups of persons belonging to a particular interest to whom, as groups, some common matters or issues are entrusted. At meetings information is communicated orally, discussed, deliberated and debated to come to a solution or decision. Meetings are supposed to be of democratic origin.

Sometimes special invitees, *ex-office.* Government nominees and institutional representatives are invited to have their specialised and technical advice for consideration. Meetings ensure collective decisions. Collective decisions are taken with oral discussions sitting in meetings, hence fear of authority being concentrated in one person is avoided.

A meeting may be informational, advisory, or problem solving. In an informational meeting the object is to present ideas, and data to the members. In advisory types of meetings the purpose is to gather and seek advice, information, suggestions relating to a problem.

The object of a problem solving meeting is to seek a decision, solution out of the collective discussion and mutual understanding of a problem. Thu is in meetings communication flows both ways. Discussion is an important object of a meeting. In this verbal form of communication the group acts as a team with responsibility since it helps in arriving at a collective decision. A rumour is an oral information circulating something. It sometimes passes unfounded news from person to person. In a rumour, communication is a piece of news or story passed from one person to another which may not be true. A verbal general talk or gossip.

A loud untrue sound. It is a talk or report of a person or thing in someway noted or distinguished. The fact of being generally talked about fosters reputation and renown. A rumour is a verbal statement or report circulating in a group, of the truth of which there is no clear evidence. A rumour once spread is not soon removed. A rumour spreads like anything and may create wonders and miracles as a channel of informal communication. The two persons involved in a rumour are: rumour spreader and rumour bearer. The originator of a rumour is also called as rumour monger. In the grapevine the leader of a group tells the message to each person in that group. A communication leader recognises rumours. The leader must be trustworthy and have credibility.

The management can use rumours for effective communication. The information can be fed into the informal channel to dispel rumours and to provide quick and easy access to the information.

Model Rumours

1. A rumour circulating that the managing director is going abroad.
2. Rumour passing from one person to another person about the change in holiday arrangements.
3. News that the secretary got a new job.
4. A person rumoured that a colleague has left the country.
5. It is rumoured that they are getting transferred.

Demonstration and Dramatisation Method: This is a method in which "doing" skills may be shown, explained and applied. Demonstration is made and dramatised as a means of giving emphasis to the subject under consideration.

Informal Manners

Informal communication is termed as grapevine. So the informal medium in oral communication, as the very name implies, is based on informal relationship of the people in the organisation. A successful management must recognise and give importance to the grapevine. It is also known as grapevine communication and means an informal communication network constituted to pass a message speedily. When an informal channel is used to communicate, it is termed as grapevine or informal communication.

It is not a deliberately created and officially prescribed channel for flow of information, hence free from all sorts of formalities. The network is formed out of personal relationships, social and group relations, but not out of position of line and authority, superior, and subordinate, or based on organisational hierarchy. It is a quick vehicle for a message. Informal communication may be conveyed by a simple glance, gesture, smile or mere silence. It is composed of a series of small groups of people linked to one another covering everyone in the organisation.

One person in the group passes the message to each person in a particular group. The individuals of the group in turn pass the message to someone in another group. Because of inter group links and chains the message quickly passes to everyone. There are communication leaders in the grapevine and the management can make use of them to communicate. On the other hand, management may create its own grapevine. L. Brown clearly describes the advantages of the grapevine to the management in the words:

> "advantages to management include expediency it saves time, gets immediate response; provides useful feedback for decision-making; generates ideas and suggestions that may prove helpful; disseminates accurate, factual information that needs to be relayed. In using the grapevine, management must be able to pinpoint the leaders and work through them, must feed in factual

information, listen to the feedback response, and be discerning in not overloading the system and using it inappropriately."

Debate in Group

In the context of group discussion it is more appropriate to quote Robert Bales who defines:

> "A small group is defined as any number of persons engaged in interaction with one another in a single face-to-face meeting or series of such meetings in which each member receives some impression or perception of each other member distinctive enough so that he can, either at the time, or in later questioning give some reaction to each of the others as an individual person, even though it be only to recall that the other was present."

In a group discussion members of the group are in interaction with one another. A group may be a small group or large group. There are no fixed norms as to the right size for a group, it all depends upon circumstances of a particular case. A group is headed by a leader generally called the chairman, controller of group discussion. A group may be a casual group, permanent group, learning group, policy-making group and action group.

For certain reasons groups are formed to take a decision or to carry out some activities. Communication in the group takes place in the form of deliberations among the leaders and group members. Group reaches decisions after discussion. Group decisions are collective opinions. Group decisions through discussions are superior and better to an individual decision which is one sided. Group discussion is a process of decision making where communication exchange on validity, reasonability, practicability, time and cost factors are interacted. Thus, group discussion involves defining a problem, generating solutions, analysing alternative solutions, identifying a balanced solution, selecting the best solution, implementing the solution and evaluating the results.

Verbal News

Oral report means presentation of written matter before a group. One must have oral communication skills for oral report presentation. This method is used in every business activity and at every level. The originator of an oral report presents an informational and analytical message. The essentials of good speaking will equally apply to cral reports. According to L. Brown:

> "The function of an oral report is to furnish he facts necessary to expedite action or to persuade someone or any number of persons to take the action the group decided on or to implement the group's solution."

Like in an oral message an oral report to be effective must carefully be planned and developed. When a report is orally read before a gathering is similar to oral presentation and should be written in such a manner. An oral report is generally drafted for a particular group of people. For instance, an oral report to a welfare committee, an oral report to a conference of salesmen and an oral report to the executives of all the departments. Like a speech oral reports have an introduction, body and ending. With a view to clarify certain things or to create interest audio-visual aids may be used.

A successful and effective oral report must follow certain essential principles. Some of the principles are:

(1) A report should be complete, clear and short.

(2) To practise report reading by imagining an audience.

(3) To set a gentle style and tone.

(4) To know the audience.

(5) To fix a time limit to read.

(6) To divide a report into paragraphs, each paragraph should give a separate central idea.

(7) Other principles of good oral communication and written communication are equally applicable.

The following are logical steps to acquire self-confidence to present an oral report, suggested by Leland Brown:

1. Preparing your talk carefully. Fear of forgetting result in stage fright.
2. Practising aloud you will know your talk better after rehearsing. Practise alone, going over it again and again, imagining your audience before you, or viewing yourself in a mirror.

3. By not memorising your talk; a tape recorder can be helpful for it allows you to hear yourself.
4. Checking your appearance. Dress appropriately for the occasion and your audience.
5. When you face your group, waiting a few minutes before you start to talk. Think of your audience as your friends. They want you to do well. Do not think about yourself.
6. Beginning slowly; do not give up once you have begun. Stage fright disappears after you start.
7. Speaking louder than ordinarily, at least at the outset.
8. Speaking as often as you can. The more practice you get, the easier it is to speak with confidence.

A medium of oral communication operates by using a television set. The television camera is connected to the receiving set. The camera scans the picture to be transmitted. The camera converts the picture into electrical signals, i.e., video, signals video amplifier applies the range of frequencies Amplitude modulated picture transmitter is a circuit which places visual information on a career wave. The microphones convert audio signals into electrical signals. The complete process gives us continuous viewing of pictures and his to listening.

Message to Public

In oral communication, the public address system is another important dimension. It is a mechanical system. It is a system adopted at meetings, shows, carnivals, meals exhibitions, gathering of employees or mass audience. Through the public address system if is possible mechanically to project the human voice spread among a large gathering. Mounted on a minitruck or any other mobile auto the PA system can be transported from place to place, presenting speakers and programmes as it goes, and reaching a widely distributed audience. Sound tracks can also be rigged up at stationary locations, providing facilities for meetings and special programmes in lieu of a permanently installed PA system. Portable bull horns afford great mobility wherever amplified sound is needed.

8

Relationship with Readers

Communication is an inter-disciplinary area of study taking within its compass the disciplines of political science, economics, literature, statistics, philosophy, psychology, sociology, linguistics and anthropology. The origins of the subject are traceable to Germany and the United States in the early-20th century. It was a time when the German sociologist, Emile Durkheim, and the Chicago School of Sociologists, began to raise questions related to the role of the press in society. In later years, with the rise of the Third Reich, both Germans and Americans were worried about Nazi propaganda, and were searching for the most effective strategies to propagate and to counter it.

Then there were American advertisers making vigorous attempts at maximum profits through manipulation of customer behaviour. The growth of the press, cinema and radio was dramatic during the pre-World War II years. It was therefore natural that some of the basic questions raised by political scientists, sociologists and psychologists at the time related to questions of attitudes, beliefs and behaviour in the new context of media persuasiveness.

By the 1960s, however, it came to be accepted in the disciplines involved that attitudes were complex phenomena, and were not subject to easy manipulation, though development communication researchers such as Daniel Lerner, Lucian Pye, Wilbur Schramm and Everett Rogers persisted in imposing their 'modernisation' model of development using the mass media. Meanwhile, the mass media grew from strength to strength and with breakthroughs in electronics and telecommunications came to regulate the whole of society. It made inroads into the home, and revolutionised social life. So all pervasive did the media become that sociologists were obliged to accept it as a 'social system' and as an 'industry' in its own right.

They went to the extent of saying that the mass media had created a 'mass' society and a 'mass' culture. This view was, however, contested by 'critical' schools of communication research in the United States, Europe and Latin America. 'Critical' schools focussed attention on the media product, the media professionals and on business/political groups that owned and controlled the media. The political and economic contexts in which media functioned was of crucial interest to them. They called into question the commercialisation and politicisation of the mass media-which they termed 'cultural' or 'consciousness' industries. The Frankfurt School of Social Research had pioneered attacks on the mass media in the 1940s. Later, two schools of 'critical' scholars that campaigned for this new approach to media studies in the seventies and eighties were:

(1) The 'Cultural Studies' School (led by Raymond Williams, Richard Hoggarth and Stuart Hall), and

(2) The 'Political Economy' School led by Peter Golding and Graham Murdock of the Centre for Mass Communication Research, Leicester University, and Nicholas Garnham of the Polytechnic of Central London. Considerable revisions in the approach of 'critical' scholars to media studies took place in the late-1980s, with the end of the Cold War and the emergence of the active viewer in reception research.

Creating Public Views

Our selection and 'reading' of components/items of the various media is influenced by the social and cultural groups we belong to. The way we see and hear and interpret programmes too depends upon the same sections. In other words, the culture, language, religion, caste and other groups we are members of provide us the frame of reference for interacting with the mass media. Thus, public opinion is formed only indirectly by the mass media, and by information from other sources like rumours, street propaganda and of course, our own interests. By themselves alone the mass media have little power in forming public opinion. Besides, it needs to be noted that the mass media are not always engaged in attempts to mould public opinion, but more often than not, in trying to meet public needs and/or to sell consumer goods and services. For commercial broadcasters, for instance, the primary aim is to 'deliver' audiences to advertisers.

In the sphere of mass communication, the public can, and often does, call the tune. Indeed, it is the responsibility of the listening, viewing, and reading public to make its opinions known to the media on reports or programmes offensive to its culture and values. Campaigns by women's organisations have, for instance, forced companies to withdraw obscene advertisements. Letters to editors and media directors too do have an impact. A strong public opinion does shape the character of the mass media for better or for worse. It is the responsibility of the public to see that the pressures brought to bear on the media are for the better. An indifferent, undiscriminating public will get what it deserves-reporting and programming of indifferent quality. Peggy Charren's movement Action for Children's Television (ACT) paid off after years of public mobilisation: every American television channel is now required to allocate at least ten per cent of the total broadcast time to children's programmes.

The hypothesis of this socialisation and learning theory is that 'the mass media by paying attention to some issues and overlooking others will affect public opinion: people will tend to know about those things dealt with by the mass media and adopt the order of priority set by media.' The term 'agenda setting' itself was coined by Malcolm McCoombs and Donald Shaw in 1976. They went on to argue that 'audiences not only learn about public issues and other matters through the media; they also learn how much importance to attach to an issue or topic from the emphasis the mass media place upon it.' For example, in reflecting what candidates are saying during an election campaign, the mass media set the agenda of the campaign. This ability to affect cognitive change among individuals is one of the most important aspects of mass communication.' These are claims for the media which are difficult to verify.

It is true that the media prioritise the news in terms of headlines and placement of stories. But it is equally true that people pay greater attention to stories of personal interest to them and their groups. Indeed, it would be nearer the truth to say that the media more often than not 'reflect' rather than 'set' the agenda. Individuals, groups, institutions, political parties and governments-all have their own agenda, and they lobby hard to set the media's agenda through press conferences, press releases, press visits, sponsorships, advertisements, gifts and other means.

The major sources of news for the media are influential elites of society, and they (together with the media proprietors' interests) usually set the agenda for what the media highlight and underplay. It must be conceded, however, that there are sections of the media which play a marvellous 'watchdog' role; truth to sell, there are other sections that play the 'lapdog' role with no concern at all for their audience's information needs. The supposed agenda-setting role of the media is related to what Elisabeth Noelle-Neumann, a German media sociologist, calls the 'spiral of silence'. From her analysis of the election scene in Germany, she assumes that individuals just hate to be isolated from their fellow-beings and so tend to follow dominant opinions rather than express their own points of view openly.

Among the most respected public opinion research organisations in the USA is the institute founded by George Gallup. The Louis Harris Poll organisation comes a close second, leaving the hundreds of other survey organisations analysing public opinion way behind. In India, ORG-MARG, IMRB, MRAS, MODE are the chief survey organisations, regularly carrying out public opinion polls. The results are reported widely in the media, and possibly exert some influence in shaping public opinion in the cities, and in providing valuable data to the government and its various departments.

An Opinion Poll selects a random sample, say a few hundred from each region, up to a total of around 2000 or 3000. With modern probability methods of sampling and statistics, it is believed that it is possible to calculate the accuracy of the sample. Yet, the margin of error ranges from 3-4 per cent. Since 1952, Gallup polls have erred by 1.2 percentage points in their predictions for national elections in United States. The polls carried out by IMRB, a research unit of the ad agency, Hindustan Thompson Associates, or by ORG-MARL, on public attitudes to various issues, and in particular election predictions based on the Gallup system are claimed to be fairly accurate.

Errors in polling occur generally because of inadequate sampling, poor phrasing of questions and the drawing of unwarranted inferences from meagre data. Errors in tabulation and analysis are not uncommon. Moreover, the variables in the analysis of human behaviour are so many that it is impossible in any survey to take all of them into account.

The demand for public opinion polls in India has increased over the years. Big publishers like to find out how the public feels about their newspapers, magazines and books. PR and advertising people like to know if they succeed in their efforts to build up a favourable image for companies and their products, through consumer surveys. Governments and political parties are interested in researching public attitudes to social and economic issues, or to the popularity of a leader. Indeed, Gallup polls themselves are now considered big news stories.

Recognising Audience

The definition of a 'media audience' depends on one's perspective of the role of communication in society. If for instance, we look upon communication as a commodity or as merchandise, and media as tools for selling that commodity, a 'media audience' for us would be no better than a potential market for products and services. On the other hand, if we consider communication to be a social good and a public service, a 'media audience' would be a participative and dialogic community, and the media as serving the educational, informational and cultural needs of the community. Further, if communication to us is a tool for persuasion and propaganda to promote certain political, religious or moral views, then a 'media audience' is 'the masses' that need to be indoctrinated.

A 'media audience' is unlike say an audience for a political meeting, a theatrical performance, a street performance, a mela or a lecture. Sociologists like to define an audience as a 'conventionalised crowd' assembled together. A media audience, however, is more than a conventionalised crowd, but rather a collectivity, an aggregate of persons who are readers, listeners, and viewers of different media or their various components. However, this 'collectivity' is not collected together at one place or even at one time.

Though, in most cases, members of the audience are attending components of one medium or another at the same time, time-shift recording (audio and video) has made it possible to listen to radio or to watch television at one's own convenience. Hence, what makes a media audience a conventional group is the fact that they are attending to the same components. That audience has come together (not in time and space) but in the common act of reading, listening or viewing.

The composition of the group is predictable in some ways; unpredictable in others. So is the reception of the audience. The quality and nature of the response too is largely unknown. While it is true that a particular component or a medium has 'caused' the audience, the audience too has in a way 'caused' the medium; the audience has influenced the form and substance of the medium, its genres and its components.

Indeed, the various genres and components/programmes are part of and have often been taken from the socio-cultural experience of the audience.

Audiences therefore, 'read' the messages of the media in terms of that experience; they 'negotiate' its various meanings, accepting or rejecting or 're-reading' the open and the latent (explicit and implicit) layers of meaning. Audiences generally do not interact with media messages as a 'mass' (as Raymond Williams observed the 'mass' exists only in the minds of the elite) but rather as a family, a cultural group, a social class, a caste or tribal group. The media, therefore, are not out there unrelated to their audiences, but an integral part of the social history and cultural values of the audience.

The Consumers

Mass media audiences are the subject of much research in India. Most of the research, however, is what is aptly termed 'market research.' The primary objective of market research is to provide advertisers and advertising agencies with quantitative data about the access and exposure of selected ('segmented') audiences to the various mass media or to their various components. Such collection of data rarely goes beyond 'head-counting' though tall claims are generally made about 'qualitative' methodologies also being employed.

Armed with such 'reliable' data (believed to be 'scientifically' collected), advertisers can 'slot' their advertising spots in newspapers or magazines with the highest readership among audiences that have a good purchasing power (often termed 'target audience') or the radio or TV programmes which have the highest 'rating.' Among professional advertisers and marketing managers such an exercise is known as 'media planning' or more ambitiously, 'media research.'

So, if I want to sell a new soft drink or a new brand of soap to upper middle class housewives, I would be advised by the 'media planner' (from the advertising agency that has also done the 'product research' and drawn up the advertisement for me) to place my advertisement in a single medium or in a combination of media (the 'multi-media' campaign) most regularly read or watched by my target audience. That potential market for my product is the 'media audience' for the market researcher. It is a deliberately selected segment of the whole audience, selected for its market value, not for its potential as an audience as such. From the perspective of the 'market researcher' and 'media planner', therefore, an audience is a 'construct', carved out of a larger group with the sole purpose of persuading (and manipulating) that segment of the audience to buy a product or service. To the market researcher and the advertiser, then, a media audience is a group of potential customers for products and services advertised in the media.

Advertisers and market researchers are not the only professional group that studies media audiences. Psychologists, sociologists, anthropologists and other social scientists too look at audiences from their own diverse perspectives. Of course, they could assist market researchers in their efforts. In fact this is how media audience research began, in the first place, in the United States. Academics were funded by business and government to look at the 'effects' of the mass media; changes in attitudes, opinions and beliefs were scrutinised to study the role of the media in bringing about changes in consumer behaviour.

Later, this selling out to business and government came to be termed 'administrative research' as against the more serious 'critical' research of social science. Thus, research for the purpose of exploiting the media for persuasion and propaganda was 'administrative'; research which questioned and challenged the status quo, which looked at the media as a social system, an institution and an industry, was 'critical.' Administrative research focussed on media audiences as 'consumers', as passive receivers; critical research turned the searchlight on the media themselves, studying their hidden meanings and their production processes. In recent years, communication researchers have begun looking at families, women, children and other groups in terms of their interactions with TV and with other members of the group. The methods used for such research have been largely qualitative, such as ethnographic observation, participant-observation, and in-depth group discussions.

Mind and Psychology

Group Influences: A group is a collection of people who share some common characteristics, and who interact with one another. A social group is 'any number of persons who share a consciousness of membership and of interaction.' Thus, we belong to social groups like the family, the community, the caste, the trade union, the professional associations, political parties, student bodies, graduates, teachers and the like. No man is an island; he is a member not of one group alone, but of many groups, and many move from one group to another through one's long life and career.

No matter how strong-willed an individual one is the pressure of groups shapes to a large extent one's attitudes, beliefs, values and opinions. Groups are a vital social reality from which there is little escape. They, much more than the mass media, are the agents of change as well as of resistance to change. Group-leaders (or opinion leaders) play an important role in the behaviour of the group. It is only the rare individual who defies the group and sets off on his or her own no matter what the consequences. But then he or she goes on to become a member of some other group or groups.

Types of Groups: The group that is most intimate and close is known as the primary group. Such for instance are the family, the peer group, the gang or the clique. The three conditions that give rise to primary groups are: (a) a close physical proximity, (b) the small size of the group, which makes for face-to-face association and cooperation, and (c) the lasting nature of the bond or a relationship like that between a husband, wife and children.

The secondary or peer group, on the other hand, is characterised by a less close relationship between members. Although, secondary groups sometimes provide pleasant human relationships, sociability is ordinarily not their goal. So, while primary groups are relationship-oriented, secondary groups are goal-oriented and much less cohesive. Examples of secondary groups are: the college, the school, the various organisations and unions, the army, film and other entertainment societies, and clubs and political parties. Then there are castes. tribes, religious and linguistic communities, and regional groups. These groups, like the primary groups, exercise a strong influence on our thought and behaviour even determining the prejudices with which we watch mass media programmes. The influence of a group on the attitude of an individual is generally treated in terms of the concept of 'reference group.' A more specific concept than secondary group, it is a group that an individual takes as a frame of reference for self-evaluation and attitude formation. Such a group has the function of setting and enforcing standards of conduct and belief. It also serves as a standard against which people compare themselves and others.

But our 'reference group' differs from situation to situation. For instance, when we watch a cricket test match our reference group is the nation we belong to, not usually the religious group we are members of. So also, for the middle-classes the reference group would be the upper class whose riches they aspire to. Consequently, reference groups are not necessarily the groups of which we are members, but rather the groups we long or wish to be members of. It is these groups that provide us the 'frame of reference' in terms of which we respond to communication. This is not to discount the role of primary and secondary groups in our understanding of and response to communication. The term 'interpretative communities' perhaps comes closest to describing the groups that shape and influence our reaction to the messages of the various media.

Whole Audience, an Entity

The large number of members who are supposed to make up 'the mass' come from all walks of life. They are, therefore, a heterogeneous group or groups with little interaction among themselves. If they are organised at all, the organisations are loose and flexible. Further, the members comprising 'the mass' are anonymous not only to each other, but to the communicator himself. They are united only by the medium and the message. It is in other words, a 'mass media audience'-yet another indefinite concept in the infant discipline of mass communication. A 'mass audience' is larger than an audience for a lecture, or for a musical or theatrical performance. But what about a 'mass meeting' or a 'mass rally' addressed by a political leader in Mumbai or Delhi? The term 'mass', therefore, lacks precision in meaning and becomes intelligible only when used in a specific context and related to certain kinds of behaviour, institution or structure. It is in fact an elastic epithet devoid of any precise scientific content and more likely to reveal the point of view of the person using it, than to clarify the phenomenon in question.

A 'mass' audience is, consequently, a very large (another imprecise word) audience that is the creation of the modern electronic mass media. It is the result of a new technology that is directed at mass production and wide dissemination of communication. The exact size of audience or readership which gives rise to mass communication cannot be specified, but it must be large relative to audiences for other means of communication such as a lecture or play, and large in relation to the number of communicators.

Indeed, this audience is a collectivity unknown prior to the age of electronics. It is as McQuail writes, 'an aggregate of individuals united by a common focus of interest, engaging in an identical form of behaviour and open to activation towards common ends; yet the individuals involved are unknown to each other, have only a restricted amount of interaction, do not orient their actions to each other and are only loosely organised or lacking in organisation. The composition of the audience is continually shifting; it has no leadership or feelings of identity.'

Such 'very large national mass media audiences' exist in the countries of the developed world, but have yet to take shape in developing countries like India. What we do have, however, are 'local audiences' which are largely urban in character, and which function as social groups, the small groups within the amorphous larger groups directly influencing the interactions with the mass media. The 'local audiences' in India have a dynamic of their own. The pulls and pressures of the family, the caste, religion, community, language, and profession are much stronger than any power of the mass media to institute a new way of thinking or a new way of life, except perhaps at a superficial level. The expectation of great persuasive power, says McQuail, from the new media has been largely misplaced. The fault lies partly in a failure to appreciate that the selection of communication content by whatever means disseminated, and its significance to the audience, will both be governed by existing mechanisms of social control, and partly in a tendency to regard the audience member as isolated and abstracted from his social environment. From the first of these stems a false assumption of discontinuity and novelty of content, and from the second a misleading conception of the vulnerability of the individual to mass persuasion.

Views of Audience

A public is a dispersed group of people interested in and divided about an issue, engaged in discussion of the issue, with a view to registering a collective opinion which is expected to affect the course of action of some group or individual. Or, as Kuppuswamy defines, a spontaneous collection of people in response to a certain kind of situation. What unites the members of a public is an issue or controversy, not their togetherness, either physical or intellectual. Indeed, the members may hold different views on an issue, belong to as many publics as they like, and be involved only slightly in an issue. Further, a 'public' has no fixed size, and no fixed place where its members gather. The 'spontaneous collection' is largely intellectual and takes place now through the mass media. Divided though its members be the movement of the public is in the direction of a collective decision but always through discussion in various forums. It is goal-oriented, wanting to take society along with its collective view, or what is properly called 'public opinion.'

A public, however, is not one composite group, but a number of interest groups, often working at odds with one another. The large majority of the groups are indifferent, disinterested and detached unless the issue at stake radically affects their way of life. Shopkeepers, for example, will generally remain uninvolved in the affairs of state, but when a legislation on hoarding of essential commodities or on Octroi is passed, they will assert their strength through a 'bandh' call. Students are up in arms when college or examination fees are raised. The small interest groups, therefore, aim at promoting their own causes by mobilising the public in their favour. The better organised they are, the greater is the pressure they bring to bear on the public, and on 'public opinion.'

Public Opinion: There are few political fantasies as enduring as that level public opinion', but Journalists, politicians and marketing people pursue them relentlessly. In general, however, 'public opinion' is a belief or view prevalent among a large number of interest groups (or at least their leaders) that comprise a public. It is not necessarily representative of all the people, nor is it a unanimous opinion. It is not as the ancient Romans would say vox populi, the voice of the people. The extent to which it is representative differs from issue to issue. It will depend on a number of factors, such as the cultural levels of the various groups and the methods habitually adopted by their members for resolving intra-group and inter-group disputes, the facilities available to them for forming and articulating a balanced judgement on the question at issue, the degree to which the interests affected are mutually compatible and the depths of emotion at which they are felt as vital by the groups concerned; and above all, the measure of confidence that the people have in the administration's responsiveness to public opinion expressed in a variety of ways.

Nature of Public Opinion: Since public opinion is always shifting, inconsistent and often contradictory, Shah concludes that 'generally, public opinion is likely to be a bundle of disparate, often conflicting, opinions rather than a unanimous or near unanimous judgement offered by the body of citizens for the guidance of the government. Only on rare occasions will it appear as the voice of the people, either because the issue is of transparent simplicity and cuts across sectional interests, or because it touches certain deep-seated emotions of a large majority of the people affected by it.' For instance, public opinion in India favoured the government's support of the liberation struggle of Bangladesh, but opposed the clamping of the 'emergency.' But it is divided over whether India should go in for nuclear power plants and for defence ballistic missiles like 'Agni' and 'Prithvi', and even whether the Pokhran-II tests were necessary.

The mass media play an important role in the formation of public opinion on various issues. However, the messages conveyed by the media are invariably mediated by the opinion leaders of groups. As Katz and Lazarsfeld put it, 'ideas seem to flow from radio and print to opinion leaders and from them to the less active sections of the population.' Village level workers or the Panchayat leaders are, for instance, opinion leaders in rural areas, and heads of committees and associations, the opinion leaders in the urban areas. It is they who interpret the messages of the media for their groups. But opinion leaders are usually leaders in one content area, and not in another. For example, in the matter of adopting new agricultural techniques the village level worker (VLW) may be the leader, while in political affairs, the Panchayat head may be the opinion leader. It needs to be noted, however, that the 'two-step flow' of information does not ensure that the required information reaches the people most in need. Opinion leaders are very selective in the kind of information they pass down to peasants and workers. Indeed, mass media use is a group activity involving family, friends and the local community—not an isolated, individual activity.

Electoral Role

The Election Commission has banned the publication of the results of opinion polls and exit polls for about a fortnight during which the national elections are held. This is primarily because of the possibility of opinion polls influencing voters.

Even when the results of opinion polls are made public in the print or electronic media, the Election Commission has spelt out some guidelines. These include the need for the media to state very clearly who are the sponsor/s of the poll, the size of the sample, how it was constituted, and its geographical spread. Further, the 'margin of error' should be made clear. The Press Council too has recommended similar guidelines for the publication of opinion poll results.

A section of the press has criticised these guidelines arguing that they infringe the constitutional right freedom of speech and expression. However, it is this same section of the Indian press that sponsors many opinion polls and publishes their results prominently without ever revealing the sample size and the margin of error. The results (and predictions too) are often laid out attractively in charts and graphs showing only percentages: a clear case of fraud and deception.

9

Framing the News

Free Writing

Several persons write articles, reviews, features, on all kinds of topics in several newspapers and periodicals, though they are not on the regular payrolls of these newspapers and magazines. They are know as 'Freelance Writers'. Freelance journalists are not attached to any newspaper or magazine. Newspapers have to employ reporters and sub-editors because they have to bring out their issue every day. Since periodicals and magazines come out according to their respective periodicity, many of them do not need many full time journalists. Therefore, they depend upon freelancers to a very large measure.

Freelancers quite frequently keep in touch with these magazines, and do assignments as per their needs. With a view of meeting their needs, freelancers have to complete these assignments as per the schedules of the publications.

Increased Scope for Freelancers : Magazine journalism now-a-days is not much different from newspaper journalism. Both delve in facts. The magazines and newspapers are now keener on giving more graphic details. They are in need of more absorbing contents. This also enlarges opportunities for any freelancer. A real good writer can even get a chance to write scripts for various television programmes. For a freelance writer the scope is vast, provided he/she is able to cash on it.

But to develop into a good writer, you will have to read various magazines and newspapers and understand what kind of stuff they use. To avoid rejection, a proper planning, research and a list of users-name and addresses of magazines and newspapers-is a must. As an unattached writer or a freelancer you can not depend only on one user. There must be alternatives.

Who can be a Freelance Writer? Virtually, anybody can be a freelance writer. Most freelance writers, as a matter of fact, have other jobs. A typical freelancer gives only a part of his energy and writing talent to this type of writing. In whichever profession you are, you can develop yourself into an acceptable freelance writer. Only you must have the grit, determination and willingness to work hard besides possessing a good but not necessarily high profile language.

All writers, be they in the staff, or freelancers have seen their pieces being rejected at one time or the other for various reasons. But this does not mean that a writer who wishes to contribute to publications can not hope someday to reach the point where he has to do no other work. But it is difficult to make writing a full-time occupation, especially in the realm of fiction.

However, it is a painful job for the editor to reject a piece. He does not reject something because he doesn't like the name of a person or the subject on which he has written. Mere language doesn't make a piece good. There has to be some originality, specificity and exclusiveness, in the piece that a writer sends for acceptance. Quite often people write on topics on which the writer does not know enough. They lift one para from here and the other from there, or try to rewrite a piece they have read somewhere and try to pass it as original. Sometimes they choose good topics but don't study it to make a piece readable. There are also some who write on any subject and pieces of such writers are kept aside, and are not liked by the editors.

Thus, freelancing should be maintained as a side business. An ambitious freelancer writer should consider his work as part-time. It has to remain an extra-curricular activity.

What to Write? Acceptable freelance contributions can be divided into the following categories-articles; features; and reviews.

Articles : An article is like an essay. But it is not an essay, it is a written composition of variable length, intended to convey ideas and facts for the purpose of informing, educating, enlightening, convincing, instructing or entertaining. Articles can be written on any subject, and can begin with a catchy introduction to attract the readers.

Features : Features are often linked to current events. Feature writers are often captivated by their own graceful writing, letting their skill overshadow the fact that they are linked closely to the news. As a feature writer, you have to learn to recognise that your proper positioning is half way between news story and the feature. Good feature stories are always in demand.

Reviews : There are many events which can neither be a feature nor an article, they are called reviews. Evaluating or even descriptive pieces can be written about music, drama, ballet or such other cultural performances. Such writing, can be termed review pieces. There is yet another kind of view. This is associated with books. A book reviewer is not only paid a good sum, but is also allowed to retain the book he has reviewed. It needs an expert evaluation and the reader has to be told what kind of book it is, and you must avoid writing whether it is good or bad.

The Stringer : There is yet another kind of freelancer called "stringer", because he is attached to one or more newspapers by the string of a fixed payment. Stringers are appointed by newspapers at small places or townships. However, the cost of keeping a staff correspondent at such places is not economical and so a teacher, lawyer or any other professional with a good knowledge of the town/city is usually employed as stringer. Working as a stringer not only ensures you a regular income, but also helps you develop contacts, which may be useful even for your profession.

Freelancing for Magazines : The concept of news magazine was developed in India. The term 'Magazine' was used as part of the name of a publication in 1731. In early years, the term had to do with contents and not with the format. Thus, a publication with a newspaper format with a variety of content was considered a magazine. The magazine, as opposed to the newspaper made no effort to print up the minute news.

Following tips can be helpful for freelancing for magazines:

(a) Choose a subject and do a lot of reading on it.

(b) Draw outlines from your notes after your readings from several sources.

(c) Write a lead, build around recognised ideas, and decide whether an anecdote would be fitting to precede the lead.

(d) Your writing must have depth and background. Try to develop one idea at a time.

(e) Be selective. Don't try to put in all the knowledge you have acquired into one piece. Too many facts or figures make it an uninteresting reading.

(f) Re-read your article after writing like a critical reader.

How to Build an Article? : To build up an article or a feature and to make it readable, what is important to keep in mind is:

Story Structure : The beginners are told that a lead must catch and hold their readers. The lead is the intro and it should be startling. Do not try to devote the beginning to summing up a story.

Sentence Structure : Beginners generally like to twist their sentences. The general rule is that nearly all sentences should be simple and direct.

Sentence Length : The sentences should be short, to make it readable.

Concreteness : Use concrete words instead of abstract ones. Abstract words confuse a reader and that is considered bad for an article and a feature story.

Verb : Making the verb do the work of an adjective is preferable. The verb expresses action.

Transitions : Learning to link paragraphs in a way that pulls the readers on is a skill that distinguishes the professional from the amateur.

Style for Magazine Articles : Every writer has his own way of writing. Magazine writing is a distinct body of prose, usually made up of words the readers can understand and information he can absorb. The general style followed by most magazines consist of crisp, original phrases made up of familiar words. The general rule is that the writing flows from the beginning to the end through smooth transition. If you are writing a profile, start with his qualities.

Sticking to the Theme : There should be only one main theme. Do not deviate from it.

One Story at a Time : Do not try to mix up too many ideas into one story. Reading such a piece makes the reader disinterested.

Make it Vivid : Give a detailed and interesting description. Don't make it much spicy as it might spoil your piece.

Fiction is not Journalism : Though, magazine sometimes publish fiction, it is not journalism. A fiction is an imaginary piece which may or may not have drawn its inspiration from a real life event. Fiction is fabrication. But journalism is concerned with facts. It is regarded as a record of contemporary history and can not be confused with unreality.

However, over the years the market for fiction in magazine writing has gradually been reduced. If you want to be a fiction writer you have to develop yourself in a different way.

The Basics

To be a good writer, you must be a good reader as well. A good write-up is a study in effortlessness. It must flow freely. The ability to write well requires that the writer should have a thorough knowledge and understanding of the news event. Also, you must understand the basic structure of the news story and the customs of news writing.

A newsman looks for information in conversation, not only with top people but even with commoners. At times, even advertisements can be a vital source of information.

To be a good writer, you have to have two important tools-to gather information and then in the second stage it is important for you to know how to transform this information in an appropriate form. Once you know what this form is, you have virtually overcome the very first requirement to become a writer.

A news story requires simple, straightforward prose, clear thinking and a complete understanding of the subject on the part of the writer. Criteria on which the editors insist upon for selecting a story are-impact, timeliness, prominence, proximity, conflict bizarre and currency. Impact is the consequence a story has on the people.

Timeliness is an important factor for any event. An incident would have a worthwhile exercise soon after it has been reported.

Prominance is a factor that largely revolves around prominent people. Even their trivial actions are read with great interest.

Proximity is how close the event has taken place. Any event at home, your town, state or nation is more catchy than a happening taking place 1,000 miles away.

Conflict is always read. Conflict is one of the journalists' favourite news because it generally ensures that there is an interesting story to write.

Bizarre or unusual incidents always attract readers. This is an old fact of journalism. 'If a dog bites a man, it is not news, but if a man bites a dog it is news'.

Currency has a somewhat similar appeal like timeliness. These are ongoing events but having a continuity. Issues that have the value of currency come and go, but there are always several such issues being discussed by the people. In the late-1960s food shortage and long queues at fair price shops was such an issue.

Individually or collectively all these can give you opportunities to write a good story. You, however, should know how to structure the story so that the most important and interesting information gets to the reader in the most efficient manner.

The Inverted Pyramid : Once you have gone through the stage of information gathering, you have to decide on the structure of the story. This is the most crucial aspect, though it may look very simple, for your story.

The most common structure for writing your story would be the same inverted pyramid, which you were told to use to write a report. In this structure, the first paragraph, gives the most important information of the story. The second and third paragraphs follow up on the information by expanding on the lead and adding information that is of lesser importance.

As the story continues, more information is added, but is of lesser importance and serves to support the information given at the beginning of the story.

The inverted pyramid structure allows the readers to get as much information as possible. The better the inversion, the better the interest of the reader would be, to proceed through the story.

To Remember

— When you write, you must remember a good write-up uses short sentences and short paragraphs.

— To convey your points more forcefully use simple words and simple sentences. Better use common words.

— Paragraph lengths should be limited to 100 words, the aim is to convey the information to the reader.

— Write your stories in the third person.

— Avoid addressing the reader by second person pronoun 'you'.

— You must not give your personal opinions in your stories. Your job is to write what you see and hear.

— Also practice, not to twist the facts. A lively copy is nothing but a vivid presentation of facts in the minimum possible words.

Accuracy and Attribution : As a journalist your aim should be to achieve accuracy. Achieving is not just a matter of the technique of writing but a state of mind that you must faoster. You should not be satisfied with false information, half-baked information or about something you may have doubts about. Make sure that dates and identifications are correct, numbers in a story add up properly and locations are correct. If you are not accurate, you will lose credibility-that is you will not enjoy the trust of the readers. Once you lose credibility as a writer, you lose your market.

Correct Attribution : Misquoting or quoting out of context are very common. While talking to a source keep your ears open. Try to understand what he/she wants to say. Quotes can be direct and indirect. Your effort should be to retain the words used by the source. However, in an indirect quotation, you have the liberty to express the views of the source in different words. The caution is that it should not change the meaning.

Attribution is important. By revealing where you have got the information from, you tell the reader whether it is reliable or not. This saves you from the embarrassment of some information which may be misleading as you leave the assessment of the reliability of the information to the reader.

As attribution builds up credibility, although too much of it can get in the way of the story by affecting its flow, and too little of it can confuse the reader. You have to maintain a balance between the two.

Attribution brings accuracy. You should remember that accuracy is the building which is constructed upon the small information you supply to it. Quotes enliven a copy but they have to be woven into it. Another key for accuracy is to cross check your facts. This means you approach different sources to ensure that your facts are correct.

Ideas and Sources : A journalist is known as a person with ideas. If you want to be a good writer, you have to have ideas as well as be able to evolve new ideas to weave into your stories. One way to get new ideas is to read a lot, but read between the lines. There may be many paragraphs, which may have some idea, which can be developed into an independent story. Another way is to meet people, visit places. For writing a piece you have to have enough back up information.

Also you have to develop news sense. In going through newspapers, you can spot stories that can be developed into a good article. Ideas can not be copy-righted, only the way they are written is copyrighted. Sometimes letters-to-the editor are also a source of good articles. Before writing you must have a clear idea of what you are writing about. Thus, ideas need a firm base of information to build upon.

To categorise the sources in a simple way, there, are three basic sources-people, records and personal information. Most information would come from personal sources. As a writer, you will have to spend most of your non-writing time talking to people. The second major source is your personal observation. Whenever possible, you should attend the events you may be writing on. Sometimes, your observation during, say a public meeting, can bring out very offbeat copy, a humorous piece or an illuminating article.

The stored sources are yet another area. The records of a government department or even of some individual can prove to be important sources.

You must be careful with your sources, cross check them, give credit and attribution where it is due and tell the truth. You should do well to quote the records though you may not reveal who has supplied it to you. The more information you build up the more it would help you and your readers to understand fully.

The Devices

Writing is not simply an inherent talent that some of you may be having and some other won't be. There are steps that all of us can take to improve our writing skills. Writing is a process. It is hard work. It is physically, mentally and emotionally demanding. Good writing does not happen all of a sudden. The writing process is often slow and at times even frustrating. It is a technique and certain guidelines should be followed to improve the writing skill.

Writing Simply : Simplicity is the best way to achieve clarity. Gifted writers take to this method to convey their message. A student, a beginner in the profession of writing, will also find it easy to write in a simple manner.

Using Simple Words : Many people think big or complicated words will impress the reader. In fact it has the opposite effect. "To write clearly, not only the most expressive but the plainest words should be chosen", Benjamin Franklin once wrote.

Using Simple Sentences : It is easier to write five simple sentences than one complex or compound sentence. Long winding sentences only distract the reader.

Economy on Words : Mostly writers use too many words in their drafts. A careful editor deletes these at the time of editing.

There is no substitute for simple, straight forward prose. You should not try to use one word more than necessary. Be on the look out for phrases, words and sentences that do not add substantially to the content of what you are writing. You should also guard against those fancy phrases which draw attention to the writing and the writer, and take away the content. Do not boast while writing.

Not Using Jargon : Each group of people has a technical language of their own. This is called jargon. You may be using certain abbreviations or names in your schools, sports field or in an office. Scientists do so in their labs. These are jargons. They are understood only by the select group. As a writer, you should not use these. You should rather explain the jargon if you have to use it. Your aim should be to make your message clear to the people who have no direct relationship to such groups. You writings should not cut people off from receiving your ideas by a language that they cannot understand.

Avoiding Adjectives : Adjectives and adverbs are often superfluous. You should build up your sentences around nouns and verbs. Usage of adjectives often weaken your message. We would suggest that you write two simple sentences than use an adjective, which more often is unnecessary if your descriptions are clear and vivid. You should select good active verbs to enliven your copy. A good verb denotes action and a better verbs denotes action and description.

Tying Together-Avoiding Jolts : Quite often you might have heard that writing must be well-knit. You knit not the words alone but the thoughts as well. Readers should be able to read through a piece of writing without stops and surprises. While introducing a new idea or piece of information, do not do so without tying it to other parts of a story. Springing up with sudden thoughts jolts a reader, and like a sudden jerk on a smooth road, he is thrown off balance.

Connect any new information in a story to information already introduced. You have to develop a mental discipline and read your copy with discerning eyes.

Avoiding Repetition and Redundancies : Both these traits show lack of discipline on the part of the writer.

Be Specific : Brevity is the soul of wit. Just as you try to avoid someone who talks too much, so do readers about writings, which have too many superfluous of high-sounding words. Eliminate all that which you have said once. You have to have accuracy and clarity. But never try to sacrifice these for the sake of brevity.

Writing Features

More and more editors have begun to pay attention to features which give individuality and character to a newspaper and offer a great variety of reading material to the subscriber. If news is the life-blood of a newspaper, editorials are its heart and features is soul. Features usually play up the human interest angle.

Main Components of a Feature : A feature resembles a news story in some respects but differs from it in some others. A feature deals with facts, like a news story. But it differs from a news story as in that it may be longer than its news value justifies and it need not follow the standard form of news presentation. A news-story has two main components-the lead and the body. But a feature also has a third component-the conclusion.

The Lead : It should consist of a summary of the subject-matter. A feature writer has a great latitude in selecting his lead. The lead may be any one of the following types or a combination of two or more of them:

News Summary Lead : This is similar to the lead in a news story and should embody the 5 words-Who, Where, What, When and Why.

Short Sentence Lead : This consist of a single striking sentence e.g., Time goes by; Art is born of humiliation.

Quotation Lead : The sayings of a renowned person—poet or leader may be taken as a lead.

Question Lead : Sometimes a question may provide a feature with an attractive lead.

Contrast Lead : Conflict and Contrast many a times provide a feature with lead which may bring forth the controversial nature of the feature.

Picture Lead : This gives a vivid description of the setting of the feature or evokes a mood or feeling.

Humours Lead : A humorous lead sets the tone of a feature perfectly for the reader.

The Body : The body of a feature is developed logically and smoothly in the same way as a news-story. A feature should conform to the basic principles of good writing, that is, unity, coherence, and readability. The writer should present his material with brevity and elegance, avoiding superfluous words as well as cliches and maintaining a high standard of writing. The feature writer can make even a simple and ordinary incident into a vital happening. The news reporter informs, but the feature writer informs, entertains and educates.

The Conclusion : A news reporter does not need a conclusion, but a feature often, though not always does. The conclusion may be a summing up of the contents of a feature, or a climax as in a short-story.

Different Types of Features

Human Interest Features : The human touch is perhaps the most vital quality in the feature.

Personal Narratives : The stories of eminent men and women are worth telling. Human interest in them survives long after they are dead. Features can be written on their life and work, their achievements and their unique contribution to the nation.

Meeting Unusual People : The world is full of extraordinary persons whose life and works can make good features.

Travel Sketches : Travel fascinates most people even though they may be prevented by lack of money or time from visiting as many places as they want to. Travel features satisfy a basic human desire to know more about the world we live in.

Historical Features : These are about persons in history books or about historical places.

Interpretative Features : These are intended to inform and instruct the reader about the background and significance of political, economic, social and religious issues.

Autobiographical Human Documents : Features in this category relate to personal experiences of intimate personal matters, e.g.,

'My Experiment with Truth' is a wonderful account of the personal experiences of Mahatma Gandhi.

Science Features : Features to popularise science by explaining a scientific development in simple language for the lay reader fall into this group.

Practical Guidance Features : These are designed to tell the reader how to make, repair or collect things. Short of do-it-yourself articles.

Miscellaneous : The list of subjects that lend themselves to feature treatment is endless, ranging from mundane activities like cooking and gardening to unusual trades and profession, from fashions and good grooming to bird-watching and mountaineering. To write a feature, the author must be true to the facts. He/She must weave the facts with imagination. Use lucid style and narrate the whole thing in simple language.

Writing Editorials

Newspapers are an important source of opinion making. This is done through every aspect of newspaper writing. Though, newspapers have separate pages for news and views, opinions are at times interwoven with news items as explanations, backgrounds and interpretative paragraphs. Editorials contain essential background to support their arguments. Only a small section of readers or say quality people turn to the edit page. The 'edit page' of a newspaper is essentially an opinion page. It is the prestigious part of the newspaper which gets most of the direct attention of the editor. It reflects the policy of the newspaper and makes a major contribution to the shaping of its image.

The Editorial Page and Its Importance : All newspapers pay extra attention to the editorial page. On the edit page, generally there are two/ three edits in the first two-three columns of the page, one main article in the centre of the page, one or two small article(s) in column 7-8 position. At the centre of the page is a light article, generally humorous, of human interest or informative. Letters to the editor are also accommodated on the edit page.

If a newspaper has several editions, the same editorials generally appear on the same position at all centres. This is essential for the overall personality of a newspaper and its image. On important occasions, newspapers in India sometimes give a front page position to the editorial on that subject. In India, all reputed dailies have their editorial columns. The preoccupation of newspapers with political developments is a legacy of the days of our freedom struggle, but in course of time, this has given way to a wider perspective embracing economic, social and international developments. Since politics plays a major part in national life, its importance is reflected in the newspaper editorial pages. Social issues steal the editorial highlight on benchmark occasions such as the eruption of a caste or communal conflict. On such occasions, while presenting his views, the editor not only express his concern and anguish over the development, but also suggest remedies to prevent a recurrence of the problem.

On political issues, the line which each newspaper takes depends on its policy, outlook and political prediction. Newspapers' political leanings are reflected in the comments which they offer.

Definitions and Characteristics of Editorials : A conventional editorial may be defined as a critical interpretation of significant, usually contemporary, events so that the publication's typical reader will be informed, influenced or entertained.

An editorial may also be defined as a journalistic essay which either (a) to intorm (b) to persuade (c) to stimulate insight in a humorous manner. It has an introduction, a body and a conclusion.

According to Joseph Pulitzer newspapers should be 'both a daily teacher and a daily tribune'. Newspapers also carry on their opinion pages from the contributions of columnists, who present a particular point of view. One columnist might differ completely with another on the same subject and interpret the same development differently.

Type of Editorials : An editorial writer's job is to study and write the piece according to the style of their newspapers. The University Journalism schools of United States classify editorials in different ways-the classification could be according to the purpose of editorial i.e. it may be informative, argumentative or entertaining. It may also be classified on the basis of its form of composition i.e. it may be narrative, descriptive or expository. An editorial may also be classified on the basis of its appeal to readers, emotion or intellects or on the basis of its contents which may be political, social, historical, scientific etc. Interpretative and explanatory editorials seek to expand the dimensions of the news reports, which fulfil the requirements of a busy reader as well as of the well-read person with a critical mind.

An informative editorial about a major foreign development would also provide the background to understand the development and explain to the reader what it means for the rest of the world. The historic background is useful in appreciating the significance of the development.

The argumentative editorial tries to convince the reader about its point of view. To influence and mould public opinion has been one of the major objectives of editorial writers.

There are also editorials that amuse and entertain. The light pieces are usually published as the third edit by major English newspapers. Humour on the editorial pages adds to their appeal for the reader whose interests are not confined to politics and economics.

Policy, Style and Guidelines : When the editorial represents the policy of the newspaper, the selection of articles of opinion from writers outside does not depend on endorsement of their views by the newspaper concerned. The edit page articles are meant to broaden the horizon of news and opinion coverage.

The cartoon is also a sort of opinion piece. The cartoonist enjoys a wide latitude in depicting big personalities as ordinary men and punching the baloon of lofty statements. In selecting news as well as opinion pieces, certain standards have to be maintained. The elementary principle is that they should not be defamatory or offend good taste.

Certain guidelines are provided by the Press Council of India which would be helpful both to the reporter and the leader writer.

— While dealing with the communal and regional matters, the press is expected to exercise due care and caution so that unhealthy and communal passions are not aroused.

— Sensational headlines with incorrect innuendos lend an unethical character to publications.

— Editor is expected to verify facts before publishing any article.

— Editorials should not use irresponsible, or filthy comments.

— Any comment against the administration or any person must be based on information, the accuracy of which has been carefully checked and verified from authentic sources.

— Contradiction pertaining to defamatory articles containing personal allegations should be published promptly with due prominence.

Letters to the Editor : Letters to the editor are published usually in the opinion columns. Though, an editor can not be expected to publish all letters representing various points of view on a controversial matter, he is expected to make an honest endeavour to select and publish a balanced gist of these letters on the issue.

If in the opinion of an editor, an article or news items submitted for publication could be liable to legal proceedings or any future complications, its publication would rest on the discretion of the editor since it is he who is answerable for anything published in the paper.

The-editorial is a journalistic essay, its title should aim to inform the reader about the subject of the editorial and arouse his interest. The simplest form of editorial structure is to state the subject and to comment on it.

Bibliography

Ajay, S. Jasra: *Information Technology in Journalism*, A.&M. Publishers, Delhi, 2002.

Almond, G.: *Art of News Editing*, Princeton University Press, Princeton, 1960.

Altschull, J.H.: *Agents of Power: the Role of the News Media in Human Affairs*, Longman, New York, 1984.

Andal, N.: *Communication: Theory and Model*, Himalaya Publishing House, Delhi, 1999.

Andrews, C.F.: *Mahatma Gandhi's Ideas*, MacMillan, London, 1949.

Aruna, Z.: *Media Power: People, Politics and Public Interest*, Kanishka Publishers, New Delhi, 2001.

Astor, J. J.: *Art of Modern Journalism*, Anmol Publications Pvt. Ltd., New Delhi, 1996.

Baran, J.: *Introduction to Mass Communication: Media Literacy and Culture*, Mayfield, New York, 1999.

Bella, M.: *Designing Messages for Development Communication*, Sage, New Delhi, 1991.

Berger, C.R.: *Handbook of Communication Science*, Sage Publications, London, 1987.

Bhatt, S.C.: *Indian Press Since 1955*, Publications Division, Government of India, New Delhi, 1997.

Bloom, B.S.: *Taxonomy of Journalistic Objectives*, Mackey, New York, 1965.

Brank, S.M.: *Journalism Characteristics and School Learning*, Harper, New York, 1976.

Carey, W.: *Communication as Culture: Essays on Media and Society,* Routledge, New York, 1992.

Chaturvedi, J.F.: *The Indian Press at Crossroads,* Media Research Foundation, New Delhi, 1992.

Dennis, K.: *British Social Life in India (1608-1937),* Routledge & Kegan Paul, London, 1938.

Desk, R.: *Media Technology in Curriculum Development,* Harper and Row Publishers, London, 2001.

Entman, R.: *Media, Power and Politics,* Free Press, New York, 1981.

Gadi, W.: *Media and Political Conflicts: News From the Middle East,* Cambridge, London, 1997.

Gandhi, V.P.: *A first Course in Practical Journalism,* Kanishka Publishers, New Delhi, 2000

Garret, A.: *Interviewing: Its Principles and Methods,* Family Service Association of America, New York, 1942.

Grey, E.: *The Story of Journalism,* Longmans Young Books, London, 1968.

Gupta, Om: *Media aur Samaj,* Manohar Publishers, Delhi, 2002.

Hachten, W.A.: *The World News Prism: Changing Media of International Communication,* Iowa State University Press, Iowa, 1996.

Holsti, O.R.: *Content Analysis,* Amerind, New Delhi, 1969.

Hough, George A.: *News Writing,* Kanishka Publishers, New Delhi, 1999.

Hynds, C.: *American Newspaper in* 1980s, Hastings House, New York, 1980.

James, C.: *Point of Departure,* Oriel Press, London, 1978.

Jan, R. H.: *Print Media Communication,* Anmol Publications Pvt. Ltd., New Delhi, 1999.

Jeremy, C.: *Grammatical Man: Information Entropy, Language and Life,* Simon and Schuster, New York, 1982.

Jhingan, M.L.: *The Economics of Development and Planning,* Konark Publishers, New Delhi, 1994.

John, A.: *The Asian Newspaper's Reluctant Revolution*, The Iowa State University Press, Iowa, 1977.

Kamath, M. V.: *Professional Journalism*, Vikas Publishing House, New Delhi, 1997.

Kelley, H. H.: *Prime Time—The Life of Edward R. Murrow*, Little Brown, Boston, 1958.

Kiran, M.: *Studies in Educational Broadcasting*, Deep & Deep Publications, New Delhi, 1996.

Krippendorff, K.: *Content Analysis: An Introduction to its Methodology*, Sage, California, 1980.

Lawrence, R.: *Investigating Communication: A Introduction to Research Methods*, Prentice Hall, New York, 1991.

Leland, D.: *Editing the Day's News*, The MacMillan Co., New York, 1947.

Madhavan, P. K.: *Careers in Publishing*, Vikas Publishing House, New Delhi, 1997.

Marvin, B.: *Survey of Broadcast Journalism 1970-71: A State of Siege*, Grosset and Dunlap, New York, 1971.

McCully, C.H.: *The Media—Instrument of Change*, National College Record, Bombay, 2001.

Mehta, D.S.: *Mass Communication and Journalism in India*, Allied Publishers, Bombay, 1979.

Melkote, S.R.: *Communication for Development in the third World: Theory and Practice*, Sage, New Delhi, 1991.

Merton, R.K.: *Social Theory and Social Structure*, Free Press, Glencoe, Illinois, 1957.

Michael, A.: *Codes for Media*, Rashmi Publications, Chennai, 2002.

Mishra, M.: *Press and Political Socialization*, Dominant Books, New Delhi, 2003.

Moraes, F.: *Witness to an Era*, Vikas Publishing House, Delhi, 1977.

Mumtaz, N.: *Journalism Guidance, Measurement & Statistics*, Takshashila, 1996.

Murthy, D.V.R.: *Developmental Journalism*, Dominant Books, New Delhi, 2001.

Murty, K.N.: *Indian Journalism*, Mysore University Press, Mysore, 1966.

Natrajan, J.: *History of Indian Journalism*, The Publications Division, Government of India, New Delhi, 1999.

Natrajan, S.: *A History of the Press in India*, Asia Publishing House, Bombay, 1962.

Ottaway, A.K.C.: *Press and Society*, Routldge and Kegan Paul, London, 1962.

Panickkar, K.M.: *The Foundation of New India*, George Allen & Unwin, London, 1963.

Parikh, R.D.: *The Press and Society*, Popular Prakashan, Bombay, 1965.

Phillips, W.: *Mass Communication Research: Major Issues and Future Directions*, Praeger, New York, 1974.

Rai, U.: *Women and Print Media: Portrayal and Performance*, Chanakya Publications Pvt. Ltd., New Delhi, 1992.

Rastogi, T. N.: *Encyclopaedia of Professional Journalism*, Anmol Publications Pvt. Ltd., New Delhi, 2001.

Rati, B.: *The Working Journalist's Guide to Substance and Style*, Dominant Books, New Delhi, 2003.

Roland, E.: *Journalism in Modern India*, Asia Publishing House, Bombay, 1964.

Ross, A.: *The Media Society: Basic Issues and Controversies*, Butterworths, Vancouver, 1987.

Rostow, W.W.: *The Stages of Economic Growth: A Non-communist Manifesto*, Cambridge University Press, Cambridge, 1960.

Sanders, D.: *Handbook of Political Communication*, Sage Publications, Beverly Hills, 1978.

Sanjay, B.P.: *The Eighteenth Elephant: Udayavani's Experiment in Development Journalism*, Udayavani Press, Manipal, 1990.

Saraswat, R.K.: *Mass Media*, NCERT, New Delhi, 1998.

Sharma, G.D.: *Methodologies of Journalism*, Popular Press, New Delhi, 2001.

Singh, J.K.: *Media Cultural and Communication*, Manohar Publishers, Delhi, 1999.

Snow, R.P.: *Media Power*, Sage Publications, Beverly Hills and London, 1984.

Sovati and Navin Chandra: *Foundations of News and Journalism*, Kanishka Publishers, New Delhi, 1999.

Srivastava, K.M.: *News Reporting and Editing*, Sterling, New Delhi, 1997.

Stevenson, R.L.: *Communication Development and Third World*, Longman, Maryland, 1988.

Thorndike, R.L.: *Media Psychology and Education*, Wiley Eastern Pvt. Ltd., New Delhi, 2001.

Vajpayee, R.: *Press: Inside Outside 2002*, Gyan Books Pvt. Ltd., New Delhi, 2003.

Verma, J.S.: *Media and Cultural Environment*, Methuen, London, 1969.

Viner, George: *The Practice of Journalism*, Heinemann, London, 1963.

Vittal, N.: *Media and Information Technology*, A.& M. Publishers, Delhi, 2001.

Whinnie, D.: *The Art of Broadcasting*, Faber & Faber, London, 1961.

Wingate, P.: *Newspaper History: From the 17th Century to the Present Day*, Constable, London, 1978.

Woollacott, J.: *Mass Communication and Society*, Edward Arnold, London, 1977.

Yadav, J.S.: *News Editing of Indian Newspapers*, ABC, New Delhi, 1998.

Young, J.: *The Manufacture of News*, Constable, London, 1973.

Zaller, R.: *The Nature and Origins of Mass Opinion*, Cambridge, New York, 2001.

Index

N

❑❑❑